ARCHI-NEERING

ARCHI-NEERING
HELMUT JAHN   WERNER SOBEK

Herausgegeben von Susanne Anna

Mit einem Text von Susanne Anna
und einem Gespräch von Nicola Kuhn
mit Helmut Jahn und Werner Sobek

Hatje Cantz Verlag

Impressum *Colophon*

Katalog

Diese Publikation erscheint anläßlich der Ausstellung »ARCHI-NEERING Helmut Jahn Werner Sobek« vom 6. Juni bis 12. September 1999 im Städtischen Museum Leverkusen Schloß Morsbroich.

Herausgeberin: Susanne Anna

Ausstellungskonzeption: Susanne Anna, Helmut Jahn, Werner Sobek, Oliver Zybok

Katalogkonzeption: Susanne Anna, Werner Sobek

Redaktion: Oliver Zybok

Bearbeitung: Anja Thierfelder

Lektorat: Karin Osbahr

Übersetzung: John S. Southard

Gestaltung: Lothar Krauss, Frankfurt am Main

Reproduktionen: Repro Mayer, Reutlingen

Gesamtherstellung: Dr. Cantz'sche Druckerei
Ostfildern-Ruit bei Stuttgart

Erschienen im Hatje Cantz Verlag
Senefelderstr. 12
73760 Ostfildern
Tel. 0711/44 05 0
Fax 0711/44 05 220
Internet: www.hatjecantz.de

© Städtisches Museum Leverkusen Schloß Morsbroich,
die Künstler und die Autoren
Stadt Leverkusen ◀▶

Die Deutsche Bibliothek – CIP-Einheitsaufnahme
ARCHI-NEERING, Helmut Jahn, Werner Sobek : [anläßlich der Ausstellung ARCHI-NEERING, Helmut Jahn, Werner Sobek, vom 6. Juni bis 12. September 1999 im Städtischen Museum Leverkusen Schloß Morsbroich] / hrsg. von Susanne Anna. Mit einem Text von Susanne Anna und einem Gespräch von Nicola Kuhn mit Helmut Jahn und Werner Sobek. [Übers. John S. Southard]. – Ostfildern-Ruit : Hatje Cantz, 1999

ISBN 3-7757-0852-9

Ausstellung

Organisation: Keith Palmer, Anja Thierfelder, Oliver Zybok

Sekretariat: Doris Eitner

Öffentlichkeitsarbeit: Oliver Zybok

Verwaltung: Uwe Rheinfrank, Barbara Wojaczek

Restaurierung: Rolf Küpper

Technik: Thomas Gattinger, Wolfgang Gierden, Sascha Wolf

Catalogue

This catalogue is published in conjunction with the exhibition entitled »ARCHI-NEERING Helmut Jahn Werner Sobek«, presented from 6 June to 12 September at the Städtisches Museum Leverkusen Schloß Morsbroich.

Editor: Susanne Anna

Exhibition concept: Susanne Anna, Helmut Jahn, Werner Sobek, Oliver Zybok

Catalogue concept: Susanne Anna, Werner Sobek

Editorial director: Oliver Zybok

Research: Anja Thierfelder

Editing: Karin Osbahr

Translation: John S. Southard

Design: Lothar Krauss, Frankfurt am Main

Reproductions: Repro Mayer, Reutlingen

*Printing and binding: Dr. Cantz'sche Druckerei
Ostfildern-Ruit near Stuttgart*

*Published by: Hatje Cantz Verlag
Senefelderstr. 12
73760 Ostfildern
Tel. 0711/44 05 0
Fax 0711/44 05 220
Internet: www.hatjecantz.de*

*© Städtisches Museum Leverkusen Schloß Morsbroich,
the artists and the authors
City of Leverkusen ◀▶*

*Die Deutsche Bibliothek – CIP-Einheitsaufnahme
ARCHI-NEERING, Helmut Jahn, Werner Sobek : [anläßlich der Ausstellung ARCHI-NEERING, Helmut Jahn, Werner Sobek, vom 6. Juni bis 12. September 1999 im Städtischen Museum Leverkusen Schloß Morsbroich] / hrsg. von Susanne Anna. Mit einem Text von Susanne Anna und einem Gespräch von Nicola Kuhn mit Helmut Jahn und Werner Sobek. [Übers. John S. Southard]. – Ostfildern-Ruit : Hatje Cantz, 1999*

ISBN 3-7757-0852-9

Exhibition

Organisation: Keith Palmer, Anja Thierfelder, Oliver Zybok

Secretariat: Doris Eitner

Public relations: Oliver Zybok

Administration: Uwe Reinfrank, Barbara Wojaczek

Restoration: Rolf Küpper

Technical support: Thomas Gattinger, Wolfgang Gierden, Sascha Wolf

Mit freundlicher Unterstützung durch/ *With the generous support of:*

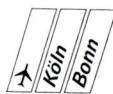

Inhalt *Content*

Susanne Anna
7   Vorwort *Preface*

Susanne Anna
10 »Form follows Force«
    – Archi-Neering als Performance der Zukunft
    – *Archi-Neering as Performance of the Future*

24 Architektur heute
    Nicola Kuhn im Gespräch mit Helmut Jahn und Werner Sobek

84 *Architecture Today*
    Nicola Kuhn in Conversation with Helmut Jahn and Werner Sobek

Projekte *Projects*
26 Sony-Center am Potsdamer Platz in Berlin
36 New Bangkok International Airport
48 Shanghai-Pudong International Airport (Wettbewerb / *Competition*)
56 DIFA am Kurfürstendamm in Berlin
62 Flughafen Köln/Bonn: Fassade Terminal 2, Parkhäuser 2 + 3 und Bahnhof
74 Flughafen München Terminal 2 (Wettbewerb / *Competition*)
80 Street Furniture Designer Line für J. C. Decaux
86 Illinois Institute of Technology, Campus Center (Wettbewerb / *Competition*)
92 Generaldirektion Deutsche Post AG, Bonn
100 Neue Konzernzentrale der Bayer AG, Leverkusen
114 Transrapid-Stationen für Hamburg, Schwerin und Berlin
120 Kaufhaus Kaufhof in Chemnitz
122 HA-LO Corporate Headquarters in Chicago
124 Neue Messe Shanghai-Pudong
130 Bürogebäude für Andersen Consulting in Sulzbach

133 Catalogue Raisonné

141 Biographien / *Biographies*

142 Bibliographie / *Bibliography*

Diese Ausstellung steht unter der Schirmherrschaft
des Ministerpräsidenten des Landes Nordrhein-Westfalen Wolfgang Clement.
This exhibition is being presented under the patronage of Wolfgang Clement,
Ministerpräsident of the state of Nordrhein-Westfalen.

Eines der Fundamente der Morsbroicher Bewegung war zweifelsohne die Auseinandersetzung mit zeitgenössischen richtungsweisenden Strömungen von Baukunst und Urbanistik. Udo Kultermann, der sich in diesem Bereich wissenschaftlich profilieren konnte, begann seine Museumsarbeit mit der Darstellung jener utopistischen Ansätze der Gläsernen Kette um Bruno Taut, die Anfang des Jahrhunderts in ihren Theorien des transparenten Bauens eine bessere Welt postulierten. Zu Hochzeiten des Kalten Krieges folgte in Leverkusen jenseits des Eisernen Vorhangs die erste Schau von Sergej Eisenstein, dem konstruktivistischen Baumeister des modernen Films. In den 70er Jahren interessierte Rolf Wedewer das hoch brisante Thema deutscher Urbanistik; er organisierte die damals richtungsweisenden Ausstellungen *Profitopoli$* und *Stadtgestalt* und mischte sich damit als Museumsmann in die von Soziologie und Politologie geprägte brandaktuelle Stadtentwicklungsdiskussion auch vor der eigenen Haustür ein.

Die Auseinandersetzung mit Fragen um zeitgenössische Architektur und strukturelle, gesellschaftliche, wirtschaftliche und ästhetische Veränderungen der globalen Stadt wird auf Schloß Morsbroich fortgesetzt. Im Jahre 1997 begann hier eine Reihe monographischer Werkschauen bedeutender Baukünstler mit dem Tessiner Mario Botta. Retrospektiven von Richard Meier, Norman Foster und Daniel Libeskind stehen gleichsam wie eine Gruppenausstellung internationaler Dekonstruktivisten zur Realisierung an. Gemeinsam mit Stephan Schmidt-Wulffen ist für kommenden Herbst eine Fotoausstellung zur Nachkriegsentwicklung bundesrepublikanischer Urbanistik in

Vorwort

Preface

One of the fundamental pillars of the Morsbroich Movement was undoubtedly the focus upon contemporary, pioneering tendencies in architecture and urbanistics. Udo Kultermann, who has earned acclaim for his scholarship in this area, began his museum work with a presentation of the utopian ideas of the "Glass Chain", the circle associated with Bruno Taut, who postulated a better world in their theories of transparent architecture that appeared around the turn of the century. In the midst of the Cold War, the first exhibition of the work of Sergei Eisenstein, the Constructivist architect of modern cinema, on this side of the Iron Curtain was presented in Leverkusen. Rolf Wedewer was concerned during the seventies with the volatile subject of German urbanistics. He organised the seminal exhibitions "Profitopoli$" and "Stadtgestalt" during those years and involved himself as a museum specialist in the then current debate on urban development, with its decidedly sociological and politological overtones, practically outside his own front door.

These studies on issues related to contemporary architecture and structural, social, economic and aesthetic change in the global city is being pursued further at Schloß Morsbroich. A series of monographic exhibitions of the work of significant architectural artists was initiated in 1997 with the show featuring Mario Botta of Tessin. Planning for retrospectives on the work of Richard Meier, Norman Foster and Daniel Libeskind as a kind of group exhibition of international Deconstructivists is currently in progress. Preparations are now being made in co-

Vorwort *Preface*

Vorbereitung. Dieses Projekt dient dem Museum als weitere Basis für seine kontinuierliche Untersuchung des öffentlichen Raumes am Beispiel von Leverkusen als Vorzeigestadt typischer Problemstellungen.

Vor dem Hintergrund der Diskussion um die neue Berliner Mitte bleibt die aktuelle Architektur- und Urbanismusdebatte auf der Schwelle zum nächsten Jahrtausend auch für die Leverkusener Museumsarbeit von Bedeutung. Hierbei kristallisiert sich seit Jahren immer stärker eine Baukunst im Dialog mit neuesten High-Tech-Erfindungen des Bauingenieurwesens als richtungsweisend heraus. Ein prägnantes Vorbild auf diesem Sektor ist sicher die Arbeit von Helmut Jahn und Werner Sobek, deren höchst intelligente und philosophische Architektur auf Schloß Morsbroich erstmalig in einer Ausstellung vorgestellt wird. Am Beispiel fünfzehn internationaler Bauprojekte der letzten fünf Jahre zeigen sich hier deutlich die graduell verschiedenen Phasen einer Zusammenarbeit, die von ihren konventionellen Anfängen kontinuierlich über additive Verschränkung von Technik und Poesie zum organischen Miteinander jenes Archi-Neering schöner, funktionaler und effizienter Lösungen fand.

Dieser Dialog wird nicht nur in der Ausstellung, die den Prozeß von Architektur in Skizzen, Plänen, Modellen, Fotos, Filmen und Materialbeispielen skulptural visualisiert, deutlich. Zusätzlich legt Nicola Kuhn in dieser Publikation ein Gespräch mit Jahn und Sobek vor, das über den Diskurs von Bau- und Ingenieurkunst berichtet. Außerdem ist erstmalig ein entsprechender Catalogue Raisonné erarbeitet worden.

Schon im Vorfeld deutscher Bauvorhaben von Jahn und Sobek hat auf verschiedenen Ebenen der kritische Dialog um gesellschaftlich relevante Fragen, deren kulturelle Technik-, Ökologie- und Urbanismusdebatte in der Ausstellung mit Vorträgen und Kamingesprächen weiter gefördert werden soll, Wogen geschlagen. Durch den glücklichen Umstand eines Neubaus der Bayer-Konzernzentrale durch Jahn/Sobek erleben wir die Wirkung

operation with Stephan Schmidt-Wulffen for a photo exhibition on post-war developments and urbanistics in the Federal Republic of Germany in the coming autumn. This project will provide the museum a broader basis for its continuing studies on public space in Leverkusen as a showcase of typical problems.

Within the context of the discussion revolving around the new Berlin Centre, the current debate regarding architecture and urbanism at the threshold of the next millennium remains of great importance to museum work in Leverkusen as well. Over the years, a dialogue of pioneering significance has emerged between architecture and the most recent high-tech inventions in the field of engineering. One particularly noteworthy example of this development is certainly the work of Helmut Jahn and Werner Sobek, whose highly intelligent, philosophical architecture is now being presented in an exhibition for the first time at Schloß Morsbroich. In a presentation of fifteen international building projects, the exhibition clearly illuminates the gradually changing phases of a cooperative relationship that has produced beautiful, functional and effective solutions along a continuum leading from its conventional beginnings through the additive linking of technology and poetry to the organic interaction of Archi-Neering.

This dialogue becomes evident not only in the exhibition, which visualises the process of architecture sculpturally in sketches, plans, models, photos, films and sample materials. Nicola Kuhn also presents a first interview with Jahn and Sobek in this publication, a conversation focused upon the discourse between the arts of architecture and engineering. In addition, the first catalogue raisonné of the works of Jahn and Sobek has been compiled.

Even in advance of the German building projects undertaken by Jahn and Sobek, the critical dialogue concerning socially relevant issues, the debate on the technical, ecological and urbanistic aspects of which is to be

aktueller hochkarätiger Architektur hautnah vor Ort. Eingedenk der einstmaligen Utopie der Gläsernen Kette begreift die Institution Museum Archi-Neering denn auch als Chance, zwischen Architektur und Gesellschaft zu vermitteln.

Zuerst möchte ich Helmut Jahn und Werner Sobek für die fruchtbare und spannende Zusammenarbeit, ihr dynamisches Engagement – trotz zahlreicher weltweiter Baustellen – sowie die Zurverfügungstellung persönlicher Materialien für Ausstellung und Katalog ganz herzlich danken. Ohne die generöse finanzielle Unterstützung der Bayer AG Leverkusen und der Flughafen Köln/Bonn GmbH wäre die Ausstellung nicht zustande gekommen. Dafür sei hier ausdrücklich gedankt. Ebenso gilt mein Dank der GKD – Gebr. Kufferath GmbH & Co. KG, der BGT Bischoff Glastechnik GmbH sowie den Leihgebern, die ihre Modelle für die Schau ausgeliehen haben. Nicola Kuhn bin ich für die Vorlage des sorgfältigen, historisch gewichtigen Gesprächs mit Helmut Jahn und Werner Sobek sehr dankbar wie auch Keith Palmer vom Büro Murphy/Jahn und Anja Thierfelder vom Büro Werner Sobek Ingenieure für ihre organisatorische Mitarbeit. Natürlich freue ich mich über den unermüdlichen Einsatz der KollegInnen vor Ort und möchte ihnen hiermit wieder einmal herzlich Dankeschön sagen. Abschließend sollte der langjährige Dialog mit Werner Blaser nicht unerwähnt bleiben; für seine Beratung bin ich ihm zu Dank verpflichtet.

Susanne Anna
Städtisches Museum Leverkusen Schloß Morsbroich, Juni 1999

promoted during the exhibition through lectures and fireside chats, was already making considerable waves. The fortunate circumstance that Jahn and Sobek have designed the new Bayer headquarters building gives us the opportunity to experience the impact of current, first-class architecture close up. Recalling the former utopia of the "Glass Chain", the museum as an institution welcomes "Archi-Neering" as a chance to mediate between architecture and society.

I wish first of all to thank Helmut Jahn and Werner Sobek sincerely for their fruitful and exciting co-operative input, their dynamic commitment – despite their obligations at numerous construction sites all over the world – and their willingness to provide materials of their own for the exhibition and the catalogue. Without the generous funding provided by Bayer AG Leverkusen and the Flughafen Köln/Bonn GmbH the exhibition would never have come to be. Special thanks are due for this support. I am also grateful to the GKD – Gebr. Kufferath GmbH & Co. KG, the BGT Bischoff Glastechnik GmbH and the lenders, who have provided models on loan for the show. I wish to thank Nicola Kuhn for the thorough, historically oriented interview and Keith Palmer of the office of Murphy/Jahn and Anja Thierfelder of the office of Werner Sobek for their organisational assistance. I am naturally gratified to have witnessed the tireless commitment of all of my museum colleagues in Leverkusen and am pleased to express my heartfelt thanks to them. I would be remiss in concluding without mention of my many years of dialogue with Werner Blaser. I am grateful to him for his good counsel.

Susanne Anna
Städtisches Museum Leverkusen Schloß Morsbroich, June 1999

Susanne Anna

Archi-Neering als Performance der Zukunft

»Form follows Force«

Archi-Neering as Performance of the Future

Architekt – Ingenieur

In der Baukunst manifestiert sich seit Jahren der zunehmende Einfluß der High-Tech-Erfindungen. Das Resultat ist eine neue skulpturale Ästhetik, die, in zunehmendem Maße gesellschaftliche Relevanz reklamierend, wieder humanistische Komponenten in sich birgt. Unsere Ausstellung spürt an einem solch prägnanten Beispiel – der seit fünf Jahren bestehenden Zusammenarbeit des Stuttgarter Ingenieurs Werner Sobek mit dem deutsch-amerikanischen Architekten Helmut Jahn – dieser eigentlich jahrhundertealten Tradition nach: dem Phänomen integraler Ingenieurbaukunst. Hierbei sei betont, daß sich unser Interesse aus humanistischer Sicht darstellt, um indes eine Beschreibung derart komplexer Materie des Technoiden den Technik- und Naturwissenschaftlern zu überlassen. Vielleicht aber trägt gerade auch ein solches Projekt dazu bei, die Kluft jener »zwei Kulturen« (Charles P. Snow) zu verkleinern.

Bereits im 15. Jahrhundert definierte man das, was wir heute Archi-Neering getauft haben, als sogenannte »Ingeniöse Tätigkeit«: Die Erfindung von Konstruktionen im Spannungsfeld zwischen Natur, Technik und Ästhetik.

In diesem Kontext ist die Überlieferung unseres Jahrhunderts frappierend, die davon ausgeht, daß das Wissen über Technik im allgemeinen rein auf den Bereich der Natur- und Technikwissenschaften bezogen bleibt. Hierbei werden vor allem die von Technikern getroffenen, nicht wissenschaftlichen Entscheidungen oft nicht bemerkt.

Architect – Engineer

High-tech inventions have been exerting an increasingly strong influence in architecture for years. This development has spawned a new sculptural aesthetics with a growing claim to social relevance and a renewed emphasis upon humanist components. Focusing on a highly significant example – the five-year co-operation between the Stuttgart engineer Werner Sobek and the German-American architect Helmut Jahn – our exhibition seeks to investigate this tradition, whose roots actually go back hundreds of years: the phenomenon of the integration of engineering and architecture. It should be noted that our interest proceeds from a humanist standpoint, as we leave the task of describing such complex technoid material to scholars in the fields of science and technology. Yet a project of this kind may contribute to a narrowing of the gap between those "two cultures" (Charles P. Snow).

As early as the fifteenth century, the discipline we now call Archi-Neering was referred to as "ingenious activity": the invention of constructions in the field of tension between nature, technology and aesthetics.

In this context, we look with astonishment upon the legacy of our century, which schools us in the assumption that technical knowledge relates in a general sense only to the natural sciences and technical disciplines. As a result, non-scientific decisions taken by engineers in particular often go unnoticed. Indeed, although many of the objects of everyday life are affected by natural science, they have been conceived by engineers who were

Sind doch viele Objekte unseres Alltagslebens zwar gemeinhin von den Naturwissenschaften beeinflußt, doch von Technikern entworfen, die nicht wissenschaftlich gedacht haben, als sie deren Erscheinung, ihre Formen und Materialien festlegten. Leonardo da Vinci, der bereits um 1500 Dinge gezeichnet hatte, die erst Jahrhunderte später konstruiert wurden, ist ein klassisches Beispiel in der Evolutionskette des Ingenieurs, in welcher der Konnex zwischen Intuition und Rationalität von Beginn an eine entscheidende Rolle gespielt hat.

Jene Fähigkeit zu geistigem Sehen, welche Eugene S. Ferguson als »Das innere Auge« bezeichnet, ist in den Natur- und Technikwissenschaften der letzten Jahrzehnte allein schon in der Ausbildung verlorengegangen. Dies geht sogar soweit, daß »der Bauingenieur von heute [...] von den gedanklichen Auseinandersetzungen, die zu geistigem Handeln führen«, wie Knut Gabriel es rigoros formuliert, »nichts gehört« hat. Hier wird die Forderung nach dem alten Uomo Universale zunehmend dringlicher.

So ist denn auch gerade Archi-Neering ein regelrechtes Plädoyer für eine innovative interdisziplinäre Auseinandersetzung mit der angewandten Kunst des Ingenieurs. Aufgrund des dringenden Bedarfs der Vernetzung mit technisch-professioneller Progression expandiert der Diskurs zwischen Kunst und Technik auch in anderen Bereichen der bildenden Kunst, zu der wir seit geraumer Zeit – vor allem aus modischen Cross-Over-Tendenzen heraus – auch wieder die Architekur zählen dürfen.

Betrachtet man nun das heutige Verhältnis von Architekt und Ingenieur, beinhaltet deren Kooperation die gestalterischen Aufgaben des Architekten im allgemeinen eher aus der Sicht menschlicher Wahrnehmung, ohne den technischen Teil des Bauwesens zu bewältigen. Hier setzt normalerweise der Ingenieur, für die Brauchbarkeit des baulichen Artefakts zuständig, an. So hat sich das Bauwesen – verfolgen wir seine Entwicklung seit dem 19.

not thinking scientifically when they specified their appearances, forms and materials. Leonardo da Vinci, who as early as 1500 drew objects which were not built until hundreds of years later, is a classical example of a link in the evolutionary chain of the engineering profession in which the connection between intuition and rational thought has always played a decisive role.

In the course of recent decades, the capacity for intellectual vision, which Eugene S. Ferguson calls "the inner eye", has been gradually eliminated from the natural and technical sciences through the process of education and training alone. In fact, "today's architectural engineer," according to Knut Gabriel's rigorous assessment, ". . . has heard nothing about the conceptual deliberations that lead to intellectual action". We hear in such words the call for the old uomo universale voiced with increasing urgency.

Thus Archi-Neering in particular is an explicit plea for an innovative interdisciplinary exploration of the applied art of engineering. In response to the urgent need for interaction based upon a technical-professional progression, the dialogue between art and technology is also expanding into other areas of the visual arts, to which architecture – especially in view of fashionable cross-over tendencies – may once again be counted as well.

A closer look at the contemporary relationship between the architect and the engineer reveals that their cooperation generally tends to approach the creative tasks of the architect from the viewpoint of human perception without dealing with the problems posed by the technical aspects of architecture. It is here that the work of the engineer, who is responsible for the utility of the architectural artefact, begins. Thus architecture – if we trace its history from the nineteenth century to our day – has always evolved in parallel to the accomplishments of tech-

Jahrhundert bis heute – immer parallel zu den Errungenschaften der Technik entwickelt: Die Industrialisierung brauchte ihre Hallenarchitektur. Zunehmende Geschwindigkeit nach dem Motto »Time is Money« bei wachsendem Verkehr verlangte mehr Wasserwege, Straßen, Eisenbahnstrecken und Brücken. Bereits damals war es in der Architektur vor allem die technikgerechte Form, die sich visualisierte. Technik und Bautechnik waren weder beherrschbar noch menschengerecht gestaltet.

Vor dem Hintergrund der Macht der Technik kam von Charles P. Snow die Forderung nach einem neuen Humanismus, der Technik-, Natur- und Geisteswissenschaften eint. Fritjof Capra hatte denn auch die »Wendezeit« eingeläutet, die in ganzheitlich geprägtem Denkansatz dem kopernikanisch-newtonschen Weltbild zugunsten einem neuen komplexen kontemplativen Denken ohne übersteigerte Funktionalität, Ökonomie und Technizität den Rücken kehrte. Aus dem Ingenieurwesen selbst kam folgerichtig mit Frei Otto bereits in den 50er Jahren in Deutschland der richtungsweisende Impuls des »natürlichen« Bauens, dessen Konstruktionen dem Vorbild der Natur folgten.

Innovative Konstrukte

Das Bauen Helmut Jahns und Werner Sobeks steht im Kontext konstruktivistischer Tendenzen. Gleich ihrem konstruierenden Werkprozeß handelt es sich bei ihrem geistigen Ansatz um eine dem Gehirn ähnliche »neuronale Vernetzung« (Ernst Pöppel) interdisziplinärer Wissenschaftspositionen aus Technik, Biologie, Physik, Ästhetik, Soziologie, Psychologie und Marketing. Archi-Neering entsteht überhaupt nur im Diskurs von Prozessen. Schon der kommunikative Umgang mit den beiden Persönlichkeiten läßt den Ansatz zur Offenheit jenes prozessualen

nology. Industrialisation needed its hall architecture. Increasing speed, in keeping with the principle of "time is money", and the rapid growth of traffic required more water routes, roads, railways and bridges. Even in the early years it was primarily the technically sound form that architecture reflected. Technology and architectural engineering were neither entirely tractable nor suited to human needs.

With the enormous power of technology in mind, Charles P. Snow voiced the call for a new humanism that would unite the humanities and the natural and technical sciences. Fritjof Capra had declared the dawn of an "era of change" which, on the basis of a holistic conceptual approach, turned its back on the Copernican-Newtonian view of the world in favour of a new, complex, contemplative kind of thinking free of exaggerated concern with function, economy and technology. Accordingly, the pioneering impulse of "natural building" came from the field of engineering itself in Germany during the fifties through the work of Frei Otto, whose designs were based upon models from nature.

Innovative Constructions

The work of Helmut Jahn and Werner Sobek can be located within the broad field of constructivist tendencies. Like their constructive working process, their intellectual approach is a "neuronal interaction" (Ernst Pöppel) resembling the cerebral function that involves interdisciplinary scientific positions from the fields of engineering, biology, physics, aesthetics, sociology, psychology and marketing. Archi-Neering emerges only from the discourse of processes. We recognise even in communicating with these two personalities the principle of openness inherent in their form of process-oriented thinking which appears to derive from their concept of working on

Denkens, welches sich aus dem Verständnis der Arbeit an sich selbst und von sich selbst ausgehend als permanent innovativer Werkprozeß zu erschließen scheint, erkennen. Hier gilt auch das im Denken dieser Erfinder am Technischen und Ästhetischen strukturierte »Panta rhei«-Prinzip.

In einem Lebenslabor »permanenter Konferenz« (Joseph Beuys) entsteht eine Spezies von Architektur, welche sich nur aus dem Begreifen der Notwendigkeit von Offenheit als Voraussetzung für die Findung progressiver Setzungen weiterentwickelt. Dieses Denkmodell integriert eine höchst sensible Wahrnehmung des Neuen an sich. Als wesentlicher Bestandteil der baukünstlerischen Arbeit trägt sie zu deren durch technische Erfindungen permanent neu gestalteten und rezipierten Innovationen bei. Gleich dem philosophischen Ansatz ist das bauliche Artefakt Helmut Jahns und Werner Sobeks ein dynamisches und visualisiert das künstlerisch Neue im Groysschen Sinne als einer von zeitlicher Linearität losgelösten Innovation.

So liefert uns Archi-Neering eine erkenntnistheoretische Alternative zum neuzeitlichen Wissenschaftspositivismus. Nicht irrationalistisch, sondern auf einer rationalistisch orientierten Vorstellung aufbauend, weist diese Baukunst, da sie subjektabhängig die Wirklichkeitskonstruktion einer scheinbar objektiven physikalischen Welt erklären kann, gleichsam über relativistische und skeptizistische Positionen hinaus. Jahn und Sobek überwinden in ihrem Bauen europäische Denktraditionen und nehmen Abschied von absoluten Wahrheits- und Wirklichkeitsbegriffen. Ihre Architektur transformiert Objektivität in Intersubjektivität, um Wissen und Handlungen zu binden. Damit verweisen sie gleichzeitig auf die volle Verantwortung für die natürliche und soziale Welt, in der wir leben.

Den Kontext der Innovationsfähigkeit von Archi-Neering, einer auf der anderen Seite auch künstlerisch-metaphysischen, zugleich pragmatischen Orientierung, bildet die Auseinandersetzung mit dem Thema der

themselves and from within themselves as a continuous, innovative creative process. Clearly, the "panta rhei" principle of technical and aesthetic structure that informs the thinking of these inventors applies here as well.

In a living laboratory of "continuous conference" (Joseph Beuys), a species of architecture takes form which thrives solely on recognition of the necessity for openness as a prerequisite for the discovery of progressive solutions. This conceptual model incorporates a highly sensitive perception of the new per se. As an essential ingredient of their architectural work, the model contributes to the innovations they are continually redesigning and reassessing through technical invention. Like their philosophical approach, the architectural artefact created by Helmut Jahn and Werner Sobek is dynamic. It visualises the new in art as defined by Groys as an innovation entirely independent of chronological linearity.

Thus Archi-Neering offers us an epistemological alternative to the scientific positivism of the modern era. Building not upon an irrational but upon a rationally oriented concept, this architecture, because it has the capacity to explain from a subjective standpoint the constructed reality of a seemingly objective physical world, takes us beyond the positions of relativism and scepticism. Jahn and Sobek escape the bonds of European traditions of thought in their work, bidding farewell to absolute concepts of truth and reality. Their architecture transforms objectivity into intersubjectivity, uniting knowledge and action. In this way, they also call attention to our responsibility for the natural and social world in which we live.

The context for the innovative capacity of Archi-Neering, an orientation that is both aesthetic and metaphysical, on the one hand, and pragmatic, on the other, is engendered by concern with the subject of the Maturana position in autopoietics. There can be no doubt that the will to discover ever better solutions in the service of a

Maturanaschen Position der Autopoiese. Der Wille zu immer besseren Lösungen im Dienste eines zutiefst humanistisch geprägten Ökologiebegriffs steht als Motor der kreativen Erfindungsmaschine in Stuttgart und Chicago außer Frage.

Hierbei schreibt Archi-Neering eine neue Position des Ökologiebegriffs fest, bei dem die geistigen Konzepte ihrer Baumeister, jener Stuttgarter Schule, mit amerikanischem Ökopragmatismus gepaart sind. Ökologie erwächst demnach eben nicht aus einer retrospektiven Haltung, sondern eher aus der Richtung eines von Maxeiner und Miersch beschriebenen »Ökooptimismus«. Dieser reicht bis hin zum Beschützen von Mensch und Natur im Sinne der höchst ethisch, gesellschaftlich relevant formulierten »Ökologischen Kultur« (Wilhelm Schmid), die den Begriff der Ökologie auf Umweltschutz erweitert betrachtet. Archi-Neering impliziert den von Schmid vorgeschlagenen, ökologisch orientierten Entwurf – jener anderen Form von Rationalität – eines vernetzten Denkens komplexer Zusammenhänge und Wechselwirkungen. Letztendlich geht es um das konstruktive Verhältnis des Menschen zu sich, den anderen und zur Welt.

Jahn und Sobek gelingt es auch praktisch, ihre ökologischen Ideen richtungsweisend umzusetzen; ihre Gebäude sind intelligente Energiespeicher, die ein Minimum an Technik, ökologisch abbaubare, natürliche Materialien mit einem Maximum an Komfort und ökonomisch-ökologischer Effizienz verbinden.

Ihr ökologisches Denken reflektiert das Prinzip der Selbstorganisation natürlicher Organismen. Im deutschen Bauen hatte Frei Otto diesen Mainstream seinerzeit begründet. Archi-Neering kreiert solche »natürlichen Konstruktionen« hochintelligenter autopoietischer High-Tech-Architekur. Ähnlich der Entstehung eines Gemäldes geht dem eine intensive Naturbeobachtung voraus. Wie Frei Otto beschreibt, bewirken ähnlich wie in der Natur »Pro-

profoundly humanist concept of ecology is the engine that drives the invention machine in Stuttgart and Chicago.

Archi-Neering defines a new position for the concept of ecology, in which the intellectual concepts of the master architects of the Stuttgart School are coupled with American-style environmental pragmatism. Accordingly, ecology does not develop from a retrospective view but instead from the direction of "eco-optimism" as described by Maxeiner and Miersch. This also encompasses the protection of mankind and nature in the sense of a truly ethical, socially relevant "ecological culture" (Wilhelm Schmid) that expands the concept of ecology into the realm of environmental protection. Archi-Neering implicitly embraces the Schmid's ecologically oriented concept – that other form of rationality – of interconnected thinking in terms of complex relationships and interactions. Ultimately, the goal is to develop a constructive relationship that links the human being to himself, others and the world.

Jahn und Sobek also succeed in implementing their ecological concepts in a practical, forward-looking manner. Their buildings are intelligent energy-storing structures that combine a minimum of technology, ecologically degradable, natural materials and a maximum of comfort and economic-ecological efficiency.

Their ecological thinking reflects the principle of self-organisation found in natural organisms. It was Frei Otto who founded this mainstream in German architecture during his time. Archi-Neering creates such "natural constructions" of highly intelligent, autopoietic high-tech architecture. Much like the process involved in the creation of a painting, the outcome presupposes a close observation of nature. As Frei Otto explains, "processes" determine "constructive activity", much as they do in nature as well. The nature model relates both to the technical and the aesthetic manifestation of the architecture. In contrast to that of the Bauhaus, it is not constructed in

zesse das Konstruieren«. Das Naturvorbild bezieht sich sowohl auf die technische als auch ästhetische Gestalt der Architektur. Deren Konstruktion folgt nicht wie am Bauhaus einem rein geometrisch abstrakten Funktionalismus, sondern eher einer Art »Form follows Force«, welche die Form als Folge eines definierten Kraftzustandes begreift.

Archi-Neering steht folgerichtig, gestalterisch autonome und selbstbezügliche Elemente und Formen herausarbeitend, für eine Elementarisierung als Reflexionsform. Sein transparentes Arrangement als technisch vorstellbare, räumliche Gesamtstruktur wird zu einer modellhaften Vorstellung des gesellschaftlichen Handlungsraumes und entwickelt den aufklärerischen ästhetischen Impuls als Wahrnehmungsideal zu einer Konstruktion idealer Lebensformen weiter. Wahrnehmung führt so zu gesellschaftlich relevantem Handeln.

Jahns und Sobeks zeitgenössische Gestaltung überwindet alle Wertmaßstäbe und setzt gegen die Form des Bedeutungslosen auf die Bedeutung des Lebenszusammenhangs. Denunziert doch der Konstruktivismus eines Archi-Neerings die bloße Abstraktion und verneint ihre rein ökonomische Verwertbarkeit. Wie in dem in dieser Publikation vorgelegten Gespräch verdeutlicht, geht es den Baumeistern denn auch um die konkrete Vermittlung von Kunst und Gestaltung. So bleiben ihre konstruktivistischen Utopien, ihre Ideen von der Konstruktion der Gesellschaft, ihrer immateriellen Werte wie Transparenz und Demokratie eben keine bloßen Ingenieurleistungen, sondern werden zu »Paradiestechniken« (Ulrich Reck).

Glass Houses

Im Kontext autopoietischen Bauens nach dem Archi-Neering-Prinzip spielt Glas, das Material der Moderne, auch in der Zweiten Moderne eine zentrale Rolle. Hat es doch wie bei keinem anderen Werkstoff in den letzten Jah-

accordance with pure, geometric-abstract formalism but in keeping with a principle of "form follows force" in which form is understood as the consequence of a defined state of force.

Consequently, Archi-Neering, in developing formally autonomous and self-referential elements and forms, stands for a kind of elementarisation as a form of reflection. Its transparent arrangement as a technically conceivable, total spatial structure assumes model character as a concept of social action space while nurturing the enlightened aesthetic impulse as a perceptual ideal with the goal of constructing ideal forms of life. In this way, perception generates socially relevant action.

Jahn's and Sobek's contemporary design overcomes all existing standards of value, emphasising the significance of the living context in lieu of meaningless form. Indeed, the constructivist component of Archi-Neering denounces mere abstraction and rejects its purely economic utility. As becomes quite evident in the interview presented in this catalogue, the architects are concerned with the concrete articulation of art and design. Thus their constructivist utopias, their ideas about the constructions of society, their non-material values such as transparency and democracy are much more than just engineering achievements. They represent "technologies of paradise" (Ulrich Reck).

Glass Houses

In the context of autopoietic building expressed as Archi-Neering, glass, the material of the modern era, plays a central role in the second modern period as well. Glass, more than any other building material, has experienced tremendous technological advances in recent years. The following remarks will focus upon the pioneering theme

ren einen solchen Technologieschub gegeben. Dem seinerzeit von Rowe und Slutzky bearbeiteten, richtungsweisenden Thema der Transparenz gilt im Jahn/Sobekschen Oeuvre nachfolgend unser Interesse. Glas ist wohl eines der interessantesten Materialien, die der Mensch je entdeckt hat. Gleichsam zu Technik und Kunst verwendet, blickt es auf eine 4000 Jahre alte Geschichte zurück. Die gotischen Kathedralen stellen die ersten prägnanten Beispiele für die Verbindung beider Wirkungsbereiche des transparenten Werkstoffes dar. Die Utopie von Glas hat schon vor Archi-Neering die Moderne bewegt. Ausgangspunkt für unsere Betrachtungen ist die Auseinandersetzung Michel Foucaults mit dem 18. Jahrhundert, dort mit dem Panopticon Jeremy Benthams, die das Fundament der Entwicklung einer Interaktion des Sehens und Gesehenwerdens bis zum Entertainment unserer Informationsgesellschaft bildet.

Jahn und Sobek entfernen sich von jenem, in der Moderne existenten Begriff, der Transparenz als Zustand oder Eigenschaft beschreibt. Sie gehen sogar über Sigfried Giedion, der das Phänomen eher als Standpunkt auffaßt, hinaus. Gleich dem dynamischen Prinzip ihrer autopoietischen Konstruktionen kann es in ihren Glasarchitekturen nur um eine dynamische Auffassung von Transparenz, die grenzüberschreitend wirkt, gehen. Sie ereignet sich als räumliches Phänomen beweglicher Raumhüllen. Sie visualisiert die Erfahrungswirklichkeit der konstruktivistischen Architektenphilosophie. Dem gesellschaftlichen Rhythmus angepaßt, werden ihre Wände zu Bildträgern der von Virilio seit langem thematisierten Geschwindigkeit der Weltbilder.

Die Transparenz-Architektur Helmut Jahns und Werner Sobeks überschreitet die Grenzen zwischen Out- und Indoor, Öffentlichem und Privatem, Licht und Schatten, Wärme und Kälte. Im Kontext ihrer auf die Interaktion von Werk und Rezipient zielende künstlerische Konzeption evozieren beliebig pluralistische Betrachterpositionen per-

of transparency, as described by Rowe and Slutzky, in the work of Jahn and Sobek. Glass is certainly one of the most interesting materials ever discovered by mankind. Used in both engineering and art, it looks back upon a history of some 4,000 years. The Gothic cathedrals provide the earliest noteworthy examples of attempts to join the two fields of application together. The utopia of glass inspired modernists long before Archi-Neering was born. The point of departure for our reflections is Michel Foucault's study of the eighteenth century and the panopticon of Jeremy Bentham, which forms the foundation for the growth of interaction between seeing and being seen that extends into the realm of entertainment in our Information Society.

Jahn and Sobek distance themselves from the idea of transparency, already formulated in the modern period, as a state or a property. They go even further in this context than Sigfried Giedion, who viewed the phenomenon rather as a standpoint. Given the dynamic principle underlying their autopoietic constructions, their glass architectures can only embody a dynamic definition of transparency that transcends all boundaries. It is expressed as a spatial phenomenon involving moveable shells. It gives visible form to the perceptual reality of constructivist architectural philosophy. Adapted to societal rhythms, their walls become image-bearing media for the speeding images of the world that have been the object of Virilio's studies for many years.

Helmut Jahn's and Werner Sobek's architecture of transparency blurs the boundaries between indoors and outdoors, public and private, light and shadow, warm and cold. In the context of their artistic concept and its focus upon interaction between the work and its perceiver, randomly pluralistic viewer positions continuously evoke dynamically changing, visual-aesthetic states and perceived realities.

Jahn and Sobek see transparent architecture as the creation of intellectual free spaces. Non-hierarchical

manent dynamisch-veränderte, visuell-ästhetische Zustände und Erfahrungswirklichkeiten. Für Jahn und Sobek heißt transparentes Bauen geistige Freiräume erschließen. Enthierachisierte Raumstrukturen im Innenbereich, deren interaktive Transparenz offene Kommunikationsstrukturen schaffen, sollen Kreativität, Klarheit und Offenheit im Denken und Handeln fördern; die Architektur wird zur Sehmaschine und kreiert eine Atmosphäre für zeitgenössische Managementprozesse globaler Wirtschaftszentralen, deren heutige autopoietische Firmenphilosophie des »Lernenden Unternehmens« (Helmut Geiselhart) längst schon im Kontext Foucaultscher Lebenskunst als Artefakt betrachtet wird.

Bereits Sergej Eisenstein – in seinen Ideen für das Drehbuch zu Glass House vom gläsernen Hochhaus Mies van der Rohes beeinflußt – war von der interaktiven Dramatik sichtbarer Ereignisse als Transformator oder Destabilisator sozialer und gesellschaftlicher Konventionen begeistert. Eisenstein weist explizit auf die Funktionen der Sehmaschine hin: Aufklärung und Kontrolle. Das »Auge« Le Corbusiers macht gleichermaßen seine objektivierende, individuierende Qualität deutlich. Michel Foucault ist derjenige, der schließlich die Thematik erstmalig aus der Architektur ableitet.

Operative Transparenz heißt bei Jahn und Sobek, daß sie ihre Gebäude in einen eigenen Organismus tranformieren, der zu seiner Umwelt Beziehungen eingeht: Als Lichtorgan übernimmt er selbständig die Regulierung von Licht und Klima sowie die Energiegewinnung. Durch eine Schichtung von hintereinander gestaffelten Hüllen und Schleier kommt es letztendlich zur Auflösung des traditionellen Gebäudekerns. Architekt und Ingenieur fassen im Sinne von Joseph Beuys ihre transparenten Membranen als unterschiedliche Aggregatzustände auf.

Die Tendenz der Abstraktion in der transparenten Architektur setzt sich fort: Vormalige noch unter dem Ein-

interior spatial structures, whose interactive transparency engenders open communication structures, are meant to promote creativity, clarity and openness in thought and action. Architecture becomes a vision machine and establishes an atmosphere for the management processes of contemporary global business headquarters, whose current autopoietic corporate philosophy of the "learning enterprise" (Helmut Geiselhart) has long been viewed within the context of Foucault's art of living as an artefact.

Even Sergei Eisenstein – whose ideas for the screenplay for Glass House were influenced by Mies van der Rohe's glass skyscraper – was fascinated by the interactive drama of visible events as transforming or destabilising agents of social conventions. Eisenstein refers explicitly to the functions of the vision machine: enlightenment and control. In the same sense, Le Courbusier's "eye" illustrates its capacity to objectivise and individualise. Michel Foucault was ultimately the first to derive the theme from architecture.

Operative transparency in the architecture of Jahn and Sobek means that they transform their building into an autonomous organism, which then enters into relationships with its environment. It acts as a light-processing organ, regulating light, climate and the conversion of energy. The layered arrangement of building shells and screens ultimately leads to the dissolution of the traditional building core. The architect and the engineer regard their transparent membranes in Joseph Beuys' sense as a collection of different aggregate states.

The tendency towards abstraction in transparent architecture is sustained. Former functional elements of technical installations still given visual expression under the influence of the early Stuttgart School for didactic purposes are reduced to linear high-tech developments. Their future, shaped by the process of increasing dematerialisation approaches "total transparency" (Jacques Herzog), an architecture of nothingness. The disappear-

fluß der frühen Stuttgarter Schule aus didaktischen Gründen visualisierte Funktionsträger technischer Installationen reduzieren sich linear zur High-Tech-Entwicklung. Deren vom Prozeß zunehmender Entmaterialisierung geprägte Zukunft steht vor der »totalen Transparenz« (Jacques Herzog), einer Architektur des Nichts. Das Verschwinden der Architektur überwindet schließlich die konventionelle Trennung der Sphären von Drinnen und Draußen gänzlich und führt zur Einheit mit der konstruierten Erfahrungsrealität. Das Gebäude wird so zur Projektionsfläche von Lebenssimulationen.

Werner Sobek nimmt bereits heute das Verschwinden der Architektur wörtlich: Er entwirft ephemere, temporäre, recyclebare Architektur aus Textilien. Seine Formen sind zeitgenössische Geometrie: Segmente, Brüche, Falten.

Urbane Systeme

Die Architektur Helmut Jahns und Werner Sobeks ist in ihren kontextuellen und situationistischen Bezügen eng mit Tendenzen deutscher Stadtentwicklung verwoben. Die Baukünstler interessieren sich für die gesellschaftliche Relevanz des öffentlichen Raumes; die Auseinandersetzung mit Öffentlichkeit ist integraler Bestandteil ihrer Arbeit. So beziehen sie urbanistische Konzepte mit ein. Gemäß der prinzipiellen Offenheit der Architektur sind die Gebäude zumeist durchgehbar. Der öffentliche Raum wird auf diese Weise eingebunden, die Stadtstruktur Bestandteil des Bauwerks. Bei der Messe in Shanghai entsteht erstmalig ein kompletter künstlicher Stadtraum mit Park und religiösem Tempelbereich. Der Flughafen München ist um einen urbanen Bereich gruppiert; Hochhäuser übernehmen in Bonn und Berlin die zeitgenössische visuelle Funktion der mittelalterlichen Kathedrale.

ance of architecture eventually obliterates the conventional dividing line between the spheres of inside and out, thus paving the way for unification with the constructed reality of experience. In this way, the building becomes a projection screen for simulations of life.

Werner Sobek is already taking the disappearance of architecture literally: He designs ephemeral, temporary, recyclable textile architectures. His forms are contemporary geometry: segments, breaks, folds.

Urban Systems

In its contextual and situational relationships, the architecture of Helmut Jahn and Werner is closely interwoven with currents in urban development in Germany. The architectural artists are interested in the social relevance of public space; public discourse is an integral part of their work. And thus they incorporate concepts of urbanism as well. In keeping with the fundamental principle of openness in architecture, most of their buildings are open-ended, thus integrating public space and making urban structure a component of the architecture. At the trade fair in Shanghai they are building the world's first completely artificial urban setting with a park and an area comprising a religious temple. The Munich airport is arranged around an urban section. Skyscrapers in Bonn and Berlin assume the contemporary visual function of medieval cathedrals.

Archi-Neering manifests itself in the discussion regarding urban development. Jürgen Paul formulates the combination of two urban forms for Berlin accordingly – the "horizontal, spatially and physically enclosed city of the eighteenth and nineteenth centuries and the vertical city of the twentieth, the American downtown with the open, transparent architecture of the (second) modern period", in which Jahn and Sobek find their rightful place.

Archi-Neering manifestiert sich in der Stadtentwicklungsdiskussion. Entsprechend formuliert Jürgen Paul für das neue Berlin die Kombination zweier Stadtformen – der »horizontalen, räumlich und körperlich geschlossenen Stadt des 18. und 19. Jahrhunderts mit der vertikalen Stadt des 20. Jahrhunderts, dem amerikanischen Downtown der offenen, transparenten Architektur der (zweiten) Moderne –, in der sich auch Jahn und Sobek wiederfinden. Im Gegensatz zum Debis-Center, welches noch das von Josef Paul Kleihues mit skeptischem Blick auf den Städtebau der 60er Jahre formulierte Konzept der »Kritischen Rekonstruktion« verfolgt, definiert das Sony-Center bereits das andere, amerikanische Urbanismus-Konzept, das die Verknüpfung beider Typen verdeutlicht. Der in Abschnitte gegliederte Großkomplex amerikanischen Typus' mit multifunktionalem Innenleben ist die artifizielle Stadt in der Stadt, eine Plazasituation, die das Leben von der Straße in den Innenbereich zieht. Collageartig wurden hier beide Stadttypen montiert. Als Modell stehen solche Projekte von Jahn/Sobek an der Schwelle zur Simulationsstadt des nächsten Jahrtausends.

Archi-Neering-Urbanistik verabschiedet sich städtebaulich vom Modell der europäischen Stadt, da dieses im Widerspruch zu den Bedürfnissen der Gesellschaft von Morgen steht. Hierbei sehen die Baumeister ihr Hochhaus im zentralen, weit ausgreifenden System, das durch funktionale arbeitsteilige Struktur in der Horizontalen und Vertikalen ein Bild geformt hat, als Zeichen. Dabei ist ihnen die visuelle Destruktion der Illusion vom humanistischen Ideal der europäischen Stadt, die sich kontinuierlich von Innen nach Außen entwickelt hat, bewußt. Jahn und Sobek gestalten die aktuelle Entwicklung nach den Forderungen globalisierter Systeme rasanten Wachstums. Die Stadt hat für sie als Kunstwerk ihren autonomen Werkbegriff längst verloren. Sie betrachten sie nach den Prinzipien ihrer Architektur als Organismus, der sich flexibel, dynamisch, den entstehenden Bedürfnissen anpaßt;

In contrast to the Debis Centre, which still follows the principles the concept of "critical reconstruction", articulated by Josef Paul Kleihues with a sceptical glance at the urban architecture of the sixties, the Sony Centre already defines the other, American concept of urbanism that exemplifies the union of the two types. Divided into segments, the large, American-style complex with its multi-purpose inner life is an artificial city-within-a-city, a plaza setting that draws life from the streets into its interior. Here, the two urban types are juxtaposed collage-style. As models, this and similar projects by Jahn and Sobek stand at the threshold of the simulation city of the coming millennium.

As regards urban architecture, the urbanistics of Archi-Neering abandon the model of the European city, as it conflicts with the needs of the society of tomorrow. The architects see their high-rise buildings as part of a centralised yet far-reaching system whose functional structure of labour distribution forms an image, a symbol. Yet they are fully aware of the visual destruction of the illusion of the humanist ideal of the European city that has progressed continuously from inside to outside. Jahn and Sobek shape the current course of development in accordance with the demands of globalised systems of explosive growth. As a work of art, the city has long since lost its quality as an autonomous creation in their view. True to their own architectural principles, they regard it as an organism capable of adapting flexibly and dynamically to arising needs, viewing the city thus as a complex technical, economic, social and cultural construct in which the ideal of an ordered society no longer exists. In its place, they plan definitive urbanistic concepts in the context of the paradigmatic shift between rationalism and irrationalism that has been in effect since the nineteenth century. In the final analysis, each them can identify with what Mike Davis describes as the "City of Quartz", and they see an aggressive approach to that as the

die Stadt also ein Konstrukt technischer, wirtschaftlicher, sozialer und kultureller Komplexität, dessen Ideal einer geordneten Gesellschaft lange schon nicht mehr existent ist. Vielmehr planen sie gemäß des seit dem 19. Jahrhundert bestehenden Paradigmenwechsels zwischen Rationalismus und Irrationalismus urbanistisch prägende Konzepte. Im Endeffekt können sich beide mit der von Mike Davis beschriebenen »City of Quartz« identifizieren und sehen nur im offensiven Umgang mit ihr eine Chance, und zwar die, die Zukunft unseres Lebens selbst zu gestalten. Jahn und Sobek denken urbanistisch flexibel. Ihre zeitgenössische Haltung zeichnet sich durch situatives Verhalten aus, nämlich dort architektonische Strukturen vorzusehen, wo sie sich wie der Organismus der Natur ein- beziehungsweise anpassen können, um zu überleben. Diese Haltung geht bis zu den ephemeren Werken Werner Sobeks, die nur temporär für eine bestimmte Situation und Funktion existieren. Ihre Dynamik trägt der Mobilität unserer Gesellschaft Rechnung, in der global agiert und situativ entschieden werden muß. Diese lebt in einer Stadt für den von Richard Sennett definierten flexiblen Menschen, der sich den Zukunftsaufgaben, der Welt des »Drift« und der Geschwindigkeit der Entwicklung eines neuen Kapitalismus stellt. Archi-Neering komponiert Orte, wo Gemeinschaft entstehen kann, um der Sprachlosigkeit zu entkommen.

Öffentliche Artefakte

Die Baukunst des Architekten und Ingenieurs befindet sich auf dem Weg in die Immaterialisierung. Sie nimmt eine ähnliche Haltung ein, wie wir sie auch in der Entwicklung aktueller Artefakte vorfinden. Ihre ikonographisch-historischen Vorbilder sind indes Bauwerke wie etwa der geplante Gläserne Turm von Mies van der Rohe aus dem Jahre 1919, in dessen fiktiver historischer Nähe ein Hochhaus von Jahn/Sobek gebaut wird, oder aber Architek-

only chance we have to take the design of our future into our own hands. Jahn und Sobek think in terms of flexible urbanism. Their entirely contemporary approach is characterised by situation-based action; in other words, they plan architectural structures in settings in which they can integrate themselves and adapt in the manner of natural organisms in order to survive. This approach extends even to the ephemeral works of Werner Sobek, ad hoc structures created only for specific functions and situations. Their dynamic quality reflects the mobility of our society, in which action is global and decisions must be made on the basis of situations. This quality is alive in the city for the flexible human being as defined by Richard Sennett, who actively confronts the tasks of the future, the world of drift and the pace of development of a new capitalism. Archi-Neering composes places in which communities can form and liberate themselves from the chains of speechlessness.

Public Artefacts

The building art of the architect and the engineer finds itself on a path towards dematerialisation. It assumes a posture much like that which is evident in the development of current artefacts. Among its iconographic, historical models are such edifices as the Mies van der Rohe's planned Glass Tower of 1919, in whose fictitious historical vicinity Jahn and Sobek are currently building a skyscraper, or the architecture of the Bauhaus successors in Chicago, plans for territory of which have already been drawn up. Yet this integrative concept of Archi-Neering points beyond its the accomplishments of its predecessors, as it not only seeks to affect and aestheticise the rapid pace of technological development but to contextualise it as well.

Finally, taking Lucius Burckhardt's argument that design is invisible at face value, it is clear that Jahn and

tur der Bauhaus-Nachfolge in Chicago, für dessen Territorium ein Entwurf vorliegt. Das integrale Konzept von Archi-Neering weist jedoch über seine Vorläufer hinaus; indem es die rasante technologische Entwicklung nicht nur mitbestimmt und ästhetisiert, sondern auch kontextualisiert.

Um letztendlich die These von Lucius Burckhardt wörtlich zu nehmen, daß Design unsichtbar sei, wird es bei Jahn/Sobek zukünftig noch mehr um die Schaffung von Atmosphären, Situationen, Milieus gehen. Denken wir hier etwa an Visionen eines »test module for living in space« (Kevin Kelly) oder an Analogien zur virtuellen Realität des Internets als fraktale Inselvision, bei der von einer Funktion zur nächsten gesurft werden kann, wie Stephenson unsere zukünftige Welt beschreibt.

Als Mixtur aus Skulptur und Architektur sind die Arbeiten des Archi-Neering-Teams Artefakte sozialer und politischer Kontextualisierung, setzen doch die transparenten Systeme in der Tradition großer Glasbauten von Ausstellungsgebäuden bis hin zur Vitrine gleichermaßen den Betrachter in ein mediales Verhältnis zu den Dingen. In letzter Konsequenz handelt es sich hier um transparente Installationen, welche gleich dem situationistisch-konzeptuellen Arbeiten Dan Grahams, den frühen Schaufensterinstallationen, etwa Begriffe der Identität, Subjektivität und Objektivität in Frage stellen. Das High-Tech-Artefakt wird so zum Ausstellungsort und Kunstwerk, das unsere Gesellschaft analysiert.

Sobek will be even more concerned with the creation of atmospheres, situations, milieus in the future. It is appropriate to call to mind in this context the visions of a "test module for living in space" (Kevin Kelly) or analogies to the virtual reality of the Internet as a fractal, insular vision in which we surf from one function to the next, as Stephenson has described our future world.

As mixtures of sculpture and architecture, the works created by the Archi-Neering team are artefacts of social and political contextualisation, as their transparent systems in the tradition of large-scale glass structures, from exhibition buildings to showcases, place the observer in a kind of medialised relationship to the things around him. Ultimately, they are transparent installations which, like the situational-conceptual works of Dan Graham – the early showcase window installations, for example – question such concepts as identity, subjectivity and objectivity. The high-tech artefact assumes the character of an exhibition site and a work of art that subjects society to analytical scrutiny.

Nicola Kuhn im Gespräch mit Helmut Jahn und Werner Sobek

Architektur heute

KUHN: Architektur heute, am Ende des 20. Jahrhunderts: Welche gesellschaftliche Funktion kommt ihr zu? Welche Rolle spielen da der Architekt und der Ingenieur?

JAHN: Die Aufgabe der Architektur ist es, die wesentlichen Eigenschaften einer Gesellschaft zu verkörpern und ins Bauliche umzusetzen. Sie reagiert auf den Zeitgeist und muß mit den entsprechenden technischen Möglichkeiten und Notwendigkeiten umgehen. Die Architektur heute soll im Unterschied zur Moderne, so glaube ich, nicht die Gesellschaft verändern, aber sie kann sie widerspiegeln und die Gesellschaft verbessern.

SOBEK: Architektur ist gestaltete Umwelt. Somit ist sie ein Spiegel der Gesellschaft, wie sie sich verhält und was sie sich wünscht. Das ist auch Thema der aktuellen Architekturdiskussion, zum Beispiel in Berlin. Dort werden Projektionen eines Stadtbildes gewünscht, Rückwärtsprojektionen auf das vergangene Jahrhundert.

KUHN: Ist es da nicht die Aufgabe des Architekten, den Blick wieder nach vorne zu richten?

JAHN: Das ist ein grundsätzlicher Streit, wie die Architekten auf die Herausforderungen zu reagieren haben oder welche Mittel sie benutzen sollen. Unsere Architektur hat eine sehr optimistische Haltung. Werner Sobek und ich, wir glauben an den Fortschritt und daran, daß eine positive Entwicklung durch das Neue entsteht – doch nicht einfach, um etwas Neues zu machen, sondern um die Bauten und dadurch die Hüllen für unsere Situation zu verbessern. Durch die Globalisierung haben wir heute eine vollkommen andere Situation; alles steht mit allem in

einem globalen Zusammenhang; man kann in ein paar Tagen die Welt umreisen. Daran scheiden sich auch die Geister: Wie weit soll man, kann man gehen als Architekt, wie weit muß man den Ort berücksichtigen? Das widerspricht heutzutage vollkommen dem, wie sich Politik und Gesellschaft verhalten. Man versteckt sich hinter Argumenten, um den Status quo zu wahren, und bevorzugt den Rückblick auf die Geschichte. So will man in Berlin Werte wiedererwecken, die in unserer Gesellschaft gar nicht mehr vorhanden sind. Ob dieser Weg richtig ist, das wird erst die Geschichte entscheiden.

SOBEK: Sicherlich gilt auch die Qualität der Vielfalt. Helmut Jahn und ich, wir sind davon überzeugt, daß die Geisteshaltung eines Menschen durch seine architektonische Umgebung beeinflußt wird. Ob ich mich in einem Haus mit kleinen Fenstern befinde, das klimatisiert und komplett mit Steinplatten verkleidet ist oder das durch Sonnenenergie und ähnliches energetisch genährt wird, das transparent ist, großzügig ist, in dem man die Jahreszeiten wechseln sieht – das hat Einfluß auf die Haltung der Menschen, die in einem solchen Gebäude leben.

KUHN: Herr Jahn, Sie haben einmal gesagt, daß wir uns gegenwärtig in der Phase der Zweiten Moderne befinden. Was genau verstehen Sie darunter, und inwiefern verbindet Sie dies mit Herrn Sobek als Ingenieur?

JAHN: Die erste Moderne war die vom Bauhaus und Mies van der Rohe. Es war der Beginn einer rationalen, technischen Architektur, die von modernen Materialien Gebrauch gemacht hat und gedanklich eigentlich

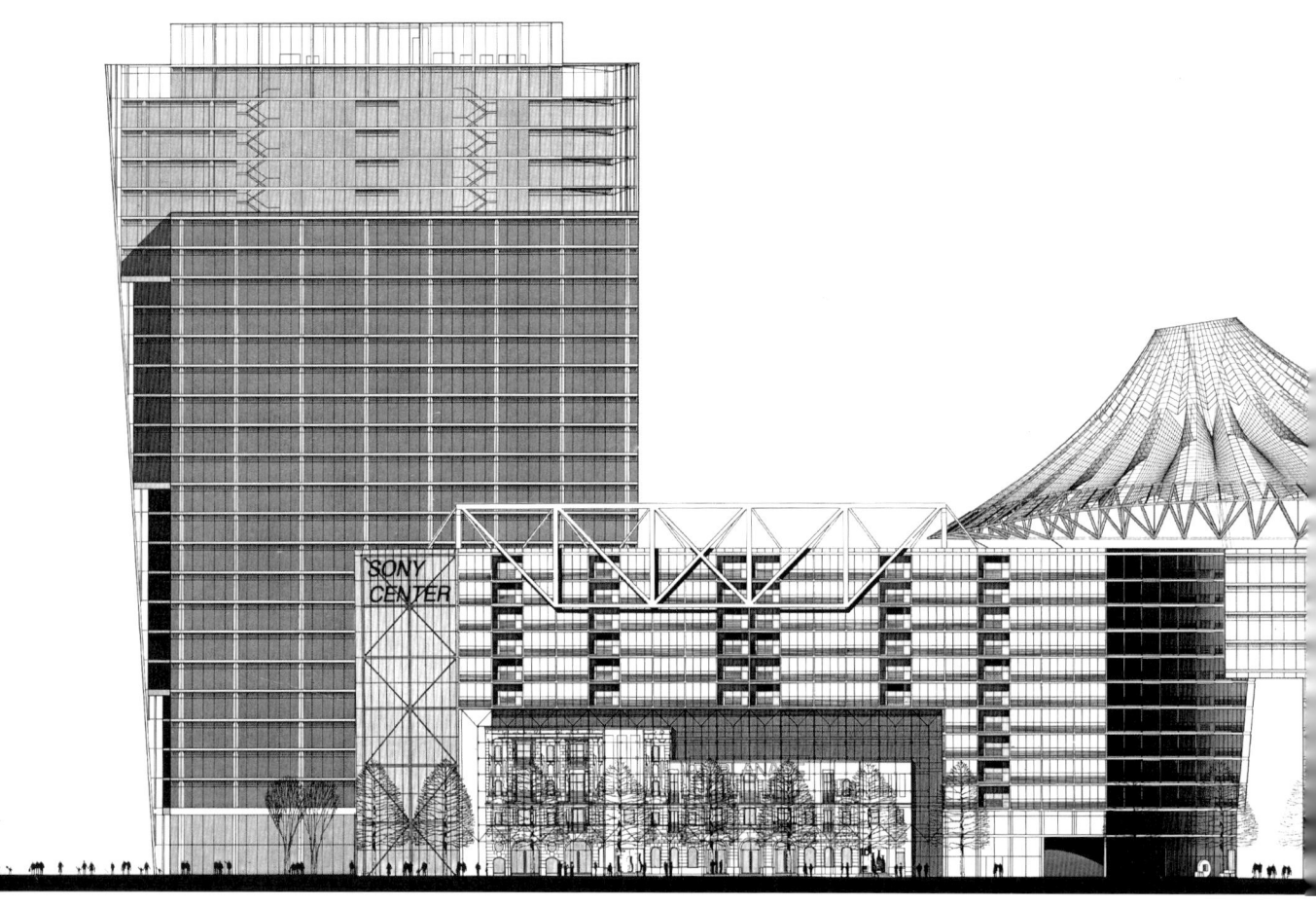

Gesamtansicht, Computerzeichnung
General view, computer drawing

immer den Möglichkeiten der Zeit voraus war. Die Apartmentgebäude von Mies van der Rohe waren vollkommen aus Glas und hatten Probleme, die man sich heute nicht mehr wünschen würde. Darin ist es zu heiß geworden, und es hat hineingeregnet. Aber gerade deswegen war Mies ein Genie. Er hat es fertiggebracht, die Menschen zu überzeugen, daß diese Dinge den neuen Bedürfnissen angepaßt werden müssen, aber daß sie an sich funktionieren. Vor allem hat er die Industrie gezwungen, entsprechende Materialien zu entwickeln, die diese Architektur ermöglichen. Durch diese Haltung hat er für die Architektur wirklich Fortschritt erzielt. Heute, in der Zweiten Moderne, haben wir viel mehr technologische Möglichkeiten sowohl bei den Materialien als auch in der Herstellung, in der Berechnung, in der Simulation. Wir können viel weiter gehen und mit einer ähnlichen Haltung eigentlich sehr viel sicherer sein. Heutzutage kann man allerdings nicht mehr solche Risiken eingehen wie diese Helden, die »heroes« der Ersten Moderne. Sie waren in gewisser Hinsicht wie Alexander der Große in der Antike oder die Könige im Mittelalter, die noch selbst ganz vorne in den Krieg ritten. Heutzutage sind wir nicht mehr vorneweg, denn wir können uns auf Kenntnisse berufen, die uns mehr Möglichkeiten geben und es uns erlauben, einstigen Visionen in sicherer Weise näher zu kommen.

Damals, als der Berliner Senatsbaudirektor Hans Stimmann zu mir gesagt hat, daß zuviel Glas an den Sony-Gebäuden am Potsdamer Platz sei, das habe nichts mit Berlin zu tun, vor allem der Turm, haben wir ihm ein Bild

Sony-Center am Potsdamer Platz in Berlin

Das städtebauliche Konzept für das Sony-Center am Potsdamer Platz in Berlin basiert auf der Überlegung einer kritischen Rekonstruktion der Stadt und geht somit weit über den vorgegebenen Masterplan hinaus. Mit dem Gebäudekomplex wird eine städtische Situation mit Plätzen und Räumen, mit Wegen und Passagen geschaffen, in welche die wenigen übriggebliebenen Teile der ursprünglich vorhandenen Bebauung integriert werden. Der architektonische Ausdruck wird durch eine Vielzahl extrem transparenter Glaskonstruktionen geprägt, die Gebäudehüllen werden in großen Bereichen zur gläsernen Haut.

The urban architectural concept for the Sony Center at Potsdamer Platz is based upon the idea of a critical reconstruction of the city and thus goes far beyond the scope of the existing master plan. The design of the building complex creates an urban setting with walkways and passages into which the few remaining elements of the original architecture are integrated. The architectural expression is shaped by a large number of extremely transparent glass constructions. Significant portions of the building shells form a glass skin.

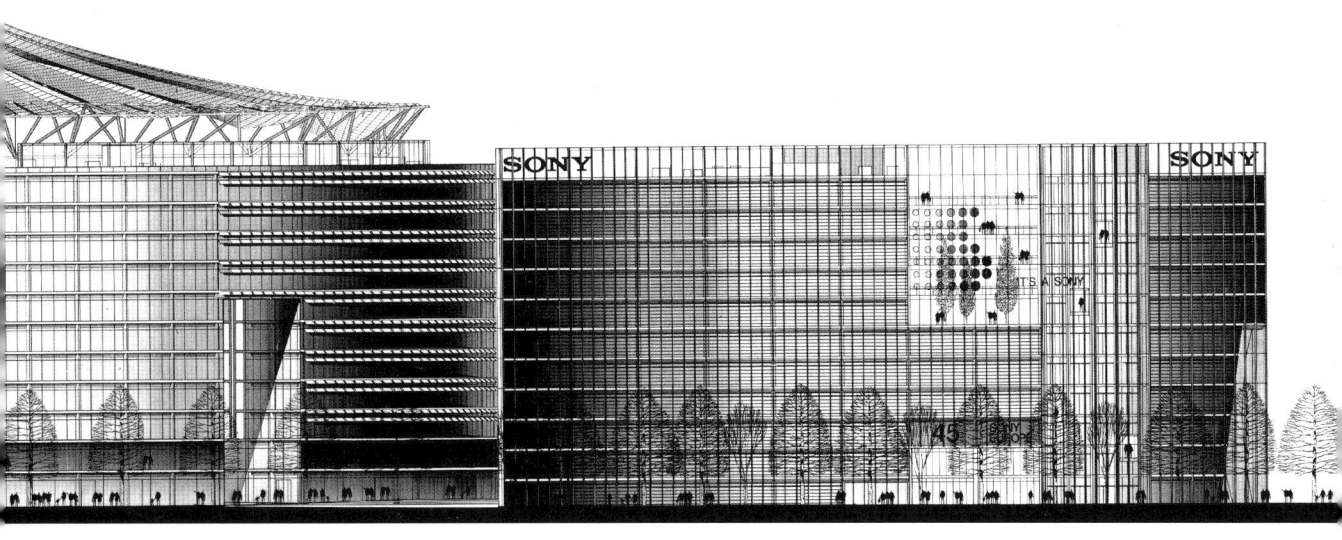

gezeigt von dem Hochhaus, das Mies 1919 in der Friedrichstraße geplant hatte. Und ich habe Stimmann erwidert: »Das ist auch Berlin, aber das ist noch nie gebaut worden.« Heute ist es erst möglich, Gebäude mit einer minimalen Technik, einer maximalen Transparenz und zugleich komfortabel zu bauen. Das ist die Beziehung zwischen Erster und Zweiter Moderne, aber auch der Unterschied.

SOBEK: In der sogenannten Ersten Moderne wurde die Industrialisierung in die Architektur eingeführt. Es wurden neue Werkstoffe wie großflächige Glastafeln, Stahlprofile, anodiertes Aluminium und ähnliches durch Mies und andere ins Bauen eingebracht, auch wenn der technologische Standard in der Planung für heutige Verhältnisse vollkommen unzureichend war. Mies hat es damals auf seinem breiten Rücken aushalten können, daß die Apartments im Sommer überhitzt waren und im Winter Eisblumen trugen. Das geht heute nicht mehr, denn nach dem ersten nicht funktionierenden Gebäude wären wir Planer ruiniert.

JAHN: Oder nehmen wir die Betonstützen: Die hatten eine Stahlverkleidung außen, aber keine Isolierung. Wir arbeiten heute wesentlich konfliktträchtiger. Alles führt gleich zum Prozeß, so daß wir kein Risiko eingehen können: Alles muß sicher, alles muß perfekt sein. Der Drang, etwas auszuprobieren, war damals viel stärker. Damals wurde mit Einfachverglasung gebaut, heute ist das nicht mehr genug. Damals wurde nicht klimatisiert, heute muß in den Gebäuden ein angenehmes Klima geschaffen werden. Genau das bringt uns beide, Werner

Sony-Center am Potsdamer Platz in Berlin

Entwurfszeichnungen zum Hochhaus und zur Integration des
Hotel Esplanade
*Design drawing for the high-rise building and the integration
of the Hotel Esplanade*

Rechte Seite: Erdgeschoßgrundriß, Lage des Forums und
des Hotels Esplanade
*Right: Ground floor plan, location of the forum and the
Hotel Esplanade*

Sobek und mich, zusammen. Wir sind der Überzeugung, daß Architektur viel mit der Lösung technischer Probleme zu tun hat und nicht nur mit Ästhetik und Form. Sicher, Ästhetik und Form sind immer in der Architektur dabei. Aber der gute Ingenieur denkt immer an die ästhetischen Konsequenzen seiner Entscheidungen, während der gute Architekt immer auch an die technischen Konsequenzen der Formen denkt, die er schafft. Wenn Frank Gehry heute ein Gebäude schafft, benutzt er im Entwurfs-, im Fertigungs- und im Bauprozeß den Computer, durch den er fast jede Form realisieren kann. Mit seiner Hilfe ist heutzutage jede Form in Einzelteile zu zerlegen, dann entsprechend auch zu fabrizieren. In diesem Fall benutzt man die Technik, um eine ästhetische Idee umzusetzen.

SOBEK: Wir sollten erklären, wie wir zu dieser Haltung gekommen sind. Unsere Idee von Architektur geht noch weiter, insbesondere bei den neueren Bauten, die auch durch Beiträge anderer entstehen. Zum Beispiel Matthias Schuler, ein Stuttgarter Gebäudeenergiefachmann: Durch ihn kommen gebäudeenergetische Konzepte hinzu, die weit über den Standard hinausweisen und mit solarer Energiegewinnung, Bodenkühlungen und ähnlichen Dingen arbeiten, so daß der Technikapparat auf das absolute Minimum reduziert werden kann. Dieses Minimum ist so simpel, daß es sich auch einfach installieren läßt. Beispielsweise bei den Betondecken: Sie werden mit kaltem Wasser durchflossen und wirken im Sommer als große Kühlflächen an dem Gebäude. Es muß keine kalte Luft mehr eingeblasen werden, man hat die Kühlrippen quasi direkt über dem Kopf. Als Konsequenz folgt, daß

EG

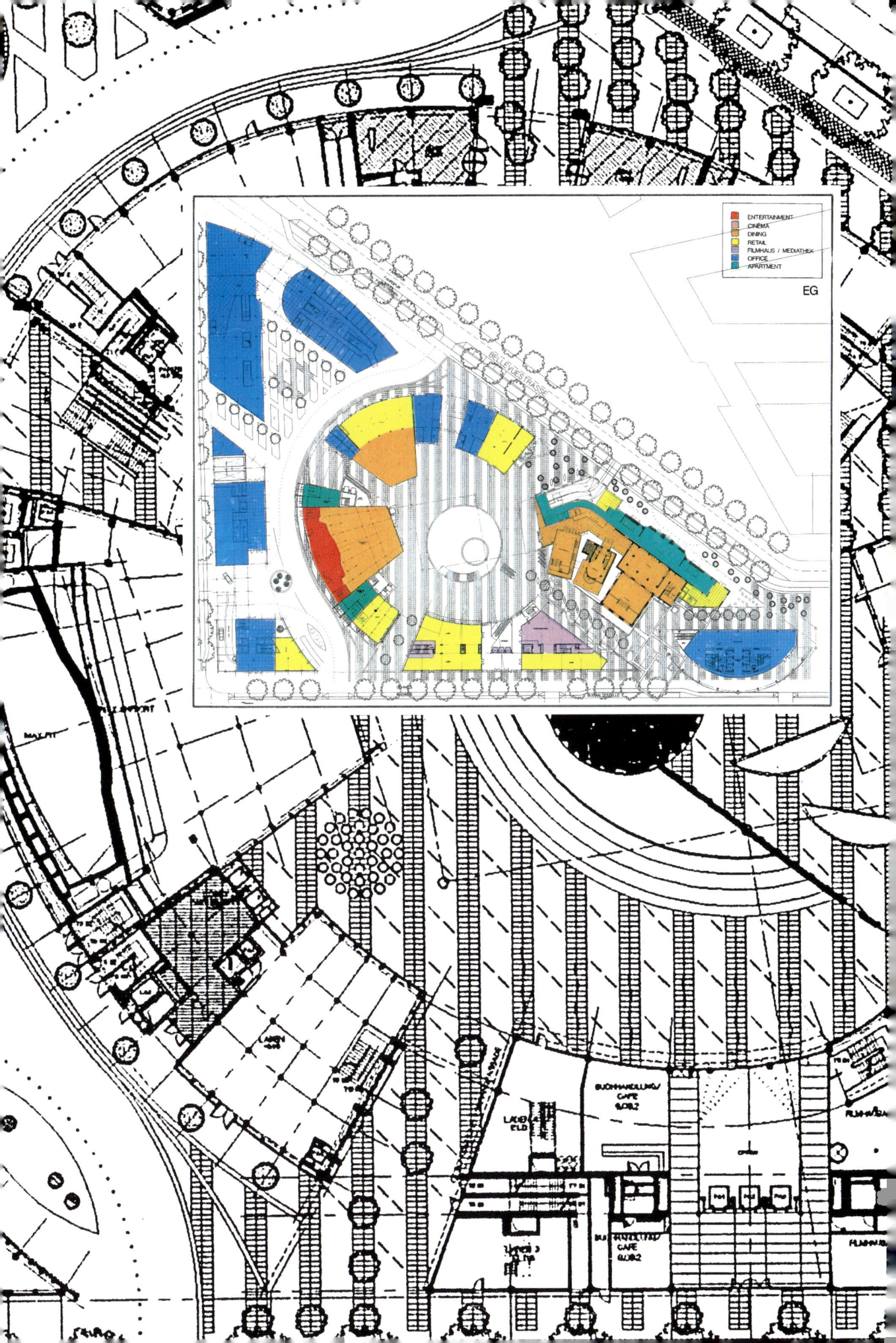

ENTERTAINMENT
CINEMA
DINING
RETAIL
FILMHAUS / MEDIATHEK
OFFICE
APARTMENT

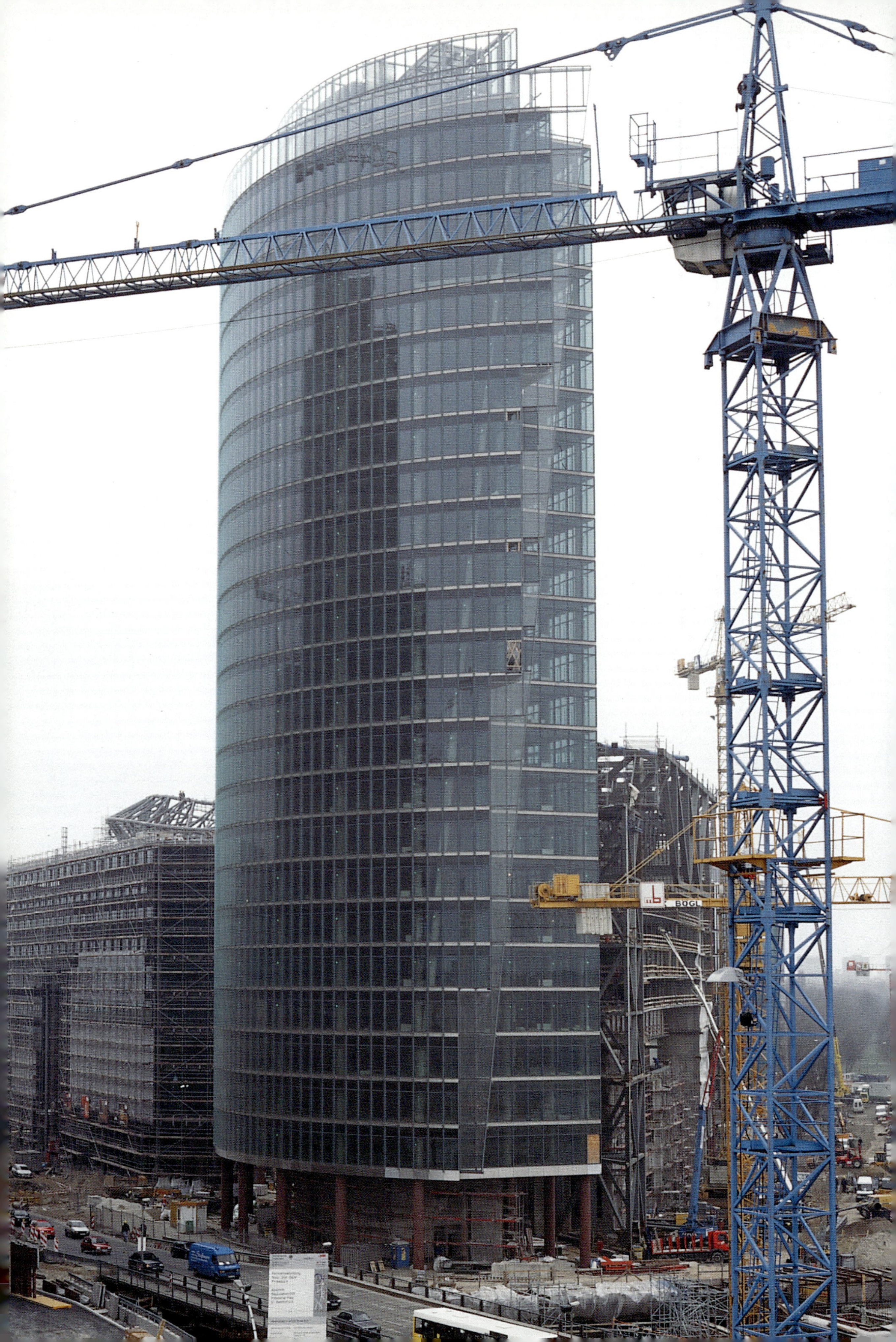
BÖGL

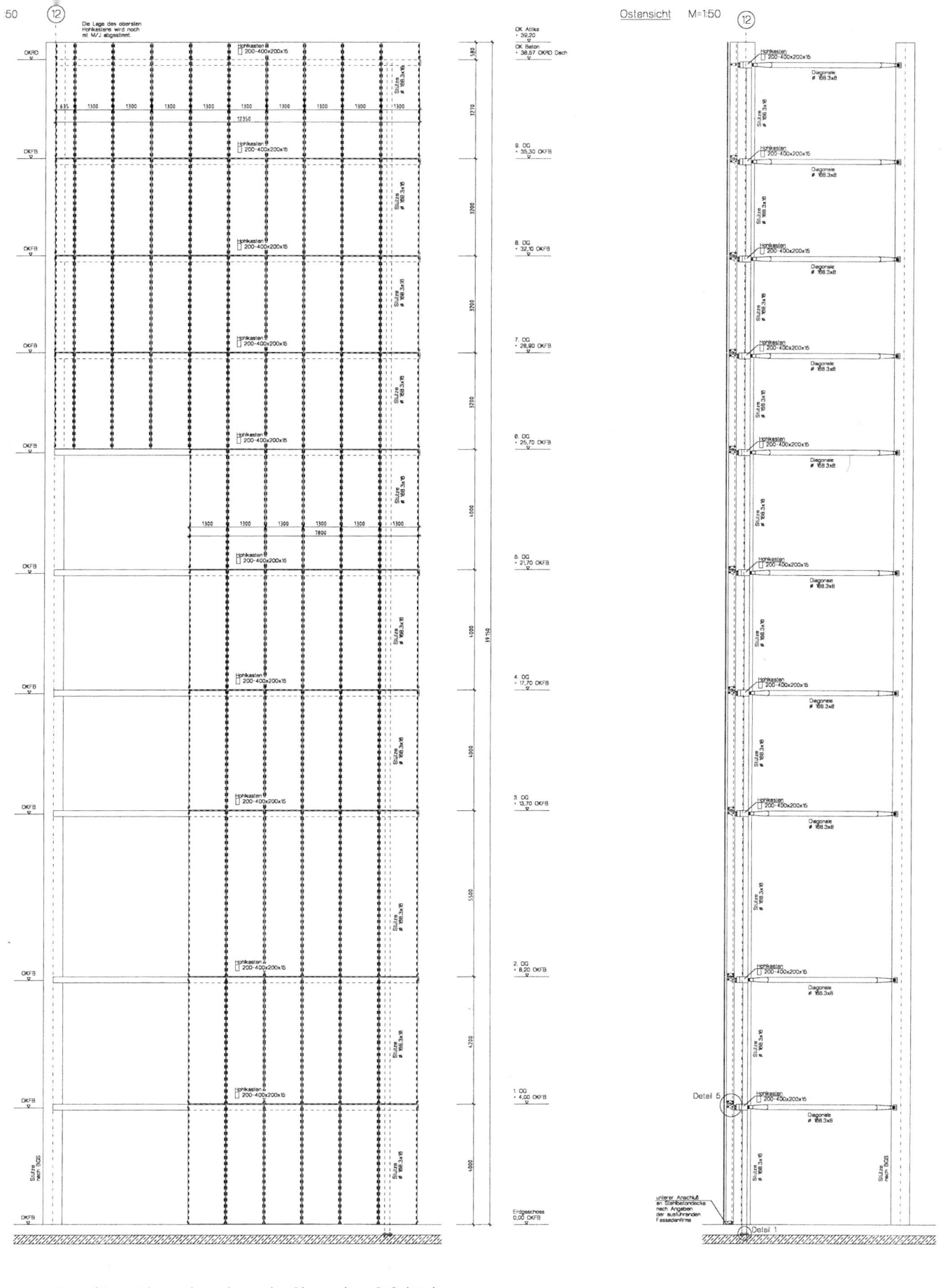

Konstruktionszeichnung der auskragenden Glaswand am C-Gebäude
Construction drawing for the overhanging glass wall on Building C
Linke Seite: Hochhaus A-Building kurz vor Fertigstellung der Fassade
Left: High-rise Building A shortly before completion of the facade

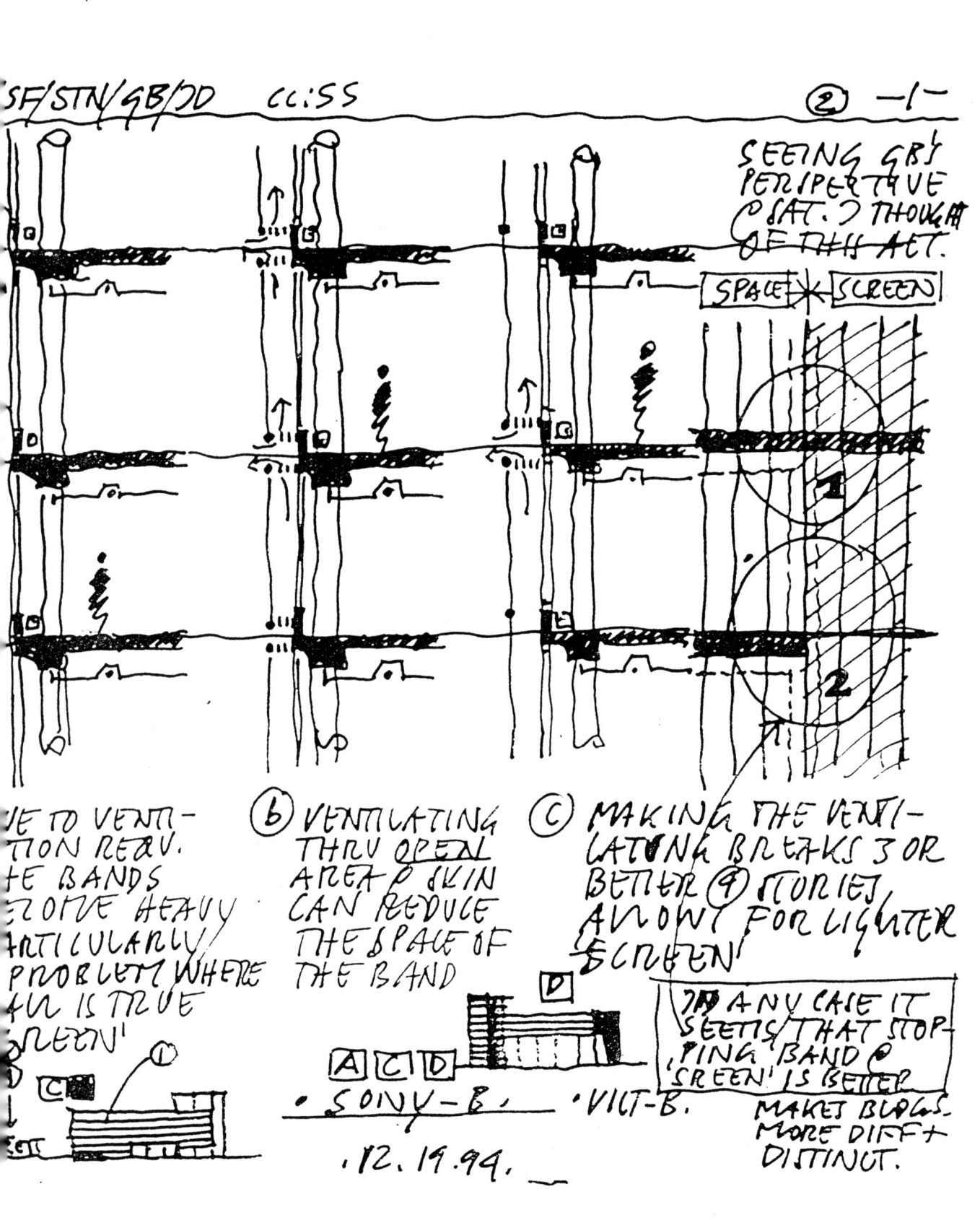

Entwurfsskizzen zur Fassade und zum Lüftungssystem
Design sketches for the facade and ventilation system

SONY—B
12.19.99

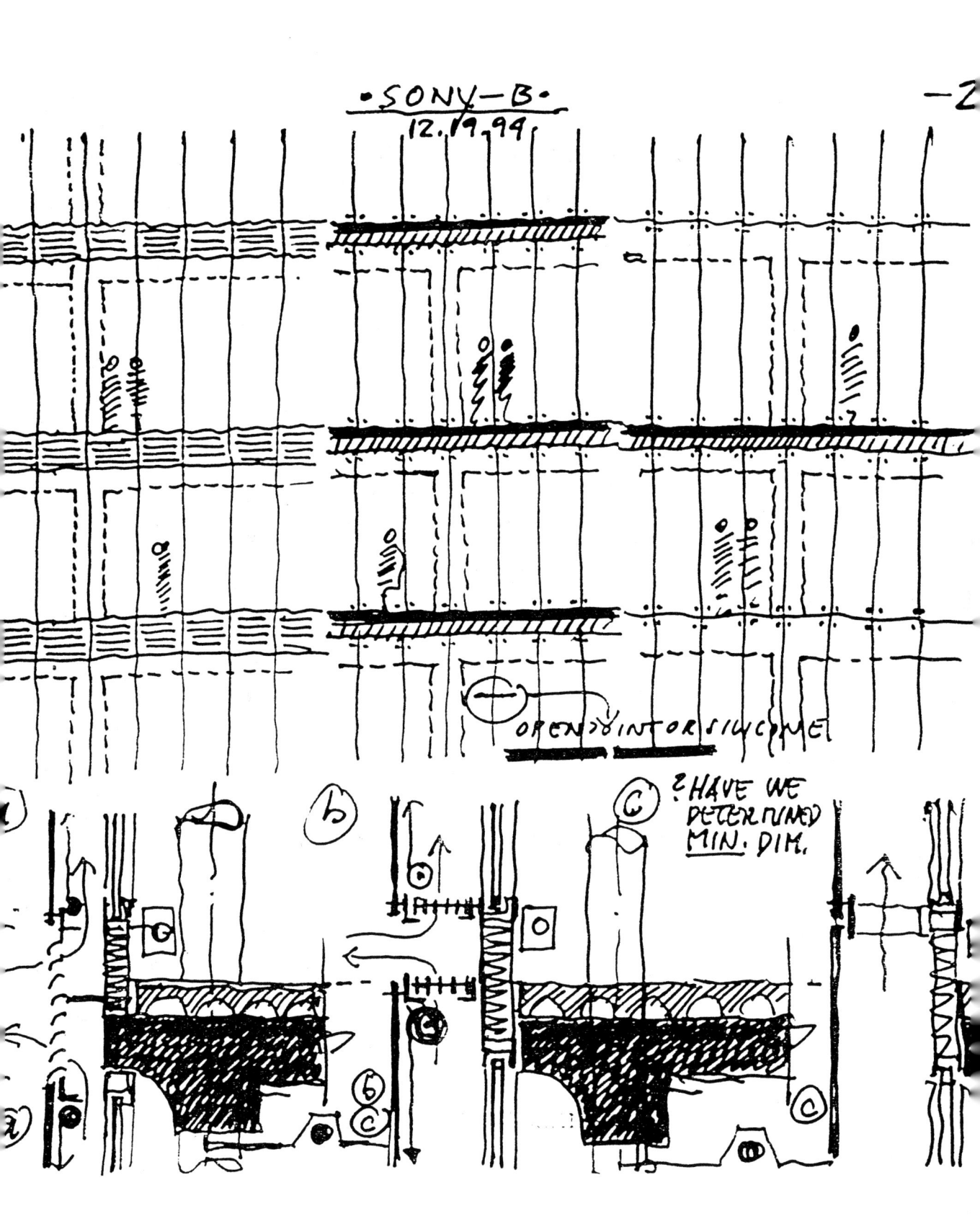

OPEN JOINT OR SILICONE

? HAVE WE DETERMINED MIN. DIM.

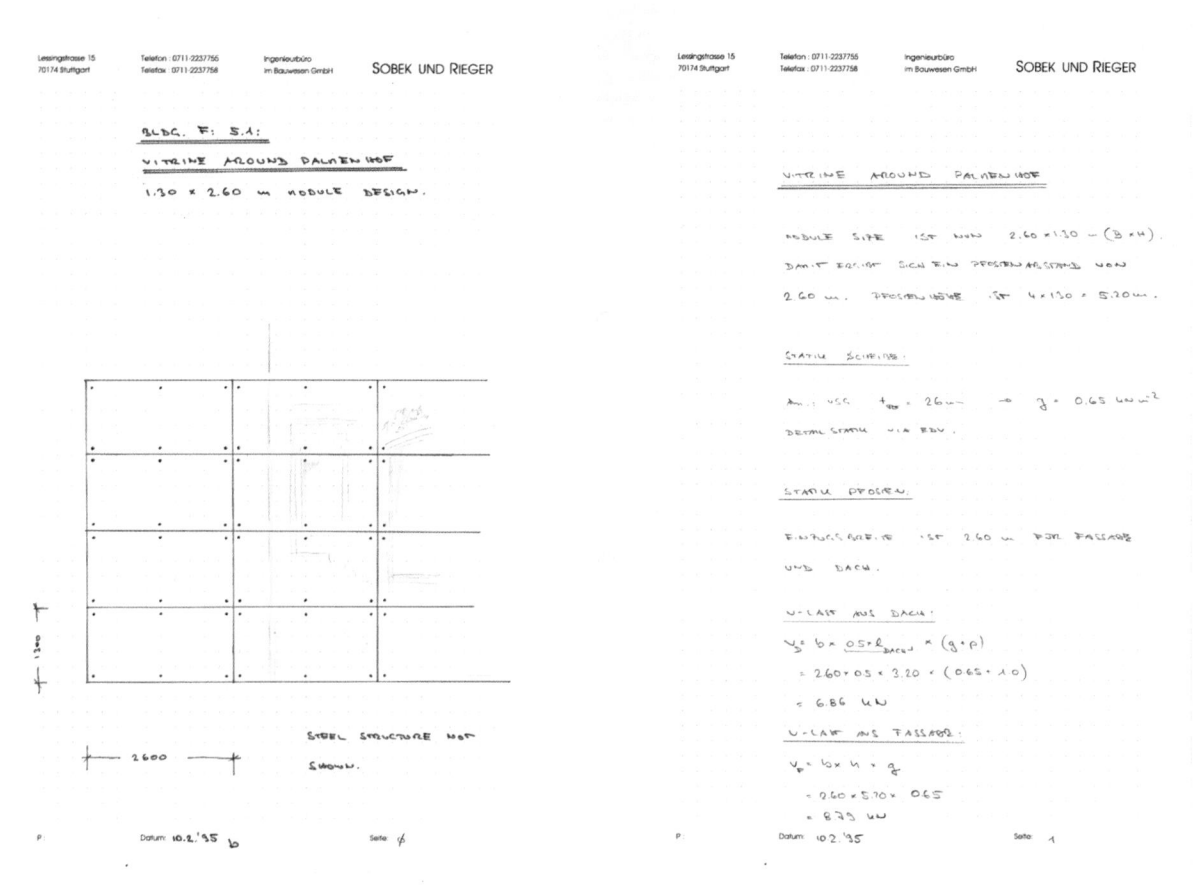

Entwurfsskizzen zu den filigranen Stahlbauteilen der Sonderkonstruktionen
Design sketches for the filigree steel elements of the special structures

es keine abgehängten Decken mehr gibt. Das führt wiederum zu einem gewissen Purismus, so daß die Gebäude in ihrer Technik letztlich immer einfacher werden. Unser Ziel ist es, daß die Dinge so einfach werden, daß man nichts mehr wegzunehmen und nichts mehr dazuzutun braucht. Bei einigen Gebäuden, die wir gerade sozusagen auf dem Reißbrett haben, auch wenn wir beide keine Reißbretter mehr benutzen, sind wir jetzt langsam soweit: Alles wird ganz einfach und dann auch leicht begreifbar. Da kommt die Luft nicht mehr aus einem Schlitz irgendwo in der Decke, und keiner weiß dann, warum die Luft jetzt warm oder kühl ist, weil alles versteckt ist. Bei uns gibt es stattdessen eine Zweite-Haut-Fassade. Man kann das Fenster öffnen, hat eine Kühldecke und kleine Heizrippen. Mehr nicht!

KUHN: Das kommende Jahrhundert wird von einigen Prognostikern als das Jahrhundert der Ökologie, des Naturschutzes vorausgesagt. Was kann die Architektur dazu beitragen, die sich bisher scheinbar auf der Gegenseite befunden hat? Ihr Entwurf für das Bonner Hochhaus der Deutschen Post hat viel Lob als Beispiel für ökologisches Bauen bekommen, und im Februar wurde Ihnen von der European Landscaping Contractors Association und dem Bundesverband Garten-, Landschafts- und Sportplatzbau der »Internationale Trend-Preis Bauen mit Grün 1999« verliehen. Demnach scheinen sich ökologisches, umweltverträgliches Bauen und eine dezidiert modernistische Architektur doch zu vertragen.

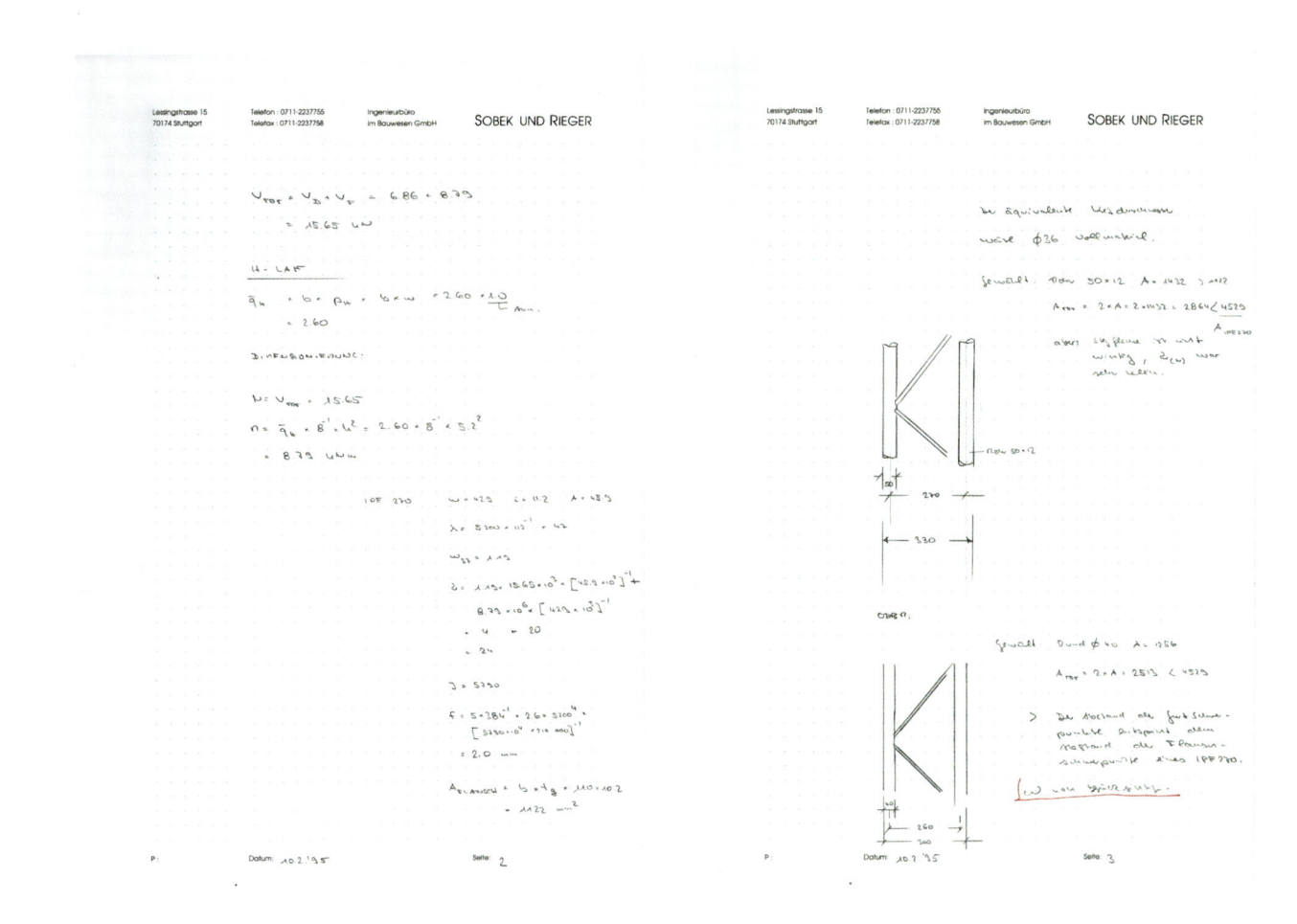

JAHN: Da könnte man wieder unser Motto aus dem IIT-Wettbewerb zitieren: »Mies was ahead of his time. He used materials and techniques, which pushed the limits of available technologies.« Auch unsere Haltung ist es, daß es nicht mehr genügt, nur konventionelle Materialien wie Ziegelstein und Stahl zu verwenden, sondern auch solche, die aus neuartigen Produkten und Prozessen entstehen, die sich ändern, die Energie erzeugen und dadurch eine neue Ästhetik schaffen. Diese Materialien sind hochtechnisch, um am Ende doch wieder einfach zu sein. Das Ergebnis ist die totale Integration zwischen Architektur und Ingenieurwesen.

SOBEK: Wir bemühen uns nicht mehr nur um Hüllen für Gebäude oder Bauteile mit konstanten physikalischen Eigenschaften. Wir sind jetzt peu à peu in der Lage und werden es zukünftig immer mehr sein, daß diese Gebäudehüllen steuerbar sind. Diese Hüllen reagieren dann ganz natürlich auf die Veränderungen des Außen und Innen. Das bedeutet aber, daß sie in einer ganz bestimmten Technizität gemacht werden müssen, die vom Engeneering her sehr anspruchsvoll ist und die auf die architektonische Gestaltung durchschlagende Wirkung hat. Souverän gehandhabt, führt diese Technik zu ganz neuen Lösungen. So gibt es beispielsweise sich selbst verdunkelnde Fassaden oder solche, die Energie gewinnen können, oder Zweite-Haut-Fassaden, die als Scheibe vor der eigentlichen Scheibe plaziert sind, so daß man in dem entstehenden Luftzwischenraum mit Hilfe solarer Einstrahlungen Wärme gewinnt, die dann nach Innen geleitet werden kann.

New Bangkok International Airport

Der auf einer Ebene neu zu errichtende Großflughafen erhält sein weithin sichtbares Wahrzeichen durch sein in 40 m Höhe schwebendes, nahezu 1000 m langes Dach. Das eigentliche Terminalgebäude befindet sich unter dem über ihm schwebenden Schattendach, ist weitestgehend entmaterialisiert. Seine Fassade ist vollkommen verglast und wird nur durch wenige Seilverspannungen gehalten. Es entstehen Transparenz, Reflexion und Lichtwirkung in einer bisher nicht gekannten Größenordnung.

The expansive airport to be built on a single level is given a prominent symbol in the form of its 40-metre-high suspended roof measuring nearly 1000 metres in length that is visible from a great distance. The terminal building itself lies beneath the suspended awning roof and is substantially dematerialised. Its facade is composed entirely of glass and held in place by only a few stretched cables. The building is characterised by unparalleled transparency, reflection and light effects.

Gesamtansicht des Flughafens, Modellaufnahme
General view of the airport, model photo

JAHN: Durch diese Komponenten, diese technischen Teile wird auch das Aussehen des Gebäudes bestimmt. Durch die Steuerbarkeit der Hülle wird eine Ästhetik geschaffen, die selbst dynamisch ist, veränderbar ist. Gerade dies ist unser Glaube, daß die Architektur am Ende nicht allein von der Ästhetik bestimmt wird, sondern auch durch solche Faktoren.

SOBEK: Um auf die Ökologiefrage noch einmal zurückzukommen: Es ist natürlich per se ökologisch, wenn wir nicht nur die Klimaanlage abschaffen, sondern auch den Energieverbrauch reduzieren, weil bei hoher Wärmeeinstrahlung nicht mehr stark gekühlt oder bei geringer Wärmeeinstrahlung geheizt werden muß.

Hinzu kommt noch ein anderer Aspekt, der mir sehr am Herzen liegt und der in unsere gemeinsame Arbeit eingegangen ist. In dem Augenblick, in dem wir die Dinge immer einfacher machen, auch im Sinne ihrer Funktionsweise auf den Punkt bringen, arbeiten wir zunehmend mit Ein-Werkstoff-Komponenten. Das heißt, es gibt eine Decke aus Beton, die gekühlt wird, und dadurch werden keine abgehängten Decken mehr benötigt, auch keinen Spritzputz, keine Tapeten. Diese Betondecke ist vergleichsweise einfach abbaubar und recyclebar im Gegensatz zu gängigen Decken, die eher als Sondermüll zu bezeichnen sind. Diese sind Mehr-Werkstoff-Bauteile, die nicht mehr trennbar und damit recyclebar sind. In unseren Bauten kann alles einfach gefügt und entfügt werden. Dadurch ist alles einfacher veränder- und entsorgbar. Das ist nicht nur ein positiver Nebeneffekt, sondern auch

eine ökologische Grundhaltung.

JAHN: Man sollte sich ohnehin vor Schlagworten hüten. Ökologie ist heute ein solches Schlagwort. In der Architektur hat es immer diese Schlagworte gegeben, die dann einen gewissen Zeitgeist repräsentierten. Der einzige Weg, ökologisch zu bauen, ist doch der, daß man das Gebäude von Grund auf – vom Entwurf, der Form, den Systemen her – so anlegt, daß es sich verantwortungsvoll der Umgebung gegenüber verhält. Deshalb bringen wir alle Experten an einen Tisch: nicht nur Architekt und Ingenieur, sondern auch den Physiker. Der konventionelle Haustechniker wäre gar nicht der richtige Ansprechpartner für uns, weil er nur ausrechnet, wieviel Luft benötigt wird. Ein Physiker beurteilt jedoch sowohl das Wohlbefinden des Menschen als auch die Qualität der Hülle. Im Zusammenwirken zwischen Wohlbefinden des Benutzers, der Hülle und den Außen- beziehungsweise Innenkonditionen besteht der Spielraum für die technischen Systeme. Eigentlich ist das absolut ökologischste Gebäude ein Gebäude, das überhaupt keine Haustechnik benötigt. Doch dafür braucht man einen hervorragenden Ingenieur. Das endgültige Ziel ist eigentlich die Überflüssigmachung von Ingenieur und Haustechniker.

KUHN: Sie beschreiben damit beinahe den Endpunkt einer Entwicklung. Gehen wir zurück an den Anfang Ihrer Zusammenarbeit. Wie sind Sie zueinandergekommen?

SOBEK: Vor fünf Jahren saßen einmal John Durbrow, ein Mitarbeiter von Helmut Jahn, und Bill Baker, ein

> • SOBEK • 10.25.95 — ⑨ —1—
> FAX→ GB/BOC/MW/SP/PC/SGB/STC/RJCH
>
> RE: CLM
> GB — WENT OVER DRWGS. + CHANGES
> DISCUSSED W/ GB. G FORWARD
> DRWGS. TO SOBEK.
> IF NEC. SOBEK'S ASST. WILL
> COME TO NOV. MTG. @ BRUSSELS
> YOU COORDINATE + DETERMINE.
>
> RE: SBIA
> BOC — SOBEK WILL HAVE NEW #'S RE
> MW   WEIGHT BASED ON REVISED SPAN.
>   TRUSS-GEOMETRY FAVOURS SCHEME 2.
>   — TERMINAL/CONCOURSE LINK REQUIRES
>   MORE TIME TO STUDY.
>   — GENERALLY ALL DRAWGS. LOOK
>   FEASIBLE.

Notizen und Skizzen in der Vorentwurfsphase des Daches und der Concourses
Notes and sketches for the preliminary phase of roof and concourse design

Freund von mir aus Chicago, zusammen, als die Frage nach jemandem aufkam, der Helmut einen Tip geben könnte zum Bauen mit Glas. Es gab damals ein kleines Problem. Mein Freund hat mich angerufen und gesagt: »Melde Dich doch mal beim Herrn Jahn, die brauchen Hilfe.« Als ich dann anrief, hieß es, daß alles schon erledigt sei, das Problem hätte sich gelöst. Ein Vierteljahr später war ich zufälligerweise mit Studenten meiner Universität in Chicago auf Bürobesuch, und als wir dann im Büro Jahn waren, habe ich natürlich auch Helmut »Guten Tag« gesagt.

JAHN: Damals hatte ich gar nicht viel Zeit. Da haben wir uns nur fünf Minuten gesprochen, aber…

SOBEK: …drei Monate später habe ich ein Fax von Dir bekommen.

JAHN: Die nächsten Schritte haben sich schnell ergeben. Eigentlich war es das Flughafenterminal Bangkok, das uns zusammengebracht hat. Damals hatten wir, auf Vermittlung von Werner Sobek, auch schon den Bauenergetiker Matthias Schuler eingeschaltet. Vor Bangkok haben wir einige Detailbereiche für Sony gemacht: die Wände, die punktgehaltenen Seil- und Glaskonstruktionen. In diese erste Phase gehören neben Sony auch das Kranzler-Eck in Berlin und der Köln-Bonner Flughafen, bei dem wir noch mehr eher additiv zusammengearbeitet haben. Der nächste gemeinsame Schritt waren Messe und Flughafen von Shanghai sowie die Transrapid-Stationen für Berlin, Hamburg und Schwerin. Von besonderer Bedeutung wurde für uns der Wettbewerb für das

② SBIA

HT: SCHEME 2
HT: UNTERGURT GEOMETRIE ANPASSEN / VERBESSERN:

|X|X|X| → ⟨⟩ ODER ÄHNLICH

TONNAGE DER NEUEN DACHGEOMETRIE BIS
MONTAG 6. NOV. '85 AN BRIAN O'CONNOR. *)

CONCOURSE – TERMINAL – LINK: ENTWERFEN,
MIT ZEIT UND RUHE.

GLASBOX, WIE
BOX UNTER MAIN-
ROOF.

*) OHNE VERSTECKTE SICHERHEITEN, GEWICHTE
GUT KALKULIEREN.

Campus Center des Illinois Institute of Technology, bei dem wir die Idee der totalen Integration von Hüllenkonstruktion und Architektur weiter verfeinert haben. Diese Idee der Verbindung von Tragwerk, Haustechnik und Hülle haben wir noch weiterentwickelt beim Kaufhof in Chemnitz, dem Bürogebäude von Andersen-Consulting in Sulzbach, den Hauptverwaltungen der Deutschen Post in Bonn, der Bayer AG in Leverkusen oder von HA-LO in Chicago.

SOBEK: Diese vollkommene Verständigung, die selbstverständliche Kommunikation auf telefonischen Zuruf, wuchs mit jedem Projekt. Die ersten Projekte, wie beispielsweise Sony, waren ja architektonisch schon formuliert. Hier konnte ich nicht mehr viel ändern, sondern nur einen Beitrag leisten, habe also auf das Gesamte keinen grundlegenden Einfluß mehr gehabt. Bei Bangkok war der Wettbewerb bereits gewonnen, die Architektur in den groben Zügen formuliert, allerdings noch nicht im Detail, zum Beispiel beim Terminalgebäude, einem gläsernen Quader, für den Helmut Jahn etwas absolut Immaterielles wollte. Das haben wir dann in Stuttgart entwickelt. Durch unser gutes gegenseitiges Verständnis konnte ich das so konzipieren, daß es seinen architektonischen Anforderungen entsprach. Darüber hinaus habe ich noch andere Änderungsvorschläge gemacht, teilweise ganz vorsichtig, weil wir uns ja noch nicht so lange kannten. Aber Helmut war offen und sagte immer nur: »Her mit den Änderungen, solange die Sache besser wird.«

New Bangkok International Airport

Concourse, Seitenansicht, Modellaufnahme
Concourse, elevation, model photo

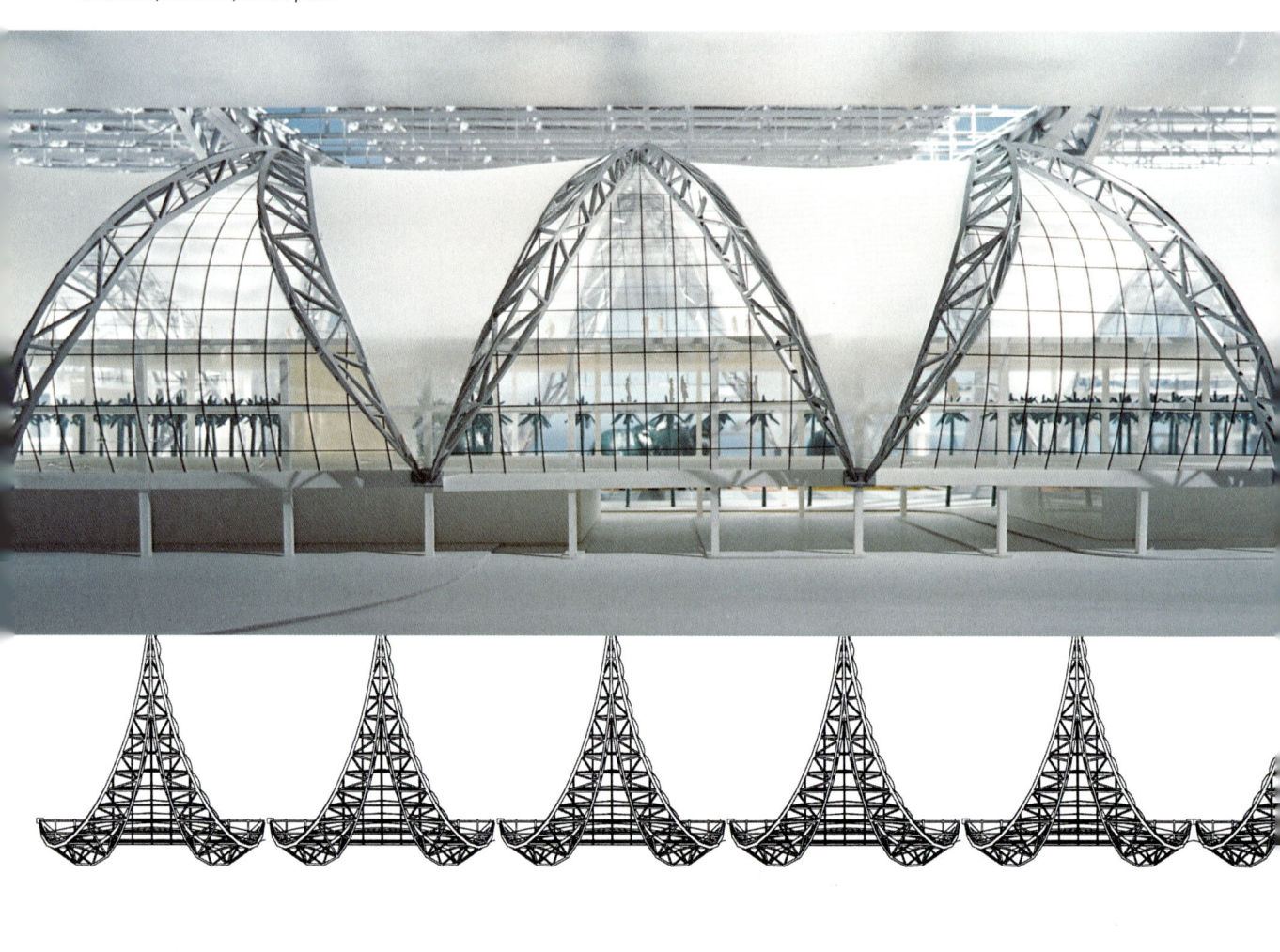

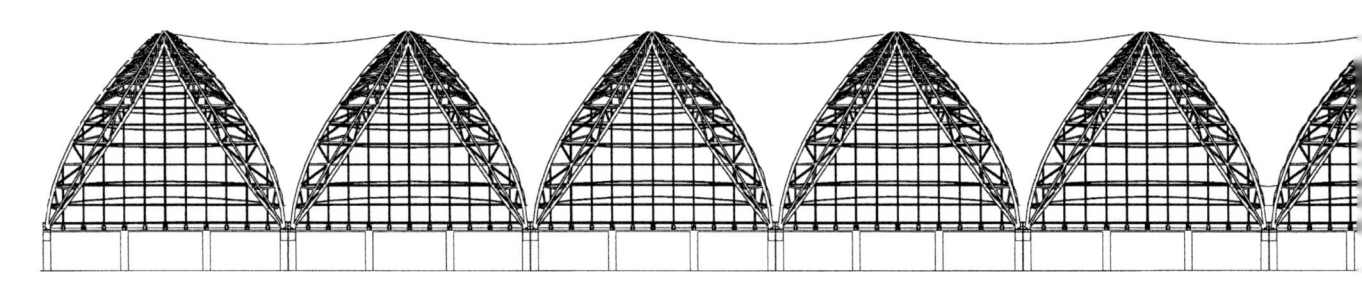

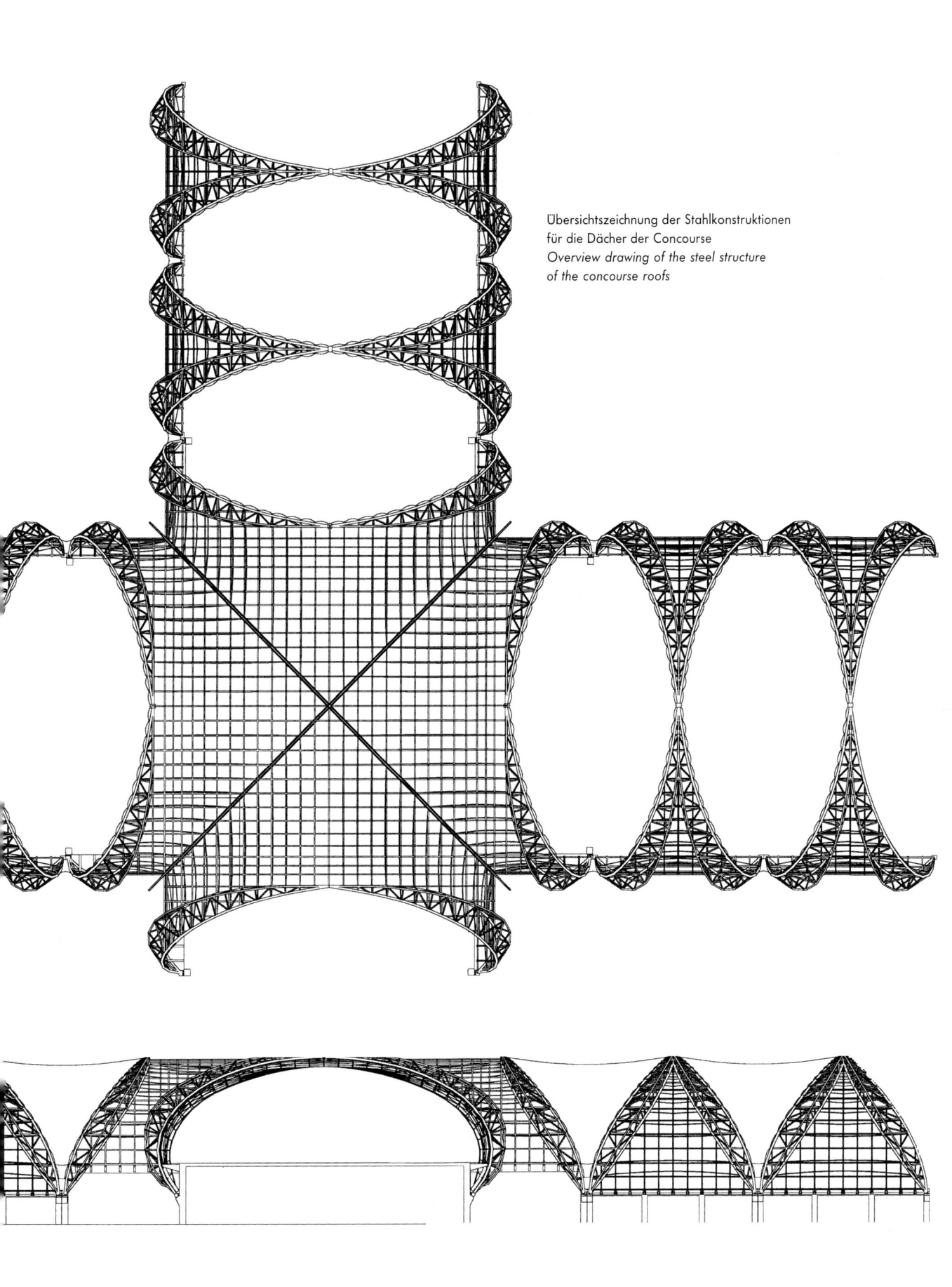

Übersichtszeichnung der Stahlkonstruktionen für die Dächer der Concourse
Overview drawing of the steel structure of the concourse roofs

New Bangkok International Airport

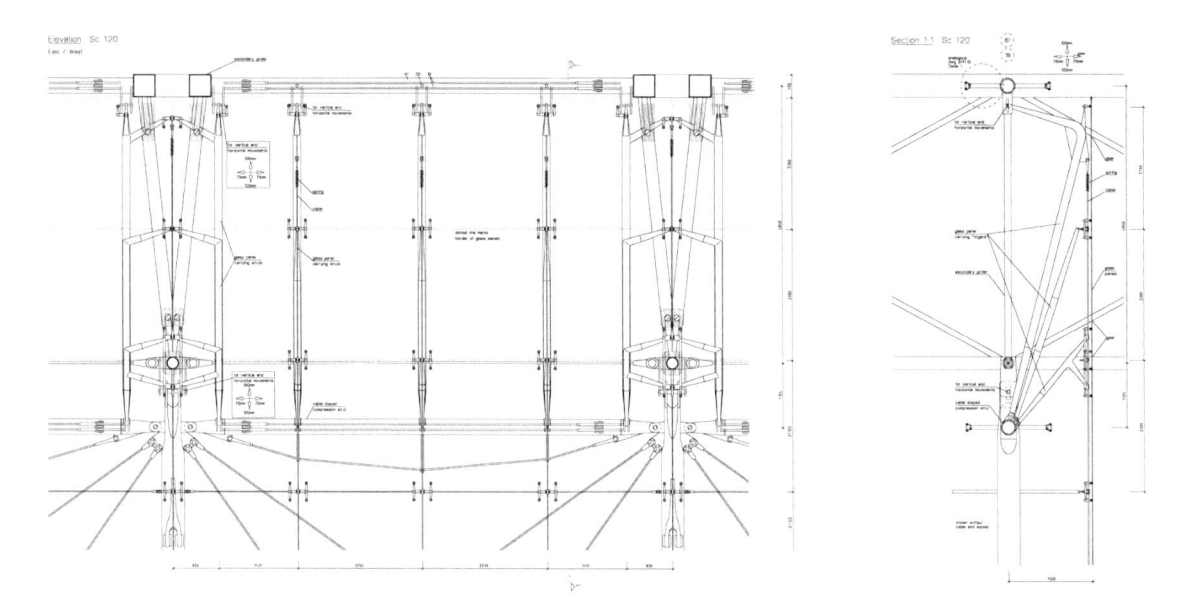

Konstruktionszeichnung, Stahlkonstruktion am oberen Rand der Terminalfassade. Rechte Seite: Glasfassade des Terminalgebäudes, Modellaufnahme
Construction drawing, steel structure at the upper edge of the terminal facade. Right: Glass facade of the terminal building, model photo

Entwurfsskizzen zur 40 m hohen Glasfassade des Terminalgebäudes
Design sketches for the 40-metre glass facade of the terminal building

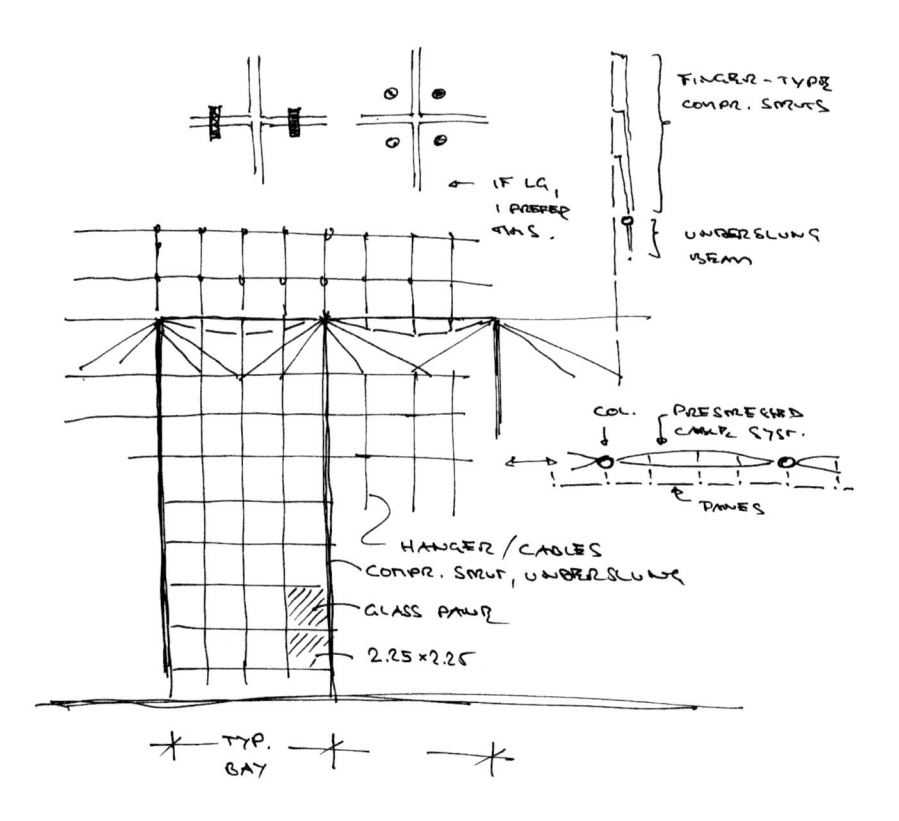

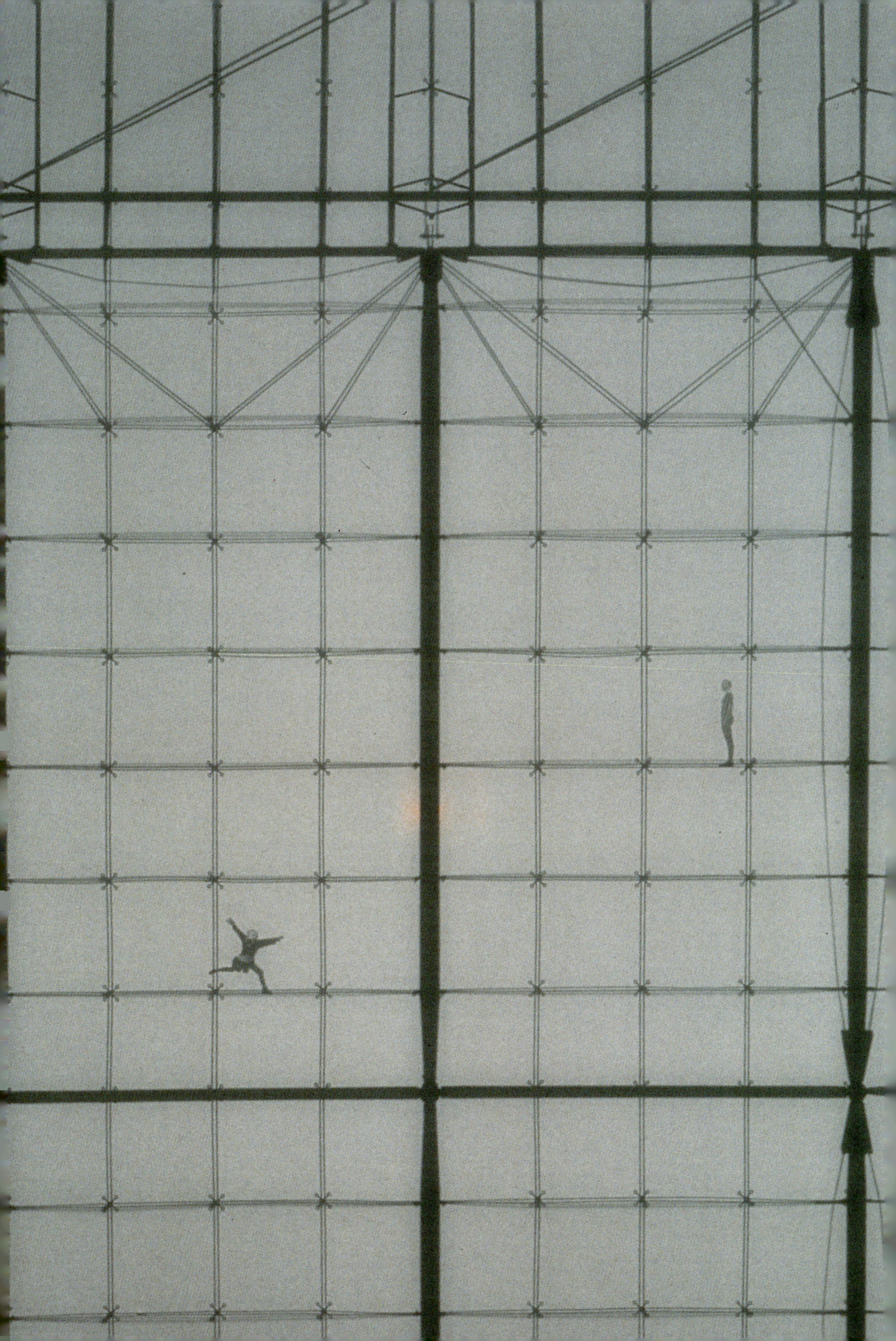

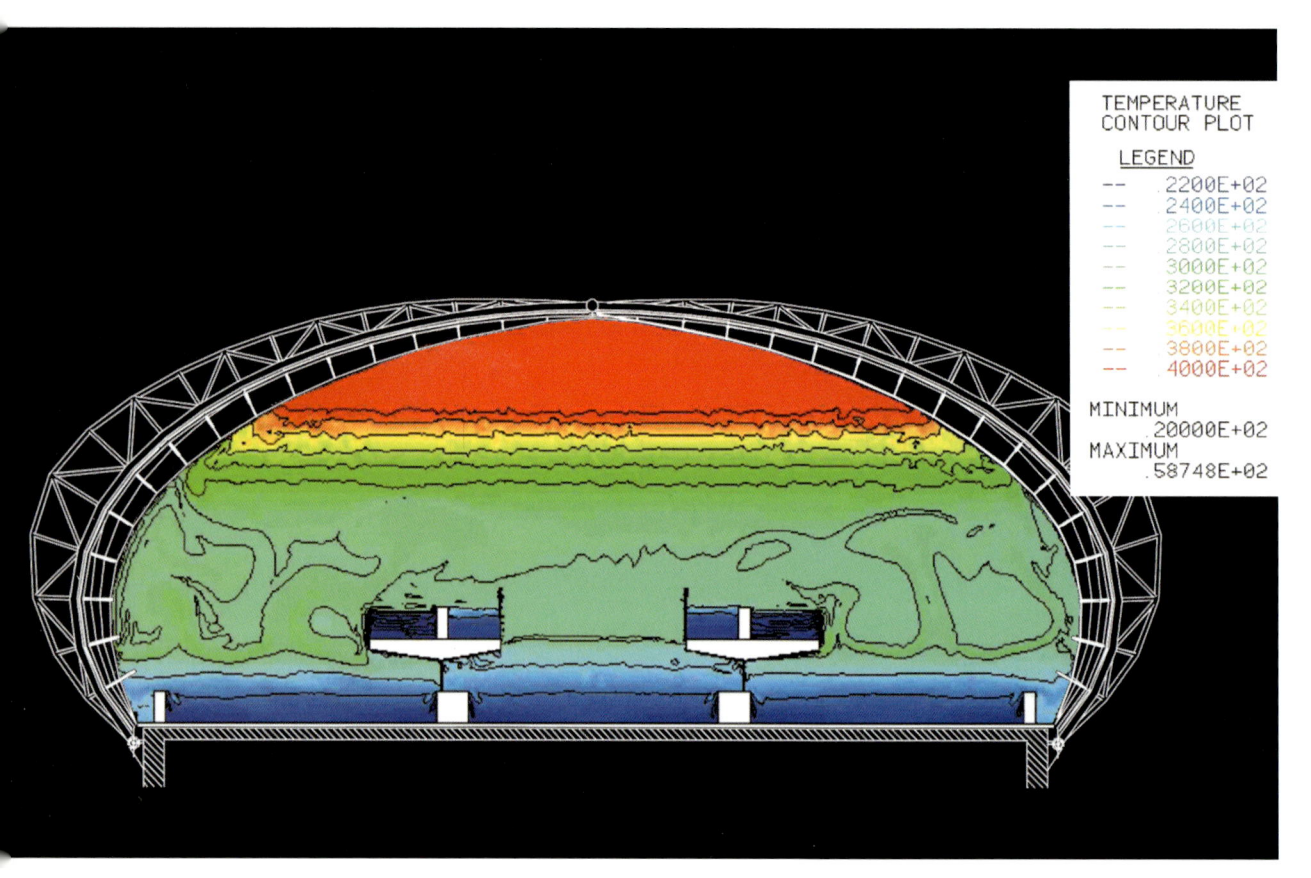

Concourse, Querschnitt, Temperaturschichtungen
Concourse, cross-section, temperature zones

JAHN: Bangkok war ein klassisches Beispiel dafür, wie es vorher immer gelaufen ist. Wir haben beim Wettbewerb Ingenieure eingesetzt, ohne mit ihnen eigentlich zu reden – wie es die Architekten meistens machen. Der Flughafenterminal sollte ein Dach haben mit einer Spannweite von 126 m Länge, 40 m Auskragung und einem sich nach unten wölbenden Fischbauch. Nachdem wir gewonnen hatten und am Gebäude zu arbeiten begannen, wurde mir erst bewußt, daß der Ingenieur eigentlich keinen echten Beitrag lieferte, weil er nur das umsetzte, was wir gezeichnet hatten. Vor allem in Amerika ist das eine typische Einstellung zur Beziehung zwischen Architekt und Ingenieur: Der Architekt denkt aus, der Ingenieur setzt um…

SOBEK: …wobei er die architektonische Idee möglichst wenig beeinflußt oder gar modifiziert.

JAHN: Er ist der Erfüllungsgehilfe. Der Ingenieur sagt vielleicht, da muß ein bißchen mehr Stahl hin, dort ein bißchen mehr Beton hinein. Mag sein, daß er tatsächlich keine bessere Idee hat und nicht die Möglichkeiten sieht, die es gibt. Schließlich ist es schwierig zu beschreiben, wie ein Entwurf im eigenen Kopf entsteht, wenn man zusammenarbeitet.

Ich erinnere mich noch gut an den Wettbewerb für die Deutsche Post in Bonn, ein offener Wettbewerb, bei dem wir um Teilnahme gebeten wurden. Wir haben uns noch gefragt, sollen wir überhaupt mitmachen? Schließlich nehmen hunderte Leute teil. Es ist wie eine Lotterie und genauso wichtig, daß man Glück hat. Werner sagte

Dachuntersicht, Modellaufnahme
View of the large roof from below, model photo

damals: »Du mußt aufpassen in Bonn mit dem Siebengebirge«, lauter Dinge, von denen ich nichts wußte. Er empfahl, etwas Weiches einzusetzen. Während des Redens haben wir Kreise und Ellipsen gezeichnet, und so ist der Entwurf entstanden. Es hat nur einer Bemerkung bedurft: »Irgendetwas Weiches machen«. Damals war ich gerade mit dem Turm von Pudong beschäftigt; schließlich braucht man immer einen Ausgangspunkt. Von dem hattest Du gesagt, er sei zu scharf, zu eckig, einfach nicht freundlich genug. Genau das machte am Ende den Entwurf so erfolgreich – diese gewisse Weichheit, diese Milde. Obwohl das Hochhaus groß ist, erdrückt es nicht. Es ist eher zurückhaltend, fast lyrisch. Durch das Licht – das sieht man auch in den Zeichnungen – wirkt es nicht abschreckend, sondern vielmehr verträglich. Es ist genau dieser Punkt, den ich vorher angesprochen habe, daß der Ingenieur denkt wie ein Architekt und umgekehrt der Architekt wie ein Ingenieur. Das ist bei allen guten Zusammenarbeiten so, daß man sich versteht, gegenseitig ergänzt und am Ende agiert wie eine Person.

SOBEK: Der eine spricht also die Sprache des anderen. Das Besondere bei uns ist, daß es sich auch auf einer gedanklichen Ebene so verhält, so daß am Ende einfach ein Stichwort – »nicht mild genug«, »zu scharf« – genügt. Das entzieht sich oft dem Rationalen des zu Bauenden. Normalerweise würde eine solche Kommunikation sehr lange dauern. Doch wir können einfach telefonieren, haben die Skizze vor uns liegen, und durch zwei, drei Wörter, die eigentlich nur eine Atmosphäre, eine Stimmung beschreiben, tauschen wir uns gegenseitig aus. Ich sage

Aufsicht auf die Gesamtanlage des Flughafens ohne Landebahnen, Modellaufnahme
View of the entire airport facility without runways, model photo

nur: »Das ist irgendwie zu wild oder zu hart«, und Helmut erwidert: »Ach ja? Ich weiß schon, was du meinst.« Umgekehrt verhält es sich genauso. Im Gegensatz zu den meisten Architekten ist Helmut Jahn ein hervorragender Tragwerksplaner und Ingenieur, so daß ich manchmal scherze: »Wenn Du so weitermachst, brauchst Du mich bald nicht mehr.« Bei diesem Kommunikationsprozeß muß man sich natürlich auch die Mühe machen, die Sprache der jeweiligen Disziplin zu erlernen, um zu verstehen, was der andere mir sagen will. Wenn ich von Beanspruchungszuständen spreche, versteht Helmut das einfach, ohne daß ich ihm lang etwas erklären muß.

KUHN: Diese Idee haben sie mit der Bezeichnung Archi-Neering auf den Punkt gebracht. Wie ist es eigentlich zu diesem Begriff gekommen?

SOBEK: Ich habe das grundsätzliche Problem, daß es für das, was ich mache, keine Berufsbezeichnung gibt. Als Tragwerksplaner fühle ich mich nur partiell abgedeckt; ein Architekt im üblichen Sinn bin ich auch keiner; Ingenieur bin ich schon ein bißchen mehr. Der Begriff Designer ist im Deutschen negativ belegt, jedoch vollkommen zu unrecht. Bei der Umbenennung meiner Firma hatte ich mir deshalb kurz überlegt, uns als »Archineur« zu bezeichnen. Genau ein Jahr später kam Helmut dann mit dem Begiff des Archi-Neering.

JAHN: Wir saßen schon vorher einmal zusammen und überlegten: Architecture and Technology, Architecture and Engeneering, Architecture and …this Technology. Wir wußten nur, daß es etwas Einprägsames sein

Planliste der Ingenieurpläne in der Entwurfsphase
Planning list of engineering plans for the design phase

sollte. Und da ich jemand bin, der nur denken kann, wenn er zeichnet oder schreibt, habe ich das auf dem Papier immer wieder ausprobiert. Dabei entstand die Koppelung des Begriffs und am Ende Archi-Neering. Das war ebenso ein visuelles wie intellektuelles Ergebnis.

KUHN: Wie ist die Reaktion auf diese Art fast intime Zusammenarbeit?

JAHN: Die Öffentlichkeit, die Presse und der Großteil der Architekturkritik hat dafür kein Verständnis. Unser gemeinsames Ziel, bis an die Grenzen zu gehen, sie manchmal sogar zu verwischen, bringt nicht nur Freunde und Applaus ein. Das macht viele nervös. Wenn ich in Amerika in Interviews mit dem gleichen Eifer, der gleichen Überzeugung wie jetzt von unserer Sache spreche, dann wird vielen richtig Angst. Ich gelte für sie als Terrorist, als Wahnsinniger, der an etwas glaubt, ob es nun die Religion ist oder die Baukunst beziehungsweise Ingenieurkunst. Auch in Deutschland interessiert dies niemanden. Man will lieber etwas Sensationelles, ein dramatisches Scheitern oder eine Kontroverse, wie es sie hier in Berlin gab zwischen Stimmann und den Architekten, die etwas anderes als er wollten.

Sony ist ein gutes Beispiel dafür, daß man doch etwas anderes machen konnte. Manche Leute nennen es gut, andere werden das absolut vernichtend beurteilen. Viele wollen aber nur ihre Vorurteile bestätigt wissen. Man nimmt den Sony-Bau nicht für das, was er ist, sondern will für Berlin eine Repräsentation der Geschichte. Das ist

结构系统描述

楼顶结构

航站楼楼顶结构系统由两相同部分组成,各部分包括支撑亮体状主梁的倾斜柱子,并沿对称轴线连在一起的,悬挂于主梁上的翅膀,两部分的连接增加了结构的稳定性,但单独一部分也能站立起。

每根主梁全长为400米,它们组成一连续的,有如飞机壳体形状的中空盒状体件。倾斜的柱子每隔50米支撑脊主梁,这些支撑体使主梁产生等向的压缩力,支撑体本身是由标准钢板组成的中空壳体。

构成屋顶面的翅膀包括间隔10至12米的悬臂桁架网格,桁架网格固定在壳体主梁上,带薄钢片盖面的波纹钢甲板横跨于悬臂的桁架间,因而可以说,结构的一部分,同时也是覆盖层,甲板上可开天窗,第二层桁架梁用于强固天窗的边缘。

楼顶的整个钢结构系统与飞机设计结构原理相同,它不仅在形式上相似,而且也具有相同的高强度和轻质设计的优点。由于整个结构系统仅由壳体梁,支撑柱子,悬臂的翅膀桁架,及波纹钢甲板四部分组成,其结构可轻易的扩展。

候机楼

候机楼结构系统与航站楼屋顶一样,也具有高强度、轻质及可轻易扩建的优点。候机楼是一固定于由柱子支撑的混凝土楼板上的钢结构,它包括间隔10至12米,由钢缆协助稳定的弧形拱,一个一单独的弧形拱内部结构与波纹钢甲板连接起来。因而整个候机楼可以解释成为由带强固脊骨的一薄钢片壳,再一次这又是飞机壳体的表现,在应力壳上开口是很容易的。

由钢缆协助稳定的弧形拱的上弦仅仅承受压力,对角及下弦由预应力拉杆组成,通过施加预应力于对角及下弦钢管而使整个弧形带有预应力,这可采用液压千斤顶来施加的预应力也可知的,所以在所有杆件上施加的预应力也是可知的。

由于整个候机楼仅由弧拱,次桁架,及钢片甲板三部分组成,这就允许轻易的预制,迅速的安装,及节资。

施工可能性的分析

航站楼屋顶及候机楼的结构可给旅客一种十分重要的,良好的第一印象,精简,轻易扩建的结构可使得用简单的技术来达到高科技的效果成为现实。航站楼屋顶及候机楼结构均为高标准钢板,受拉钢管与薄钢片组合成的钢结构,这是钢厂标准项目,所有使用钢均为标准钢材,焊剂及铆接也为标准技术。由于整个屋顶仅由四部分组成,候机楼由三部分组成,使得预制及装配这七个部件可轻易地达到最优化。根据中国桥梁及高层建筑的施工水平,这是毫无困难的。

电气

概括

航站楼与候机楼电气部分的基本设计原则是合理的根据建筑群体的组织及形态,使用最少的能量来创造出舒适的环境,这通过最大程度地利用不同种建筑因素来创造出明亮及凉爽的空间,同时最小程度地使用人工照明及机械冷却系统。

此外,机械系统将设计成节能及能简易操作,通过使用废气的能量循环系统,单区域的不同供水量系统,二次乃至三次抽冷却水及对所有机械设备采用节能马达,可以大幅度的节省。

层分作用及小气候

航站楼及候机楼的规模加强了维持舒适环境的能力,空间的高度允许使用层分原理与热对流来或创造小气候。顶部的开口能够让自然上升的热气(高密度)排除,冷空气(低密度)下沉,壳内低层冷空气的分发允许在旅客集中的地带形成凉爽的小气候。气体分发管道一般位于旅客占用的楼板的底面,这就允许通过使用建筑部件,如柱子,空气台,检查台的表面,商店,指标牌等,来把空气引进使用区域。在旅客层保持冷空气分发的层分作用,人体身上及照明散发的热量将上升并通过屋顶外出的区域排出,同时底层排出的冷空气将下沉留在旅客使用的区域。

结果是使用的冷却能量较大程度的低于使用于同类空间的规定能量,相应的,也最大程度地降低了用来抵销聚集的能量。更进一步,通过使用为冷空气直接排放空气而特制的圆筒形气窗,排放出的空气能很好的被控制住以便来满足使用空间并维持分层小气候的原理。实上,并不是整个空间,而是旅客的使用区域是凉爽的。温度梯度沿高度而很明显地上升,在顶部,温度最高的气体进入大气。另外,由于建筑尺度,体量,及空间组合方式,其对冷却要求降低到最小程度,从而增强了冷却系统的工作效率。

基本设计参数

1. 离港道路边 - 国际

总共车辆 = 3600
总小汽车/出租车 (97%) = 3492
总公共汽车 (3%) = 108
公共汽车上的全部乘客 (假定10人/汽车) = 1080
一高峰小时公共汽车上的全部国内乘客=324 (单乘)
公共汽车上的全部国际乘客 (40%) = 432 (双乘)
公共汽车上的全部国外乘客 = 216 (单乘)

---

t = 平均一辆公共汽车所占的车道边 = 14 米
t = 平均一辆公共汽车所占用车道边的时间 = 5 分钟 (假定)

公共汽车一共所需要的车道边长度

$$L = \frac{alt}{60n} + 10\% = \frac{216 \times 14 \times 5}{60 \times 10} + 10\% = 28 \text{ meters}$$

1.3 所有离港所需车道边 - 国际 = 173 米

2. 检查柜台 (中央式,很普遍的检查性式)

数据:
a = 一高峰小时的全部旅客 = 1260
b = 不前往空侧的转机旅客 = 140
t = 平均一旅客办手术所需时间 = 2.5 分钟 (假定)

所需柜台:

$$N = \frac{(a+b)t}{60} + 10\% = \frac{(1260+140) \, 2.5}{60} + 10\% = 64 \text{ desks}$$

3. 护照检查 - 离港

数据:
a = 一高峰小时的全部旅客 = 1260
b = 不前往空侧的转机旅客 = 140
t_2 = 平均一旅客办手术所需时间 = .75 分钟 (假定)

所需检查位置:

$$N = \frac{(a+b)t_2}{60} + 10\% = \frac{(1260+140) \times .75}{60} + 10\% = 19 \text{ positions}$$

4. 安全检查 - 中央式

数据:
a = 一高峰小时的全部旅客 = 1260
b = 不前往空侧的转机旅客 = 140
y = X光手提包检查器能量 = 300 (假定)
w = 平均一旅客所带手提包数 = 2 (假定)

所需X光手提包检查器:

$$N = \frac{(a+b)w}{y} = \frac{(1260+140) \, 2}{300} = 10 \text{ units}$$

5. 到港旅客检疫

数据:
d = 一高峰小时的到港旅客 = 1260
b = 不前往空侧的转机旅客 = 140
t_2 = 平均一旅客办手术所需时间 = 0.5 分钟

所需控制位置:

$$N = \frac{(d+b)t_2}{60} + 10\% = \frac{(1260+140) \times 0.5}{60} + 10\% = 12 \text{ positions}$$

6. 护照检查 - 到港

数据:
a = 一高峰小时的全部旅客 = 1260
b = 不前往空侧的转机旅客 = 140
t_2 = 平均一旅客办手术所需时间 = .50 分钟

所需检查位置:

$$N = \frac{(a+b)t_2}{60} + 10\% = \frac{(1260+140) \times 0.5}{60} + 10\% = 12 \text{ positions}$$

7. 到港海关

数据:
e = 一高峰小时出关的全部旅客 = 1400
f = 需经海关检查旅客的比例 = 0.25
t_4 = 平均一旅客办手术所需时间 = 1.5 分钟

所需海关检查位置:

$$N = \frac{eft_4}{60} + 10\% = \frac{1400 \times 0.25 \times 1.5}{60} + 10\% = 9 \text{ positions}$$

8. 到港道路边 - 国际

8.1 小汽车/出租车

数据:
a = 一高峰小时乘坐小汽车/出租车的全部国际到港旅客 = 1044
n = 平均一辆小汽车/出租车上的乘客 = 1.5 (假定)
l = 平均一辆小汽车/出租车所占的车道边 = 7.6 米
t = 平均一辆小汽车/出租车所占用车道边的时间 = 3 分钟

小汽车/出租车一共所需要的车道边长度:

$$L = \frac{alt}{60n} + 10\% = \frac{1044 \times 7.6 \times 3}{60 \times 1.5} + 10\% = 291 \text{ meters}$$

8.2 公共汽车

数据:
a = 一高峰小时乘坐公共汽车的全部国际到港旅客 = 216
n = 平均一辆公共汽车上的乘客 = 10 (假定)
l = 平均一辆公共汽车所占的车道边 = 14 米
t = 平均一辆公共汽车所占用车道边的时间 = 7 分钟 (假定)

公共汽车一共所需要的车道边长度:

$$L = \frac{alt}{60n} + 10\% = \frac{216 \times 14 \times 7}{60 \times 10} + 10\% = 39 \text{ meters}$$

8.3 所有到港所需车道边 = 330 米

1. 离港道路边 - 国内

1.1 小汽车/出租车

公共汽车一共所需要的车道边长度

$$L = \frac{alt}{60n} + 10\% = \frac{324 \times 14 \times 5}{60 \times 10} + 10\% = 42 \text{ meters}$$

1.3 所有离港所需车道边 - 国内 = 266 米

2. 检查柜台 (中央式,很普遍的检查性式)

数据:
a = 一高峰小时的全部旅客 = 1935
b = 不前往空侧的转机旅客 = 215
t_1 = 平均一旅客办手术所需时间 = 1.75 分钟 (假定)

所需柜台:

$$N = \frac{(a+b)t_1}{60} + 10\% = \frac{(1935+215) \, 1.75}{60} + 10\% = 69 \text{ desks}$$

3. 安全检查 - 中央式

数据:
a = 一高峰小时的全部旅客 = 1935
b = 不前往空侧的转机旅客 = 215
y = X光手提包检查器能量 = 400 (假定)
w = 平均一旅客所带手提包数 = 2 (假定)

所需X光手提包检查器:

$$N = \frac{(a+b)w}{y} = \frac{(1935+215) \, 2}{400} = 12 \text{ units}$$

4. 到港道路边 - 国内

4.1 小汽车/出租车

数据:
一高峰小时全部国内乘客 = 1935
a = 一高峰小时乘坐小汽车/出租车的全部国内乘客 = 16
n = 平均一辆小汽车/出租车上的乘客 = 1.5 (假定)
l = 平均一辆小汽车/出租车所占的车道边 = 7.6 米
t = 平均一辆小汽车/出租车所占用车道边的时间 = 3.0 分钟

小汽车/出租车一共所需要的车道边长度:

$$L = \frac{alt}{60n} + 10\% = \frac{1611 \times 7.6 \times 3}{60 \times 1.5} + 10\% = 449 \text{ meters}$$

4.2 公共汽车

数据:
一高峰小时全部国内乘客 = 1935
a = 一高峰小时乘坐公共汽车的全部国内乘客 = 324
n = 平均一辆公共汽车上的乘客 = 10 (假定)
l = 平均一辆公共汽车所占的车道边 = 14 米
t = 平均一辆公共汽车所占用车道边的时间 = 7 分钟 (假定)

公共汽车一共所需要的车道边长度

$$L = \frac{alt}{60n} + 10\% = \frac{324 \times 14 \times 7}{60 \times 10} + 10\% = 58 \text{ meters}$$

区域面积计算

	航站楼	候机楼 A	候机楼 B	总
层数 0	21,500			21,
层数 1	42,600	6,000	6,000	54,
层数 2	6,200	26,600	32,100	64,
层数 3	26,600	19,900	12,450	58,
总计	96,900	52,500	50,550	199,

投资估算

航站楼与候机楼   4,232,827

基础	431,225,600
大型结构	797,120,522
外墙	736,400,640
屋顶结构	149,270,400
室内结构	373,176,000
机械	621,960,000
电气	281,955,200
特殊系统	290,248,000
运输系统	248,784,000
仪器	261,223,200
场地改进	41,464,000

行李系统	281,955
飞机滑行道	808,548
停车库	348,297
航站楼前道路系统	586,135
总计	**5,742,308**

(数据单位为人民币)

Shanghai-Pudong International Airport (Wettbewerb/Competition)

Das Gebäude wird in der Konstruktionsweise der Flugzeuge selbst errichtet: das Gebaute als Symbol des Ereignisses. Röhrenartige Concourse verbinden das Terminal mit den Flugzeugen. Das Terminalgebäude selbst wird von einem großen Dach überspannt, das aus zwei aufgeständerten Rümpfen mit weit auskragenden, flügelartigen Dachflächen besteht. Die seitliche Einhüllung wird vollkommen verglast konzipiert, nur wenige metallische Seile, eher Gespinst als Konstruktion, stabilisieren die Glasfläche.

The building is to be erected in keeping with the design of the aircraft themselves: architecture as a symbol of the event. Pipelike concourses connect the terminal and the aircraft. The terminal building is spanned by a large roof consisting of two fuselage-type beams with widely overhanging, winglike roof surfaces. The sides of the building shell are designed as a full-glass construction. The glass panes are stabilised by just a few metal cables that resemble a web rather than a construction.

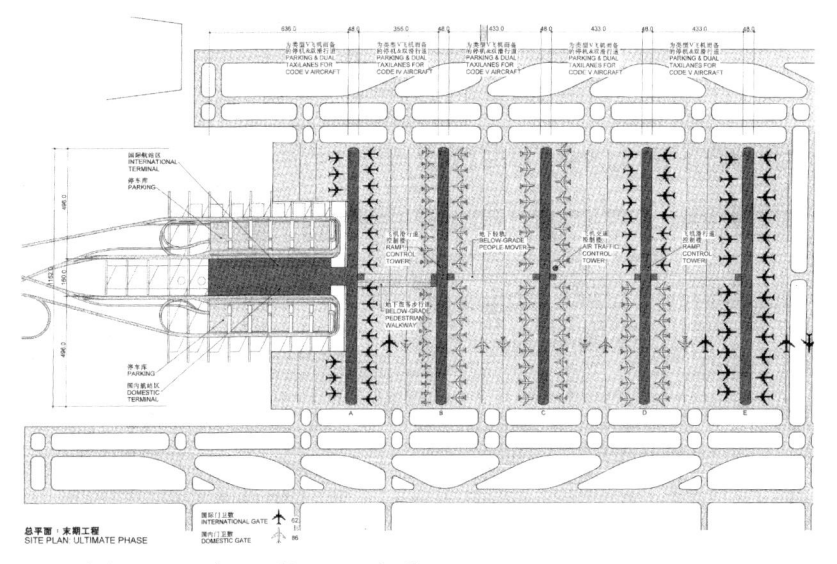

Linke Seite: Beschreibung des Entwurfskonzeptes und der tragenden Konstruktion
Left: Description of the design concept and the supporting framework structure

Grundriß der Gesamtanlage und Positionen der Flugzeuge
Ground plan for the entire airport facility with aircraft positions

in Frankreich mit den neuen Bauten anders: der Bibliothek, der Fondation Cartier in Paris, der Pyramide vor dem Louvre. Das einzige, wofür man die Pyramide kritisieren könnte, ist, daß sie zu klein ist. Im Entwurf war sie ursprünglich größer; ihre heutige Form ist ein Kompromiß. Die genannten Gebäude sind die einzigen in Paris, die den alten standhalten können. Alles dazwischen hat nicht diese Qualität.

SOBEK: So etwas wird nur möglich durch einen Bauherrn, der sich mit dem identifiziert, was er bauen will. Präsident Mitterand wollte einfach die Grand Bibliothèque und hielt seine schützende Hand über den Architekten. Dominique Perrault war damals 26 Jahre alt, als er das Projekt gewann. Und natürlich haben ihn alle sofort verurteilt und seinen Entwurf als monströs bezeichnet, zu teuer, als »bibliothekstechnischen Unfug«. Es bedurfte der Durchsetzungskraft eines Präsidenten, um das Projekt zu realisieren. Ähnlich verhielt es sich beim Grand Arche oder beim Institut du Monde Arabe. Solche Bauten sehen Sie in Deutschland nirgends. Etwas wird nur zu einem Ausnahmeprojekt, wenn Mut dahinter steckt und eine klare Haltung. Dann entsteht ein in sich geschlossenes Gebilde, das tatsächlich ein Statement ist.

KUHN: Der ideale Bauherr steht also mit Courage von Anfang an hinter dem Architekten.

JAHN: Ich sage immer, man braucht kein anderes Projekt, sondern einen anderen guten Bauherrn. Wenn ich zurückblicke auf die Gebäude, die wir gemacht haben, sehe ich die genaue Relation zwischen der Qualität der

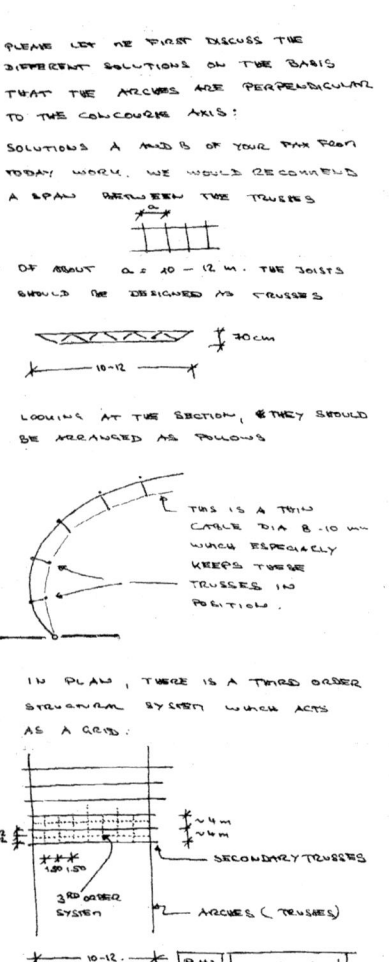

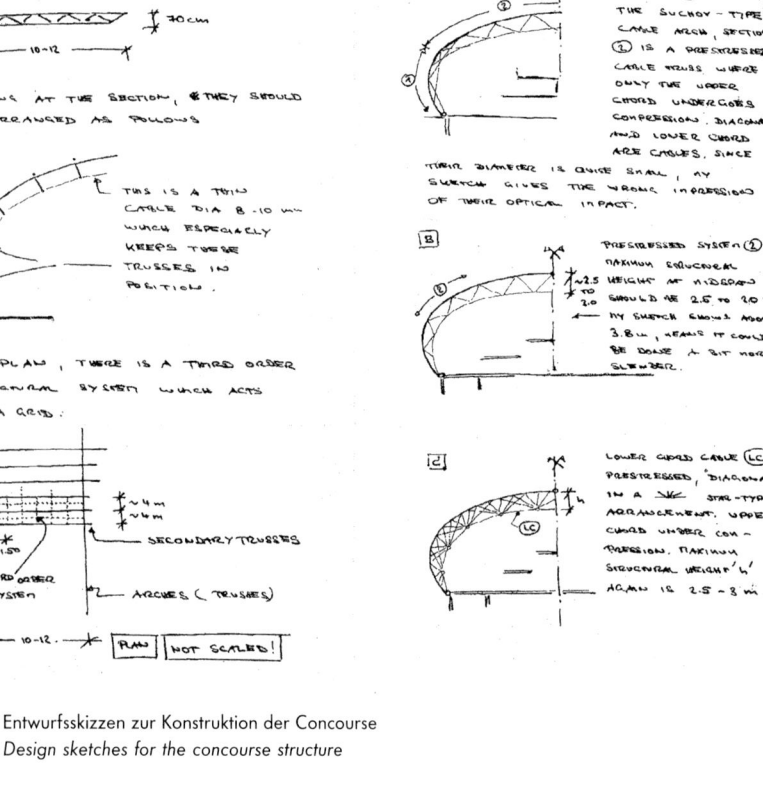

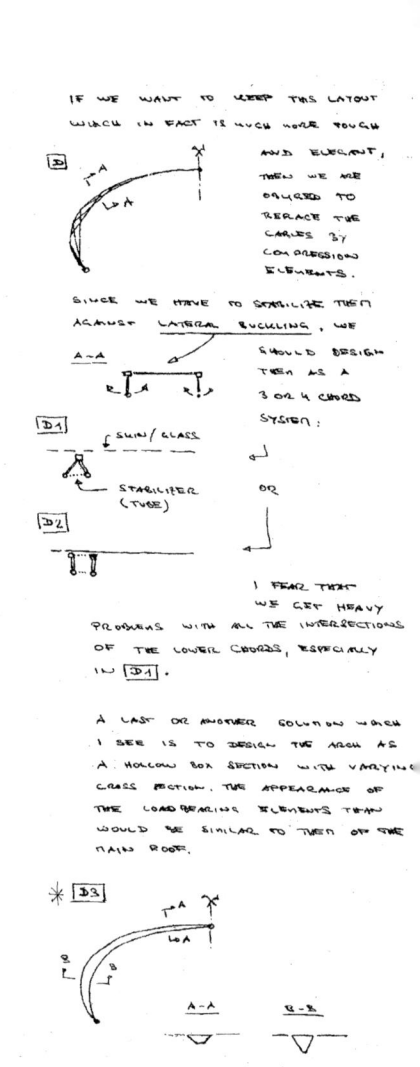

Entwurfsskizzen zur Konstruktion der Concourse
Design sketches for the concourse structure

Architektur und der Unterstützung oder auch dem positiv gesehenen Druck, den ein Bauherr ausübt, damit man etwas Hervorragendes leistet. Deswegen ist es auch so schwierig, im Bereich der kommerziellen Architektur ein großartiges Projekt zu verwirklichen. All die genannten französischen Bauten sind öffentliche Projekte. Öffentliche Architektur ist in den meisten Ländern – nicht nur in Deutschland oder Amerika – nicht annähernd von dieser Qualität, weil die öffentliche Hand normalerweise zurückschreckt, wenn etwas den Eindruck erweckt, teuer zu sein. Dann kann es nach deren Meinung eben auch nicht gut sein.

SOBEK: Hinzu kommt, daß diese Gebäude mit einem gewissen Restrisiko behaftet sind, sei es ein Kostenrisiko, ein gebäudeenergetisches Risiko oder ein Benutzungsrisiko. Wenn es an zwei Tagen im Jahr einmal 28° C im Büro werden könnten oder mehr, dann schrecken die Leute zurück, weil laut Arbeitsstättenverordnung bei mehr als 28° C in einem Gebäude nicht mehr gearbeitet werden muß. Folglich braucht der Mieter dem Bauherrn für diese Zeit keine Miete zu zahlen. Damit kommt der Salto bis hin zum Architekt, dem der Investor vorwirft, er habe einen Planungsfehler gemacht. Wir würden uns also einen Privatmann, einen Bauherrn wünschen, der sich das leisten kann, der bereit ist, na ja, einmal in zwanzig Jahren auf einen Monat Miete zu verzichten oder der seine Mitarbeiter mal ohne Jackett herumlaufen läßt. Ein Gremienbauherr, beispielsweise ein öffentlicher Bauherr, würde dieses kleine Risiko nie eingehen.

Blick in die Concourse, Modellaufnahme
View into the concourses, model photo

KUHN: Sie beschreiben den Wunsch-Bauherrn. Haben Sie nicht auch offene Wünsche, was die Bauaufgaben betrifft, die Sie gerne noch gemeinsam verwirklichen würden?

JAHN: Ich habe nie geglaubt, einen gewissen Gebäudetyp, eine Kirche oder ein Museum, unbedingt noch bauen zu müssen. Diese Serie von Bürogebäuden, die wir jetzt gemacht haben – erst das Airport-Center, dann Sony und das Kranzler-Eck in Berlin, schließlich die Bayer-Konzernzentrale in Leverkusen und der Büroturm für die Deutsche Post in Bonn –, das ist Stufe für Stufe die Verfeinerung unseres Konzepts der Integration von Architektur und Ingenieurwesen. Es resultiert aus einem bestimmten Selbstverständnis, einer Haltung, bei der man nie mit dem zufrieden ist, was man gestern vollendet hat. Man fühlt sich immer verpflichtet, morgen etwas Besseres zu schaffen. Aber das kann man nur mit Hilfe von anderen, von Ingenieuren und auch der Industrie. Darin besteht dann der Fortschritt.

Diese Serie von Bürogebäuden ist viel interessanter, als wenn ich jetzt hier eine Kirche gebaut hätte, dort ein Museum, obwohl wir etliche von diesen Bauaufgaben auch übernehmen würden. Oder nehmen wir diese Sukzession von Flughäfen: United Terminal in Chicago, der Flughafen Köln-Bonn, der Flughafen in Bangkok; das ist eine Linie. Ich sage immer etwas spöttisch: »Das United Terminal ist ein Gebäude aus dem 19. Jahrhundert, Köln stammt aus dem 20. Jahrhundert, und Bangkok wird vielleicht aus dem 21. Jahrhundert sein.« Ich glaube, darin

51

Blick durch die gläserne Fassade unter das große Dach, Modellaufnahme
View through the glass facade beneath the large roof, model photo

liegt die Herausforderung, das wirkliche Interesse: die Grenzen zu verschieben, die Meßlatte höher zu legen. Sich in jeder Sparte zu versuchen, ist stattdessen eine Gefahr. Das macht der typische Architekt, so wie ich früher auch einer war. In seiner Voreingenommenheit und Arroganz glaubt er, alles zu können. In unserem Büro in Chicago haben wir früher nie einen Consultant beteiligt. Wir haben alles selber gemacht, selbst die Landschaftsplanung, und auch dem Ingenieur haben wir noch gesagt, was er tun soll. Die Qualität unserer heutigen Gebäude ist dagegen nicht nur durch den Architekten allein bestimmt, sondern auch durch das Tragwerk, die Haustechnik, die Landschaftsplanung.

Heute Nachmittag beispielsweise war ich bei der Präsentation des französischen Lichtkünstlers Yann Kersalé für die Beleuchtung des Sony-Gebäudes, für das Dach, die Portale und das Hochhaus. Kersalés Beitrag ergänzt, ja verstärkt die architektonische und räumliche Konzeption des Gesamtkomplexes, die Idee des Übergangs von der wirklichen Stadt in die innere, virtuelle Stadt. Ich mußte natürlich sofort daran denken, wie es gewesen wäre, wenn ich ihn schon beim United Terminal oder dem Münchner Airport-Center als Consultant dabeigehabt hätte. Wie jeder Könner seines Fachs beherrscht Kersalé seine Hardware, die Mittel, mit denen er umgeht – ähnlich wie ein Ingenieur die Grenzen der Materialien kennen muß oder ein Haustechniker mit dem Komfort umgeht. Während der typische Haustechniker nur die Temperatur im Raum mißt, untersucht unser Fachmann Matthias

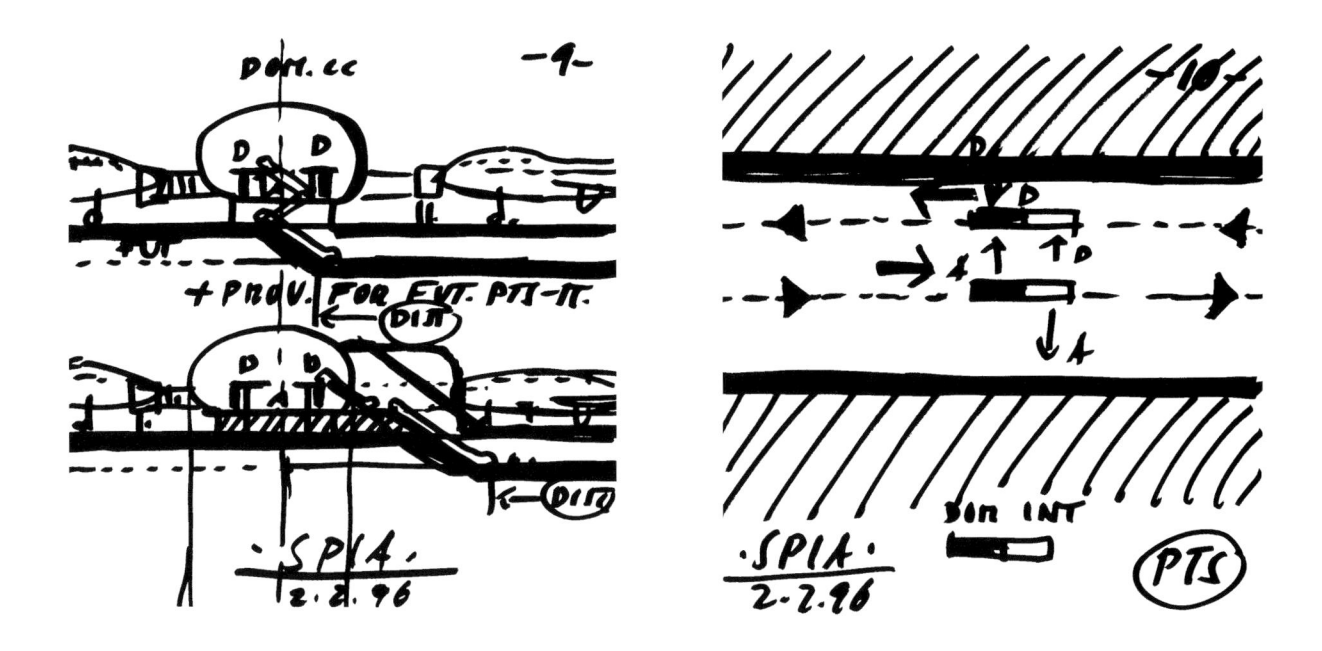

Entwurfsskizzen
Design sketches

Schuler, wie sich der Mensch fühlt, fragt nach der empfundenen Temperatur, wie die Wärme von den Wänden abstrahlt. Kersalé geht ähnlich ganzheitlich beim Sony-Gebäude vor. Bei ihm sind alle Lichter außen. Sie leuchten das Dach an wie eine große Lampe, die nicht von innen, sondern von außen leuchtet, transluzent ist. Dadurch sind die Farben außen, aber kaum innen zu sehen. Sie entstehen durch ein dichroitisches Glas, das er dreht, so daß es auf der einen Seite Rot und Blau, auf der anderen Seite Grün und Gelb leuchtet. Viele Künstler haben das »Dichroitic Glass« verwendet, aber nicht so wie Kersalé. Wir konnten kaum glauben, wie einfach das war. Wenn etwas überzeugt, fragt am Ende keiner, warum es richtig ist. Darin besteht eben die Kunst, etwas für eine gewisse Situation herauszufinden, das stimmig ist.

SOBEK: Wir sind nicht auf der Suche nach dem Auftrag für das höchste Haus, die längste Brücke oder die größte Halle. Stattdessen ist es unser Ziel, perfekter zu werden, auch durch die Beteiligung anderer. Langsam haben wir ein Team von Leuten mit einer ähnlichen Geisteshaltung zusammen, die die Sprache des anderen verstehen gelernt haben. Und auf einmal werden die Gebäude, die wir zusammen planen, klarer, einfacher, logischer. Sie bekommen immer mehr Qualität.

JAHN: Am Anfang bei Sony, beim »serious planning« 1994/95, hatte ich einfach nicht die richtigen Ingenieure an meiner Seite. Die Ingenieure wollten nicht gefordert werden, sondern arbeiteten lieber so, wie sie es

Shanghai-Pudong International Airport

Ansicht des Entwurfs, Modellaufnahme
View of the design, model photo

kannten – nach dem Motto: »Wenn Du nichts Neues ausprobierst, kannst Du auch keine Fehler machen.« Das ist, als wenn einer auf den Berg klettern will und nicht die richtigen Steigeisen hat; dann kommt er nicht hoch. Mit diesen Ingenieuren hätte ich bei Sony diese speziellen Wände nicht machen können. Ich weiß noch, wie sehr ich Überzeugungsarbeit zu leisten versuchte. Mir wurde immer nur erklärt: »But this is a facade. You are the architect. You have to do the facade.« Und ich habe dann immer geantwortet: »No, I can't do the facade.« Das war noch diese herkömmliche Teilung zwischen dem Architekten und dem Ingenieur, der eigentlich nur reagiert. Wir wollen aber einen Ingenieur, der mitwirkt. Nur der typische Architekt sieht seine Position gefährdet, wenn er sie mit jemandem teilen muß.

SOBEK: Zu mir kommen immer wieder Auftraggeber, die sagen: »Herr Sobek, bauen Sie mir doch auch so eine Wand aus Glas.« Häufig besteht dann das Problem, daß ich vielleicht die Sprache des Architekten spreche, aber er sich nicht in meiner Sprache unterhalten kann, weil er sich bisher nicht hineingedacht hat in diese eher ingenieurspezifischen Dinge oder sich auch nicht hineindenken will.

JAHN: Das Ergebnis solcher Mißverständnisse kann man an vielen Gebäuden erkennen. Die Industrie macht das Marketing dafür, indem sie erklärt: »Wir können Ihnen auch so eine Wand herstellen; den Sobek brauchen Sie gar nicht; wir können das ebenso ausrechnen.« Entsprechend sieht dann ein solches Gebäude aus, als ob es

fünf Leute entworfen hätten. Der eine hat das Vordach gemacht, der andere die große Glaswand in der Eingangshalle, der dritte die Sonnenblenden. Aber erst wenn ein Gebäude aus einem Guß entsteht, hat es seine Qualität.

Im Moment sprechen wir vor allem über Glasgebäude, transparente, dynamische Gebäude. Das gleiche gilt aber auch für Steingebäude. Das muß dann nur nach anderen Regeln, mit einer anderen Haltung beurteilt werden. Schließlich muß nicht jeder an das Gleiche glauben. Wenn ich mir aber die neuen Gebäude auf dem Pariser Platz in Berlin anschaue, dann sehe ich, wie sich die Architekten aufgrund einer übergeordneten Haltung zurückgenommen haben. Die besten Gebäude an diesem Platz sind eigentlich noch jene ganz einfachen beiderseits des Brandenburger Tors. Bei den anderen Gebäuden, die eine traditionelle Formensprache zu sprechen versuchen, gewinnt weder das Alte noch das Neue, obwohl man auf Nummer Sicher gegangen ist. Das ist das Gleiche wie beim Berliner Stadtschloß. Wenn man es so wie damals wieder aufbaut, dann weiß man genau, wie es aussieht. Aber wenn man das Wagnis eingeht, etwas anderes zu machen, ist für viele das Risiko zu groß.

KUHN: Sie sind nicht nur ein Team für große Bauten, sondern auch für sehr viel kleiner dimensionierte Projekte, wie »Street Furnitures«.

JAHN: »There is no major and no minor surgery. Every surgery is serious.«

DIFA am Kurfürstendamm in Berlin

In einem schwierigen städtebaulichen Kontext wurde das Bürogebäude für die DIFA bewußt als ordnendes Element entworfen. Die Einzelgebäude haben eine sehr ruhige Form, wenige zusätzliche Elemente wie ein großes Passagendach oder ein fliegender Träger ergänzen das Ensemble, dessen Fassaden vollkommen verglast sind. An seiner im Grundriß dreieckigen Spitze, zum Kurfürstendamm hin, löst sich das Gebäude schließlich vollkommen in Glas auf.

The DIFA office building was deliberately designed as an ordering element in a difficult urban architectural context. The individual buildings present a very calm form; only a few additional elements, including a large arcade roof and a flying buttress, complement the ensemble, the facades of which are constructed completely of glass. The building dissolves completely into glass at its pointed, flat iron-shaped top facing the Kurfürstendamm.

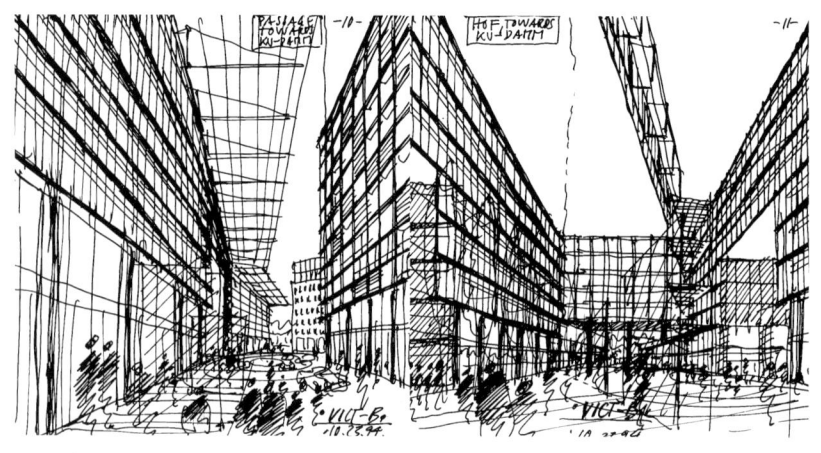

Entwurfsskizzen zur Passage und zum Innenhof
Design sketches for the passage and the courtyard

KUHN: Also gibt es für Sie keinen Unterschied zwischen großen und kleinen Bauaufgaben?

JAHN: Was ist groß, was klein? Das Ku'damm-70-Gebäude hat nur 800 qm, Sony dagegen 200 000 qm. Die Street Furnitures für Decaux waren ein Pilotprojekt, um herauszufinden, wie weit man mit Glas als tragendem Material gehen kann. Das würden wir heute schon wieder anders machen.

SOBEK: Aber es war richtig zu seiner Zeit.

KUHN: Werden diese Straßenmöbel – die Bushaltestelle, die Litfaßsäule, der Zeitungskiosk – auch verwirklicht?

SOBEK: Eine Haltestelle ist jetzt gebaut.

KUHN: Ein vergleichsweise kleines Objekt in Relation zu den meisten Ihrer anderen Bauwerke, die sich vielfach durch eine besondere Höhe auszeichnen und dadurch eine starke Auswirkung auf das urbane Umfeld haben.

JAHN: Die Höhe eines Gebäudes war für mich nie Selbstdarstellung oder ein Zeichen von Gigantomanie. Der Frankfurter Messeturm wurde so hoch gebaut, weil der damalige Bürgermeister Wallmann ihn so hoch haben wollte. Und Sony hat so viele Stockwerke, weil Debis so hoch ist. Ich war eigentlich immer ziemlich leidenschaftslos, wenn es darum ging, auf ein Gebäude mehr oder weniger Geschosse drauf zu tun. Die Qualität bezie-

Gesamtkomplex, Modellaufnahme
Entire complex, model photo

hungsweise die Haltung eines Gebäudes ist mir viel wichtiger. Ich finde die Hochhausdiskussion hat eher mit Sensationalismus zu tun. Sony ist für mich außerdem kein hohes Gebäude. Die Gebäude am Potsdamer Platz bilden zusammen einen städtebaulichen Akzent. Man erkennt sie jetzt als Gruppe und sieht, daß sie eine gewisse Berechtigung haben. Sie signalisieren wie ein Tor den Übergang von der Potsdamer in die Leipziger Straße.

KUHN: Durch den Sony-Turm haben Sie einen »point de vue« geschaffen, eine Markierung innerhalb der Stadt.

JAHN: Ein Hochhaus – ob man es will oder nicht – setzt immer ein Zeichen. Genau dies war auch die Absicht beim Messeturm in Frankfurt. Dieser Typ Wolkenkratzer war für Frankfurt ein Symbol, quasi ein Re-Import, weil das Bauhaus nach Amerika emigrieren mußte, das diese Hochhäuser gebaut hat. In Frankfurt sind sie nur noch ein Abklatsch der 50er-, 60er-Jahre-Hochhäuser Amerikas. Eigentlich sind diese alten Gebäude auch heute noch qualitätvoller als jene, die in den 80er Jahren gebaut wurden: das Civic Center in Chicago, das alte Mies-van-der-Rohe-Gebäude, IBM, Olivetti, das Seagram-Gebäude in New York. Das wird auch noch lange so bleiben, denn in Amerika ist die technologische Durchsetzbarkeit von Ideen, wie wir sie vertreten, sehr gering. Wir arbeiten zur Zeit an einem Gebäude für HA-LO Corporated in Chicago, wo wir nur Bruchteile von dem verwirklichen können – hinsichtlich Materialien, der Integration von Haustechnik –, was wir hier in Deutschland machen.

DIFA am Kurfürstendamm in Berlin

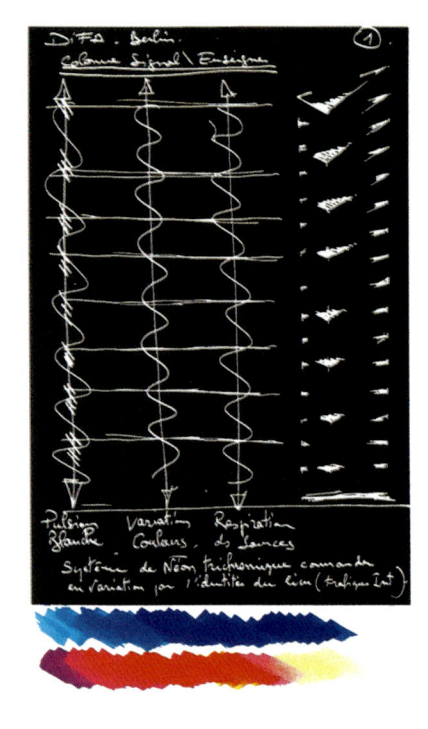

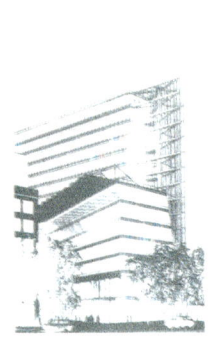

Skizzen von Yann Kersalé zur Illumination der Gebäudespitze
Sketches by Yann Kersalé for the illumination of the top of the building

Ansicht, Café Kranzler im Vordergrund, Modellaufnahme
View with Café Kranzler in the foreground, model photo

SOBEK: Im Grunde genommen hat man Probleme, wenn man an diesem Projekt für Chicago arbeitet.

JAHN: Doch zurück zum Frankfurter Messeturm, der geradezu figürlich wirkt. Das war damals die gewünschte Gestaltung, der Zeitgeist eben. Schon damals haben wir versucht, einen Weg zu finden, wie man eine traditionelle Form in einer modernen, zeitgemäßen Art verwirklichen kann. Das Material Naturstein wurde für mich in dem Moment akzeptabel, als wir herausfanden, daß die Platten nicht 4 cm dick sein mußten, sondern mit Hilfe neuer Maschinen auf 2 cm Dicke reduziert und sogar am Rand eingefräst werden konnten, wodurch sie wie Glas im Rahmen eingebaut werden konnten. Am Messeturm kann man diese Metallrahmen genau sehen. Das Ganze wurde in Paneelen vorgefertigt und mit vier Schrauben befestigt. Und obwohl das Gebäude mehr figürlich wirkt – anders als Sony, das eine viel abstraktere Ästhetik hat –, ist die technische Haltung die Gleiche geblieben: daß man im Umgang mit den Materialien sämtliche technische Möglichkeiten ausnutzt, damit sie in ihrem Ausdruck ehrlich sind. Dieser Weg führt natürlich immer zu einer Minimalisierung. Die Kunst besteht im Weglassen. Das Ziel ist dann erreicht, wenn man etwas weglassen kann.

SOBEK: Oder vielmehr, wenn man am Ende nichts mehr weglassen kann.

JAHN: Aber dieses Ziel werden wir wohl nie erreichen, so lange können wir gar nicht leben. Wir sind auf der Suche nach einer Hülle, die dynamisch reagiert, die nicht mehr aus einer schwerfälligen Konstruktion besteht.

Wir wollen eigentlich nur noch eine Scheibe, nicht mehr die zweischaligen Fassaden, bei denen die Außenscheibe nichts mehr leistet. Aber wir benötigen noch immer Kabel und Halter, die mit Hilfe der Winden das Glas von einem zum anderen Geschoß spannen. Aber irgendwann wird jemand ein Glas entwickeln, das entweder stärker ist oder sich durchbiegen läßt. Es ist nur eine Frage der Zeit, bis ein Glas kommt, das nicht mehr zerbricht. Das aber wird nur entstehen, wenn es jemand fordert.

KUHN: Glas wird also auch in Zukunft Ihr wichtigstes Baumaterial sein.

SOBEK: Wir arbeiten mit Glas aus zweierlei Gründen: erstens wegen der Transparenz, zweitens wegen der technologischen Möglichkeiten. Die Entwicklung wird bei Glas noch wesentlich weitergehen als bisher, indem es zum Beispiel schaltbar wird. Per Knopfdruck wird schon heute eine durchsichtige Scheibe undurchsichtig. Gewisse Frequenzen des Lichtes, beispielsweise die Infrarot-Frequenzen, gehen dann nicht mehr durch, sondern werden reflektiert, damit sich das Gebäude im Sommer nicht aufheizt. Oder man läßt diese Frequenzen im Winter gezielt hindurch, damit das Gebäude erwärmt wird. Glas bietet neben Textilien, die in der Architektur nicht ganz so einfach einsetzbar sind, weil noch niemand ihre Klaviatur so perfekt spielen kann, die größten Entwicklungspotentiale.

JAHN: Ton zum Beispiel kann nicht mehr weiterentwickelt werden. Der ist perfekt. Er kann vielleicht ein

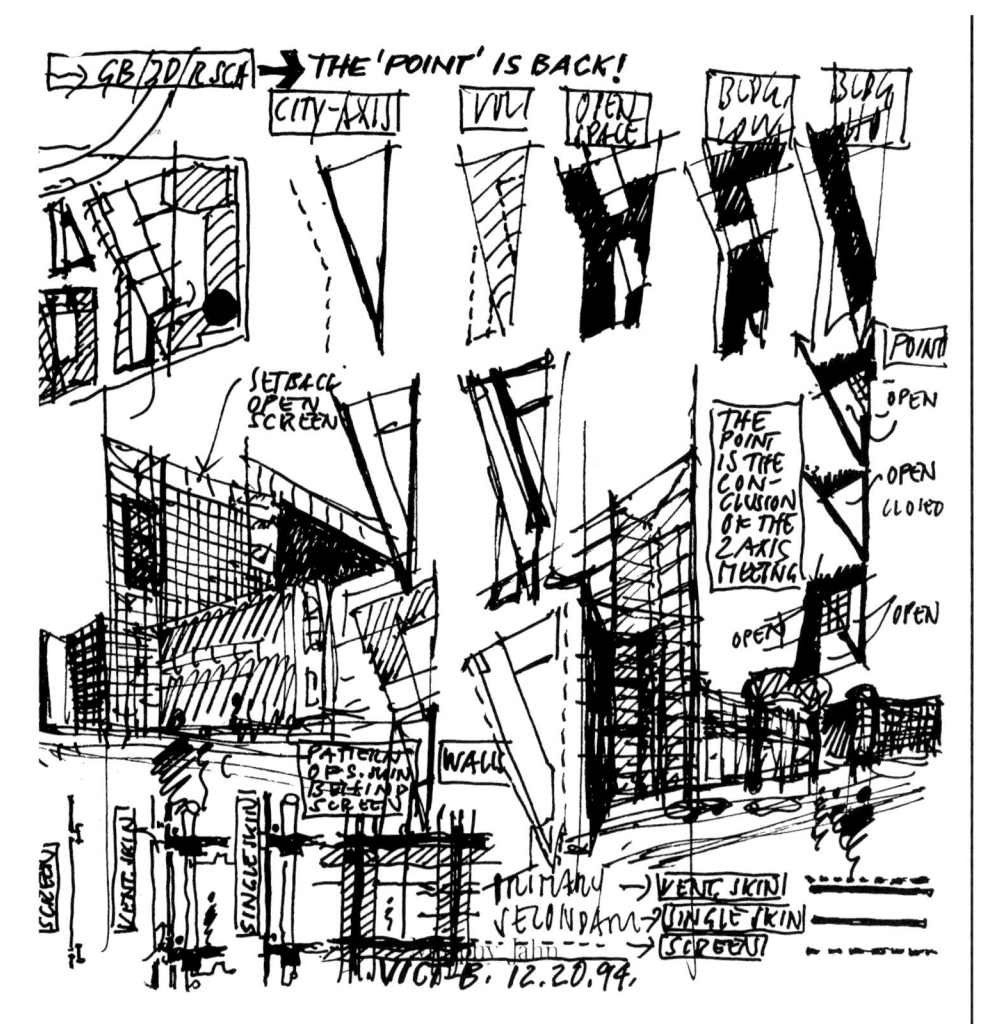

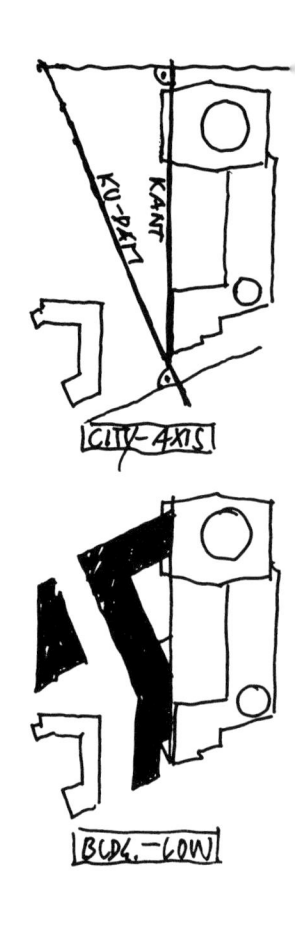

Studien zur Konfiguration der einzelnen Gebäudekörper
Studies for the configuration of individual building shells

bißchen mehr tragen, fester werden, leichter verarbeitet sein, schneller hart werden; aber die Grenze ist erreicht. Auch Stahl hat seine Grenzen, so hochfest wie er heute gemacht wird. Ziegelstein – offen gesagt – interessiert mich auch nicht, denn das ist keine zeitgemäße Technologie mehr. Das ist Handwerk; man legt Stein neben Stein. Und dennoch entstehen noch heute Gebäude, für die der Ziegelstein in der Fabrik auf Geschoßform vorgefertigt wird, weil es von den Kosten her nicht mehr zu vertreten ist, daß Maurer die Ziegelsteine legen. Auf diese Art und Weise wird der Ziegelstein eigentlich vergewaltigt, da er nicht materialgerecht verwendet wird.

SOBEK: Es stellt sich die Frage, warum eigentlich Ziegelsteine noch heute verwendet werden. Der Grund liegt in der Sehgewohnheit; man verbindet damit eben sehr viel. Früher wurde mit Ziegelsteinen gebaut, weil es für die Herstellung großformatiger Elemente keine Technologien gab. Sobald der Ziegelstein größer gemacht wurde, zerplatzte er während des Brennprozesses. Außerdem hatte man keine Baukräne; die Steine wurden auf das Gerüst hochgetragen – bis in die 60er Jahre hinein. Da die heutigen Kräne noch nicht existierten, gab es unglaublich intensive Entwicklungen für kleinteilige Baumodule. Inzwischen verfügt man über diese Hebetechnik, und darum ist es verfehlt, Modulgrößen zu benutzen, die auf die vorhandene Technologie überhaupt nicht abgestimmt sind.

KUHN: Sie arbeiten mit Glas, um Transparenz herzustellen. Hat das auch eine symbolische Bedeutung für Sie, etwa im Sinne des »demokratischen Bauens«?

DIFA am Kurfürstendamm in Berlin

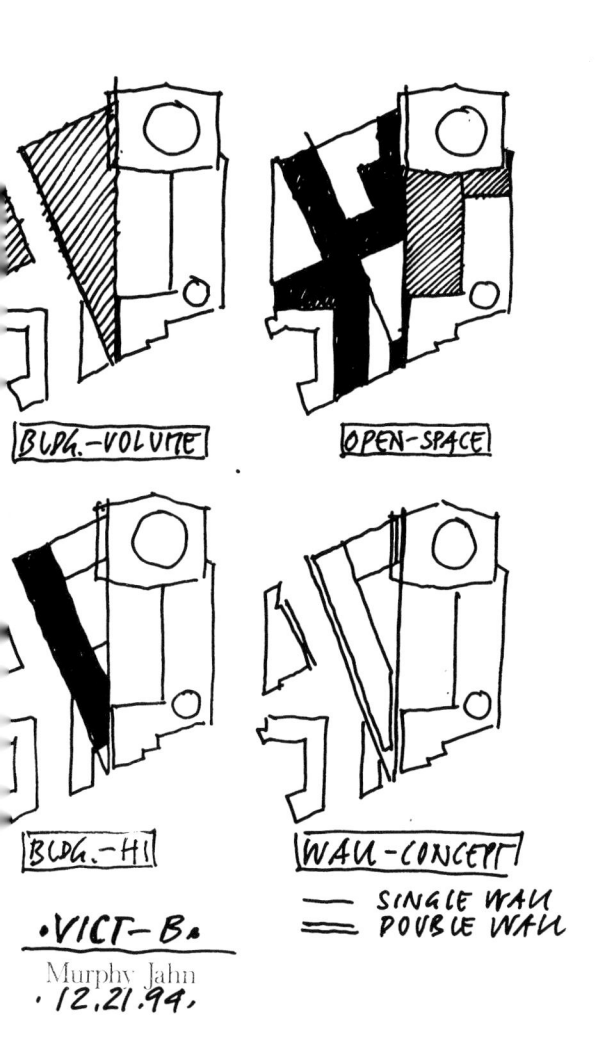

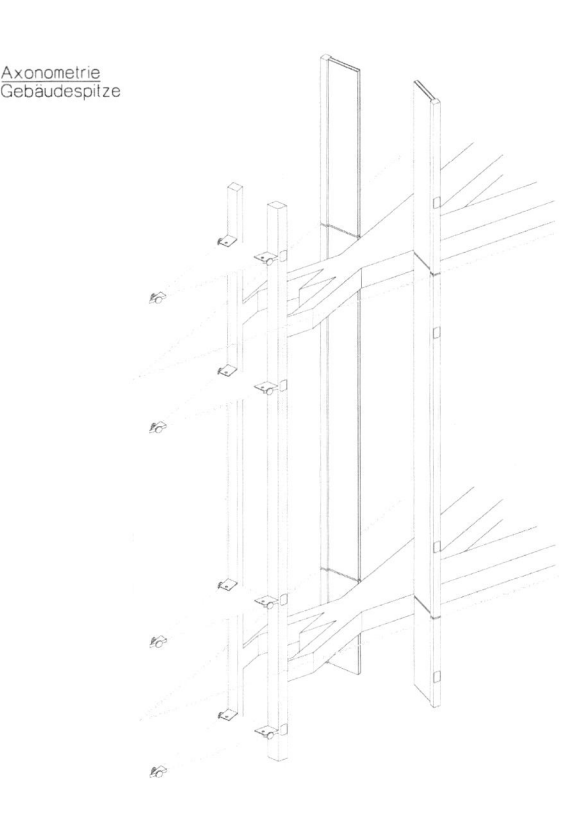

Axonometrie
Gebäudespitze

Perspektivische Darstellung der Konstruktion der vordersten Kante der Gebäudespitze
Perspective view of the construction of the front edge of the top of the building

JAHN: Vor ungefähr 20 Jahren gab es in Frankfurt ein Symposium über demokratische Architektur. Alle haben über Transparenz und Geschichte gesprochen. Nur ich habe Buh-Rufe geerntet, als ich sagte, gute Architektur sei immer monumental. Oh, da wurde vielleicht gepfiffen! Doch am Ende stimmt es doch. All diese Bauwerke – ob die griechischen Tempel, die Pyramiden in Ägypten, das Kolosseum in Rom oder die Train Stations – sind monumental. Da wollte sich nicht ein Architekt oder Ingenieur ein Denkmal setzen, sondern es war angebracht für die Situation. Demokratische Architektur ist doch nur eine andere Art Vergangenheitsbewältigung, Bewußtseinsverdrängung…

SOBEK: Der Ansatz ist außerdem reichlich populistisch, denn die Idee läßt sich allzu leicht formulieren. Manche bauen noch immer nach diesen Vorstellungen.

JAHN: Sie benutzen sie als Marketingmittel.

KUHN: Die Gleichung Glas beziehungsweise Transparenz gleich demokratisches Bauen beziehungsweise offene Gesellschaft stimmt also nicht mehr?

SOBEK: Glücklicherweise. Es gibt gewisse Grundregeln, die sind so trivial, daß man sie gar nicht erwähnen muß. Aber wenn man beispielsweise einen Bundestag baut wie Behnisch, in dem die Besucher hinuntergehen, dann betritt man einen Raum einfach anders. Man schaut von oben auf das herab, was da auf einen zukommt

Flughafen Köln/Bonn:
Fassade Terminal 2, Parkhäuser 2 + 3 und Bahnhof

Als Helmut Jahn Werner Sobek kennenlernte, hatten die Planungen zu diesen Gebäuden unter Beteiligung anderer Ingenieure bereits begonnen. Das Konzept einer absolut entmaterialisierten Fassade für das Terminalgebäude konnte aber nur mit Werner Sobek realisiert werden. Das gleiche gilt für die Screens aus Edelstahlgeweben, welche die großen Parkhäuser durch ein ständig veränderliches Spiel aus Licht und Farbe ihrer Dimension entheben.

Planning for this building with the involvement of other engineers had already begun when Helmut Jahn met Werner Sobek. The concept of an absolutely dematerialised facade for the terminal building could not have been realised without Werner Sobek, however. The same applies to the stainless-steel mesh screens whose constantly changing interplay of light and colour purge the large parking garages of their monumental dimension.

Entwurfsskizze Dach und Fassade des Terminalgebäudes
Design sketch for the roof and facade of the terminal building

– im Gegensatz zum Reichstag, wo man gebeugten Hauptes erst einmal viele Stufen nach oben laufen muß. Das sind die alten Tricks der herrschaftlichen Architektur: die Menschen in gebeugter Haltung und atemlos oben ankommen zu lassen.

KUHN: Kommen wir zu einem anderen Material, dem Holz. Herr Sobek, ich weiß, daß Sie es sehr schätzen. Wäre das nicht auch ein Material für Ihre Zusammenarbeit mit Herrn Jahn? Oder paßt das nicht?

SOBEK: Doch. Das hängt davon ab, wie man Holz verwendet. Im klassischen Ingenieurwesen wird nur mit vier Werkstoffen gearbeitet: mit Stahl, Beton, Holz und Mauerwerk. Wenn Sie in ein Standard-Ingenieurbüro in Deutschland gehen, auch zu den höherqualifizierten, und eine Konstruktion aus Aluminium andenken, dann werden sicherlich alle sagen: »Dies ist interessant, aber das beherrschen wir nicht.« Möchten Sie etwas aus Glas bauen, dann können das mittlerweile einige, aber nicht das Gros. Wollen Sie eine Fassade aus Titan, dann werden Sie keine Antworten bekommen, ebenso bei einem Konstrukt aus Kohlefasern. Ich habe mir schon als Student zum Ziel gemacht, sämtliche Materialien einzusetzen – unabhängig davon, ob es Holz, Bambus, Kohlefaser, Titan oder Beton ist. Und zwar so, daß es immer für den Ort, die zu bauende Architektur stimmig ist. Gleichzeitig will ich die Baustoffe so einsetzen und miteinander verbinden, daß sie dem neuesten technologischen Stand entsprechen, daß sie leicht wieder auseinanderzubauen und zu rezyklieren sind. Dieser Ein-Werkstoff-Gedanke –

Nachtaufnahme der Baustelle des Terminalgebäudes
View of the terminal building construction site at night

Zusammenbauen, Fügen und Entfügen, Komponieren und Dekomponieren – ist uns gemeinsam wichtig.

Holz spielt da natürlich eine besondere Rolle, auch wegen seiner hohen haptischen Qualität. In gewissen Bereichen hat es hervorragende tragende Eigenschaften. Außerdem ist Holz in energetischer Hinsicht wie auch als Wärmedämmung und Schalldämmung attraktiv. Architektonisch richtig angewandt, verfügt Holz über besondere ökologische Qualitäten, da es sich um einen nachwachsenden Rohstoff handelt, den man vergleichsweise einfach rezyklieren beziehungsweise entsorgen kann, solange er mit entsprechend verträglichen Chemikalien oder gar nicht imprägniert ist. Das große Problem beim Holz besteht aber darin, daß es in einer Achse, parallel zu den Holzfasern, ein hervorragend beanspruchbarer Baustoff ist, in der zweiten Achse, nämlich senkrecht zu diesen Fasern, die ja innen hohl sind, nahezu gar nicht beanspruchbar ist, sondern sich zusammendrücken lassen wie ein Schwamm. Das hat Konsequenzen in der Fügetechnik. Es gibt eigentlich keinen größeren Fehler, als in Holz einen Nagel einzuschlagen oder eine Schraube einzudrehen. Aus einem weichen Werkstoff darf man die Beanspruchung nicht punktuell herausnehmen. Holz ist ein sehr leistungsfähiger Baustoff, aber nur dann, wenn man die Kräfte ganz homogen ein- und wieder ausleitet.

KUHN: Kommt Holz für Gemeinschaftsprojekte mit Herrn Jahn also nicht in Frage?

SOBEK: Wir arbeiten in meinem Büro sehr intensiv an der Entwicklung von holzadäquaten Verbindungs-

Auszug aus den Konstruktionsplänen zur Fassade des Terminal 2
Excerpt from the structural drawings for the facade of Terminal 3

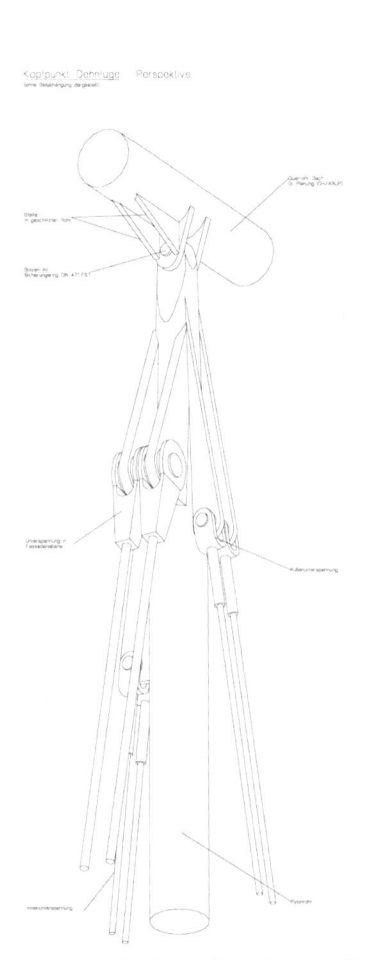

Übersichtszeichnung zur Stahlkonstruktion der Fassade des Terminalgebäudes
Overview drawing of the steel structure for the facade of the terminal building

techniken. Die heute übliche Technik – eine Reihe von Holzstäben über großformatige Stahlteile zusammenzufügen – lehnen wir ab. Für einige Bauwerke, etwa beim A-Motion-Pavillon für DaimlerChrysler, haben wir großformatige Holzteile eingesetzt, die sehr schön in ihrer formalen Qualität sind. Am Ende gibt es aber immer noch einen metallischen Beschlag, der mit Bolzen stahlbaugerecht verbunden wird. In dem Augenblick, in dem wir eine befriedigende Lösung im Zusammenfügen von Holz finden, kann ich mir vorstellen, daß auch Herr Jahn etwas in Holz baut.

JAHN: Ich habe immer gefunden, daß Holz als ein natürliches Material zu wertvoll ist. Aber vielleicht weiß ich auch nicht genug über Holz, wie man es verbindet.

KUHN: Das Gebäude der Zukunft scheint sich nicht nur durch höhere Flexibilität in der Benutzbarkeit auszuzeichnen, sondern insgesamt durch das Moment der Bewegung. Zumindest ist das bei einigen Ihrer Arbeiten zu erkennen, Herr Sobek. Verbirgt sich dahinter eine weitere Vision für die Architektur des 21. Jahrhunderts, die aus der Verbindung zwischen Architekt und Ingenieur ihre Weiterentwicklung erfährt?

SOBEK: Das Moment der Bewegung wird für uns eine zunehmende Notwendigkeit, etwa um ein Dach flexibel öffnen und schließen zu können. Vieles probiere ich aber außerhalb unserer Zusammenarbeit aus, etwa im Bereich der Messestände, da diese meist nur einen Monat oder eine Woche stehen und der Auftraggeber eher

Flughafen Köln/Bonn

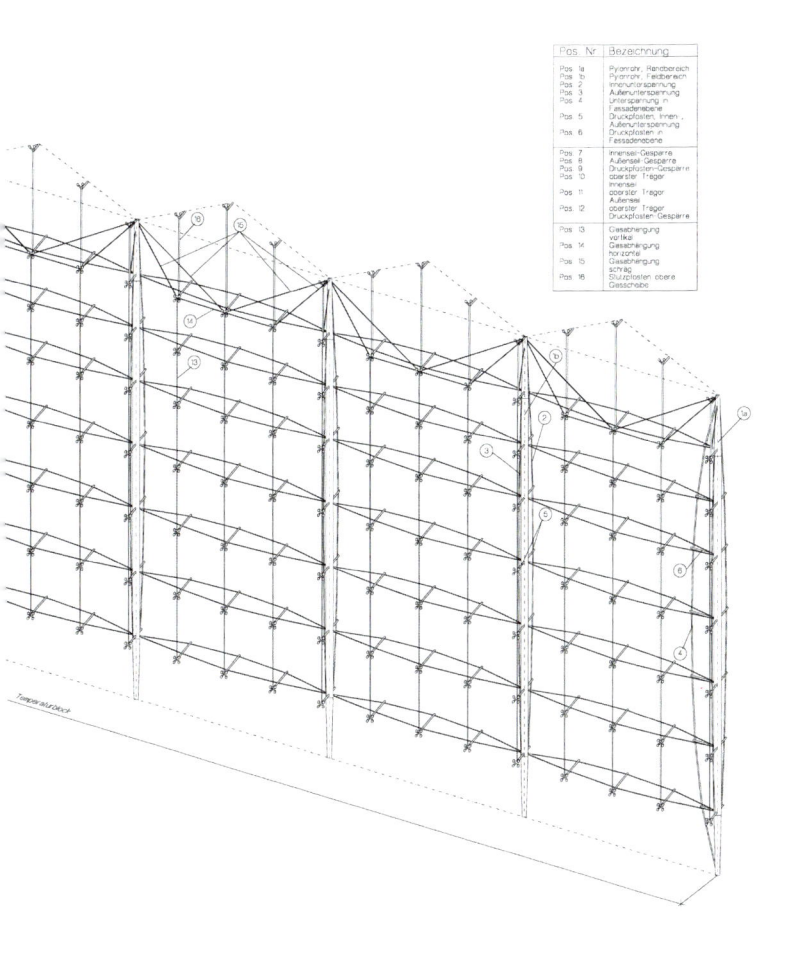

Gesamtanlage, im Vordergrund das Parkhaus 2, dahinter Terminal 2, Modellaufnahme
Entire airport facility, Car Park 2 in the foreground, Terminal 2 to its rear, model photo

FLB - PARKHAUS 2

ANSICHT:

SCREEN AUS GLD- EDELSTAHLGEWEBE.

V-SCHNITT:

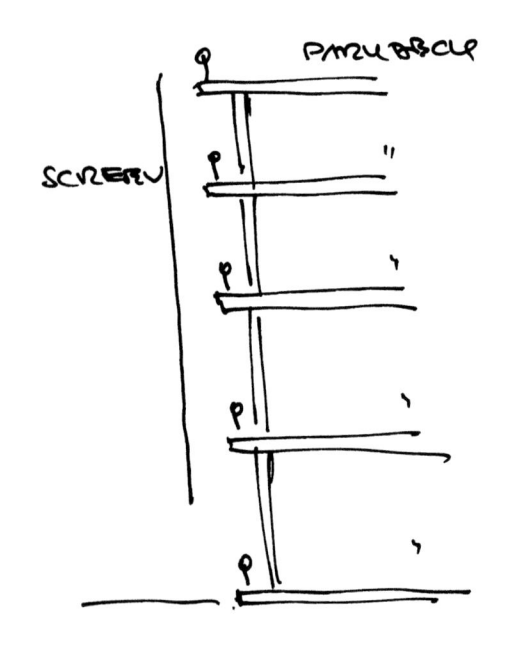

PARKDECK

SCREEN

SCREEN SCHWEBT/HÄNGT 20-40 CM VOR DER AUSSENKANTE DER PARKDECKS.

MESH 1:1

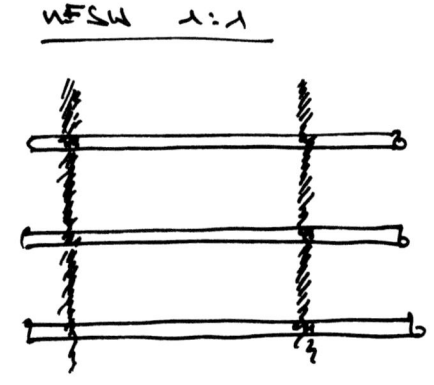

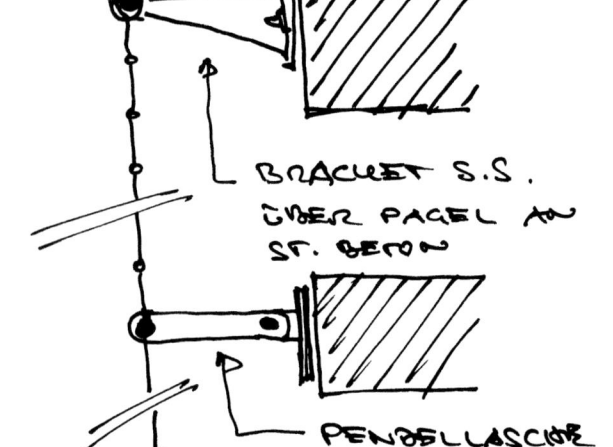

BRACKET S.S. ÜBER PAGEL AN ST. BETON

PENDELLASCHE

SPIRALFEDER, ZWILLING:

- EISLAST ANSETZEN!
- WINDLAST NUR UM 10-20% REDUZIEREN. (PERFORATION DER FLÄCHE IST VORHANDEN ABER: AERODYNAMISCHE VERSPERRUNG).

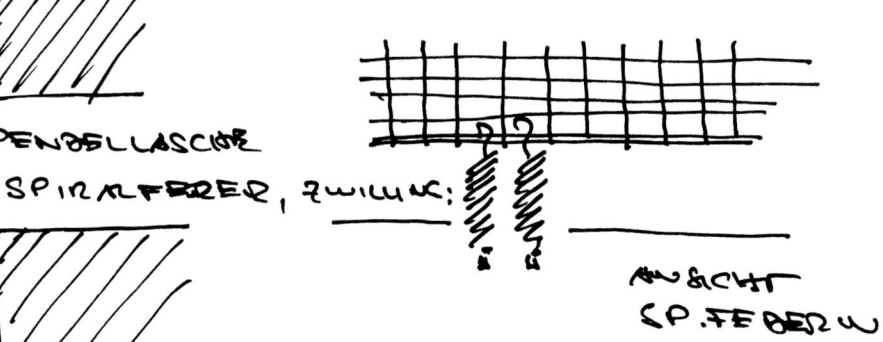

ANSICHT SP.FEDERN

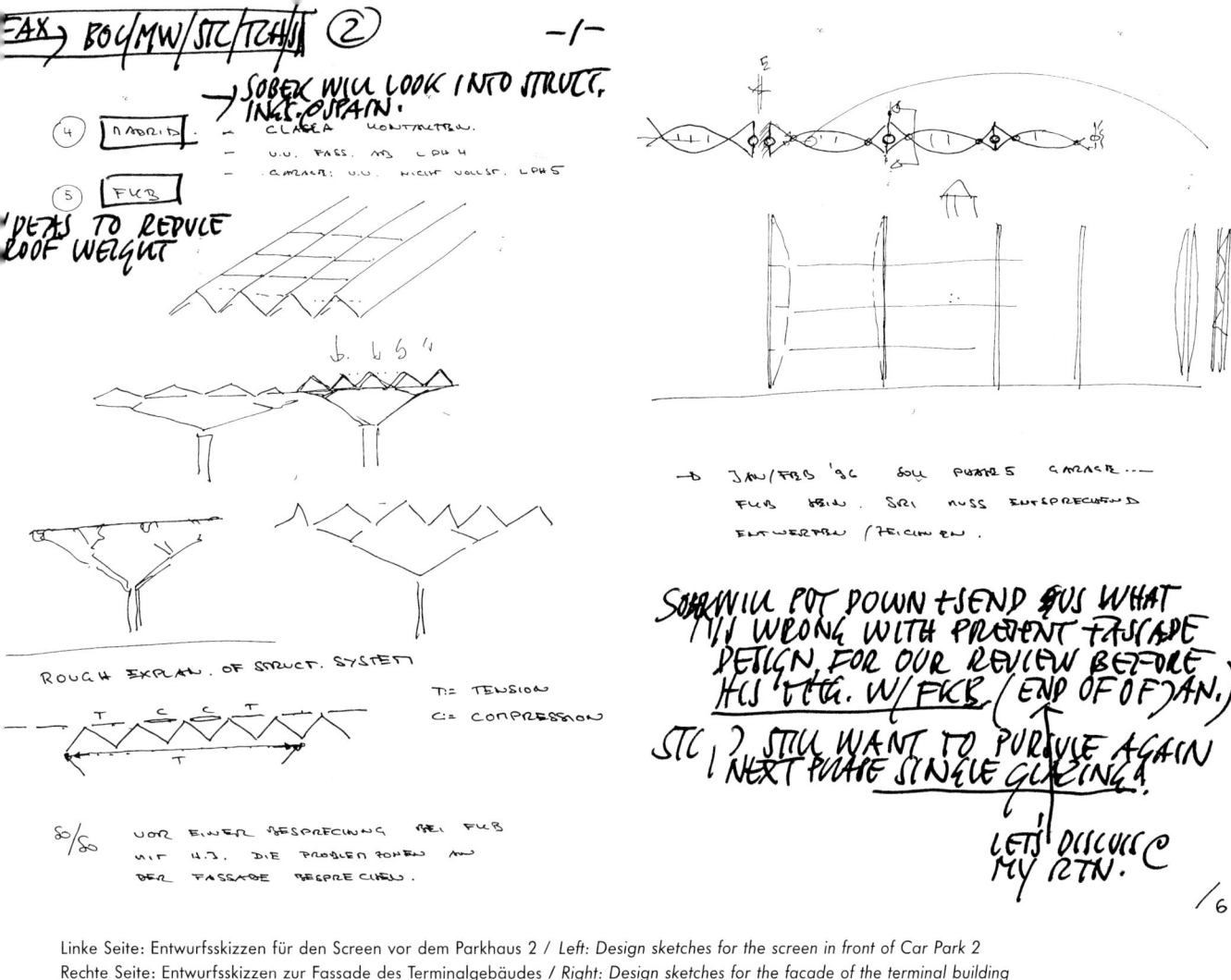

Linke Seite: Entwurfsskizzen für den Screen vor dem Parkhaus 2 / Left: Design sketches for the screen in front of Car Park 2
Rechte Seite: Entwurfsskizzen zur Fassade des Terminalgebäudes / Right: Design sketches for the facade of the terminal building

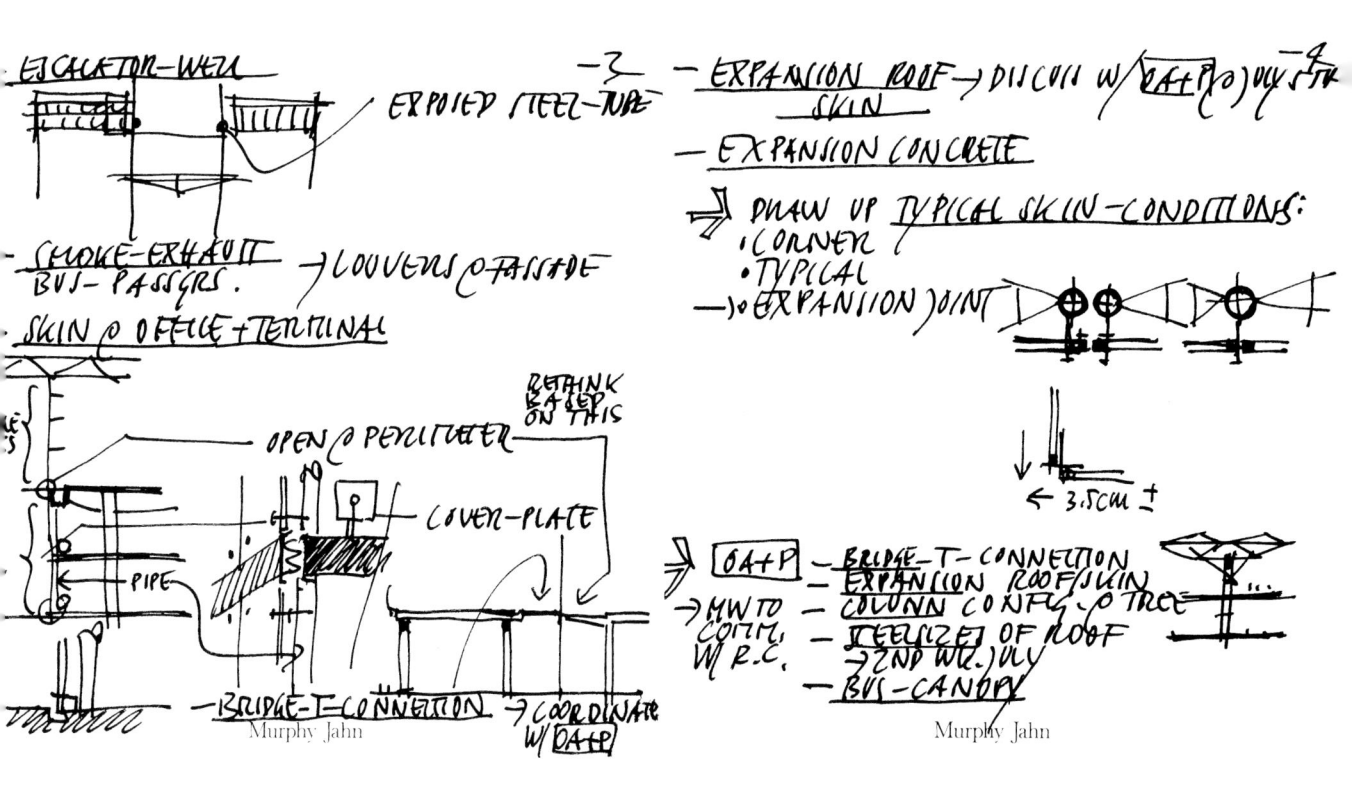

Flughafen Köln/Bonn

Schrägaufsicht auf das Glasdach des unterirdischen Bahnhofes, dahinter Terminal 2, Modellaufnahme
Oblique view of the glass roof of the underground railway station, Terminal 2 to its rear, model photo
Rechte Seite: Parkhaus 2, Blick nach oben in die Parkwendel. Folgende Seiten: Parkhaus 2, Detailaufnahme des Screens aus Edelstahlgewebe
Right: Car Park 2, upward view into the parking spiral. Following pages: Car Park 2, detail view of the stainless steel mesh screen

bereit ist, ein gewisses Risiko einzugehen. Da muß dann nicht immer alles wasserdicht sein, und man hat die Möglichkeit, etwas aus Kohlefasern zu bauen oder in Holz auszuprobieren. Das sind Experimente, um Sicherheit zu erzielen, bevor wir das im größeren Maßstab einem Bauherrn vorschlagen, der dann viele Millionen Mark investiert, dessen Existenz häufig davon abhängt und für den es die nächsten fünfzig Jahre funktionieren muß.

Helmut Jahn und ich machen ähnliche Experimente auch schon zusammen. So haben wir zu viert in Stuttgart – gemeinsam mit dem Gebäudephysiker Matthias Schuler und einem Akustiker – einen hölzernen Container bauen lassen, um die Lichttransmission unterschiedlicher Gewebelagen zu untersuchen. Natürlich kann man ausrechnen, durch wieviele Lagen Gewebe wieviel Licht hindurchgeht. Aber was sagt die Zahl 1,5 % schon? Deshalb wollten wir dies selbst erfahren und haben einen Nachmittag in diesem Container verbracht, um herauszufinden, wie sich die Helligkeit im Raum verändert.

JAHN: Heute haben wir auf diese dreischalige Konstruktion mit einer Membran außen, einer innen und akustischen Absaugern in der Mitte weltweit das Patent.

SOBEK: Natürlich gibt es nie die eine Lösung. Man hat ein Repertoire an sogenannten richtigen Lösungen. Die Kunst besteht nun darin, daß man den Fächer dieses Repertoires öffnet und weiß, welche Lösung man mit den anderen Lösungen bei einem Bauwerk zusammenbringen muß, damit der Duktus insgesamt durchgängig ist.

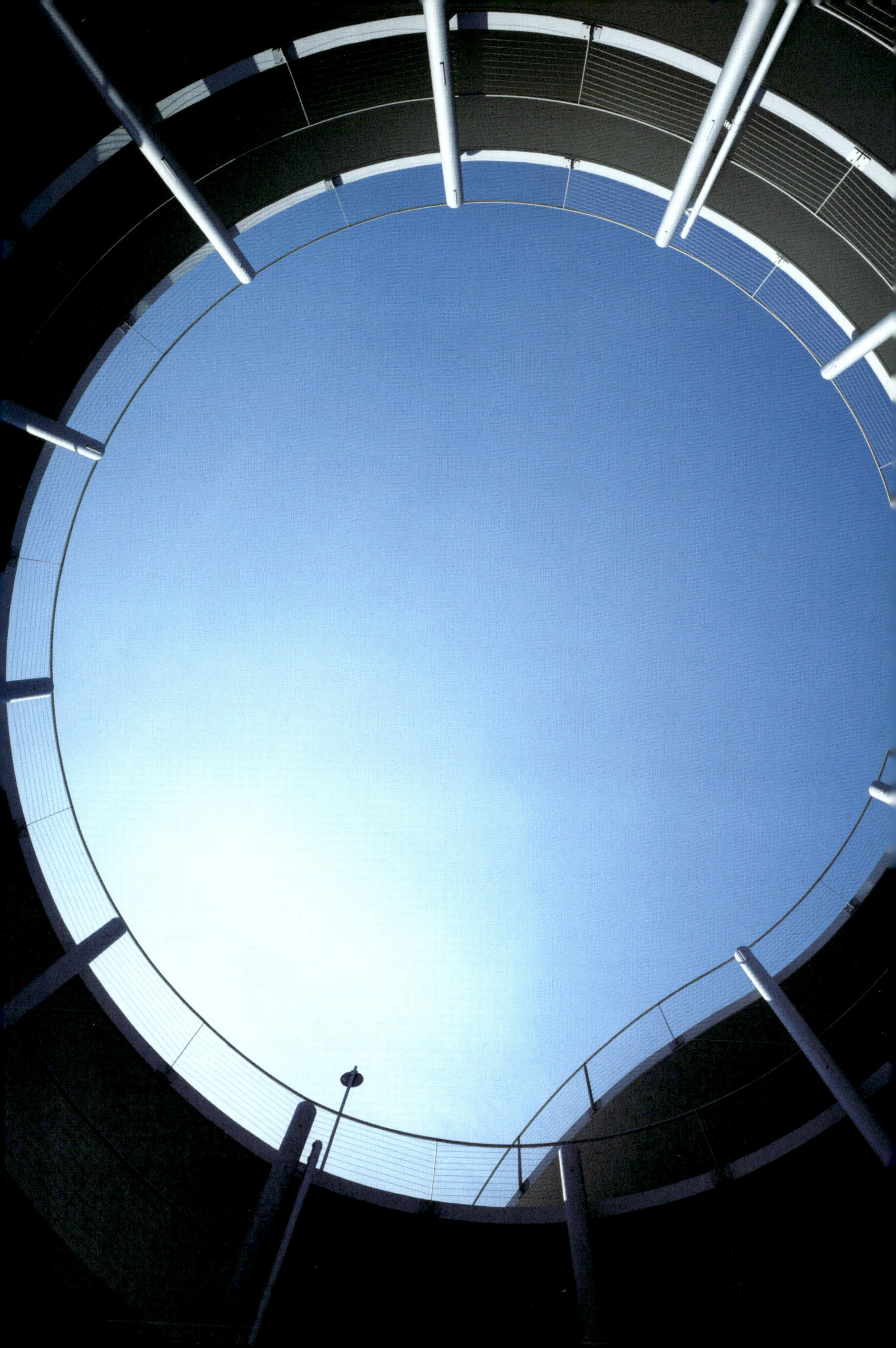

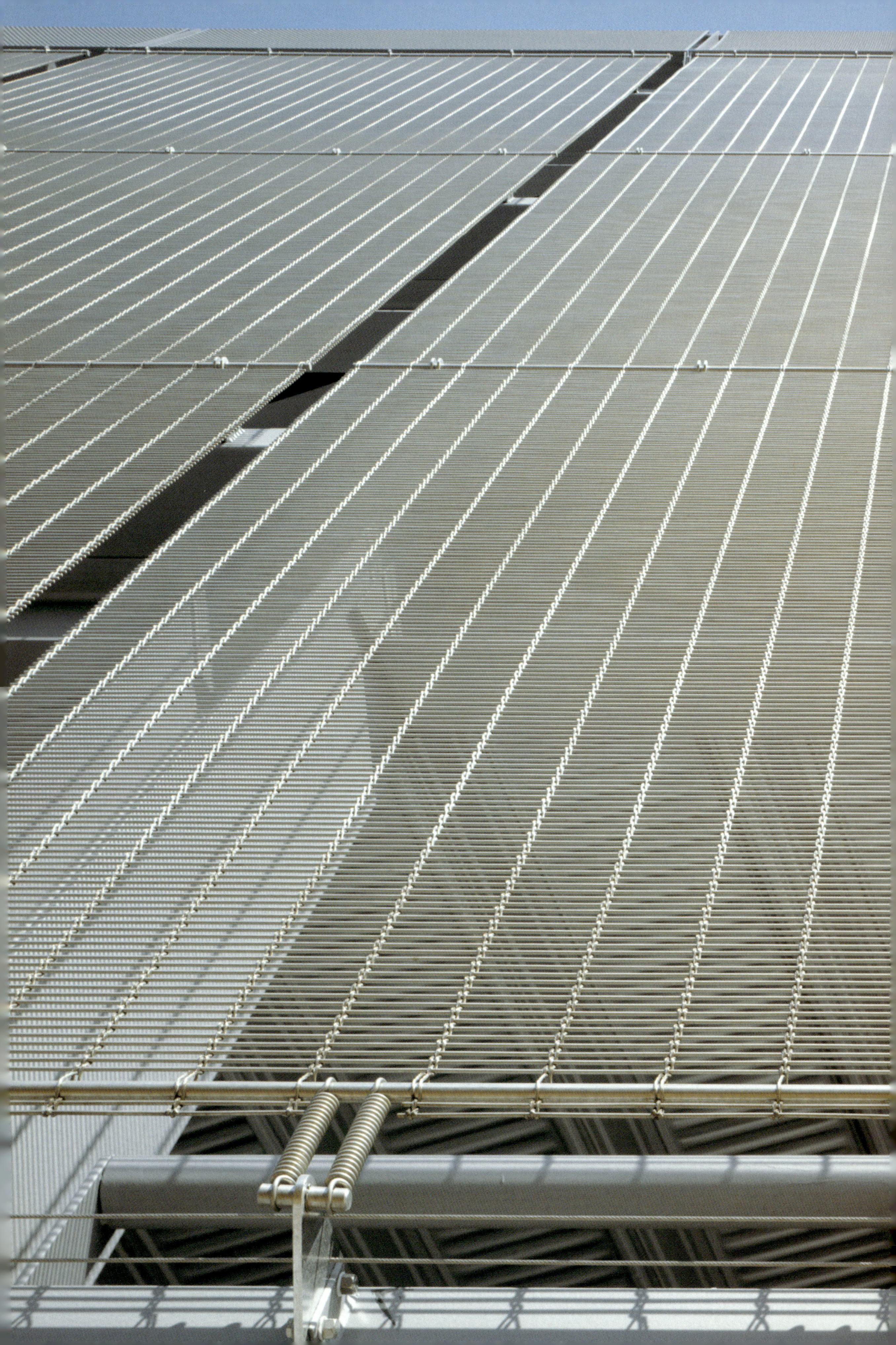

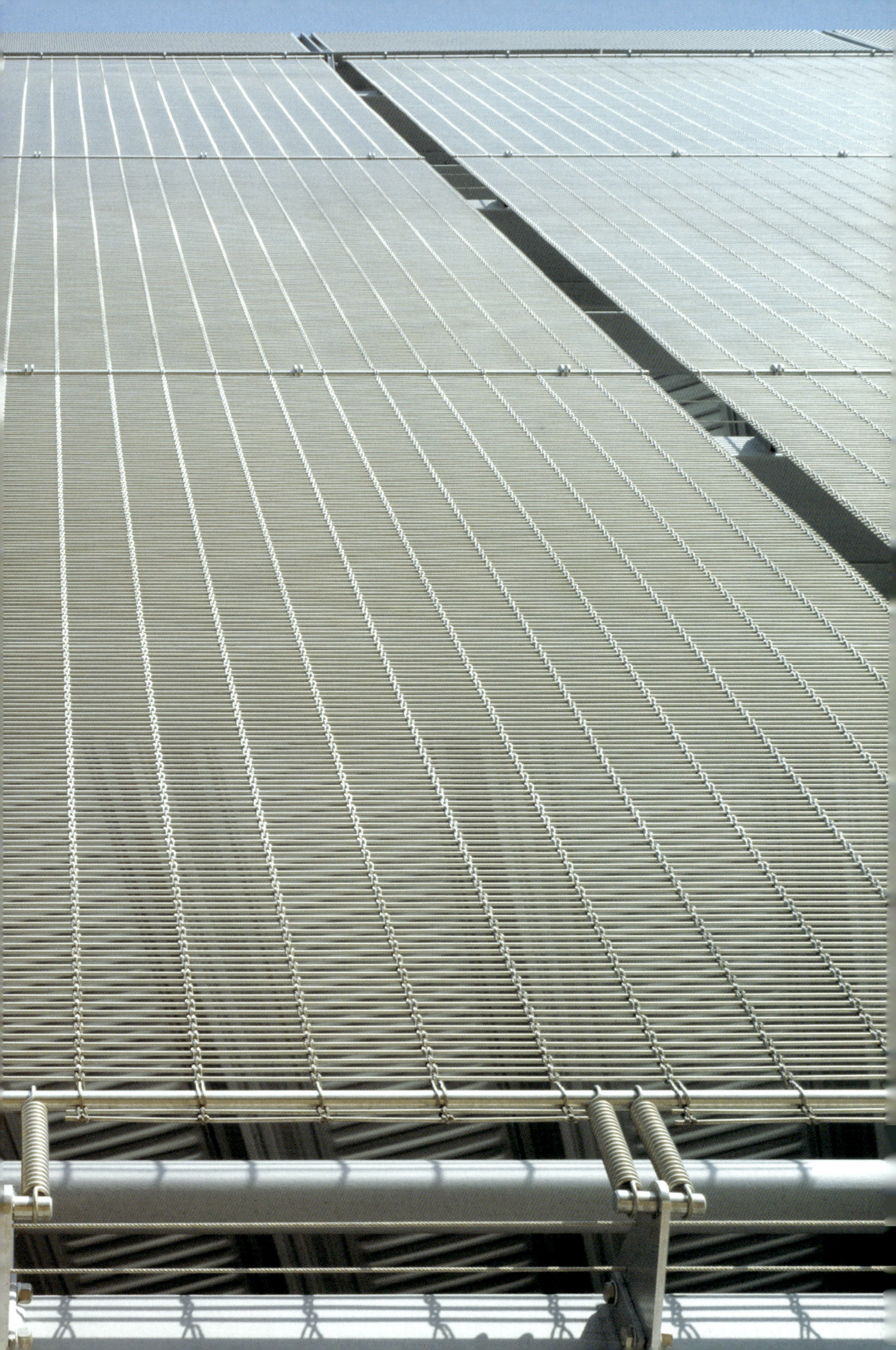

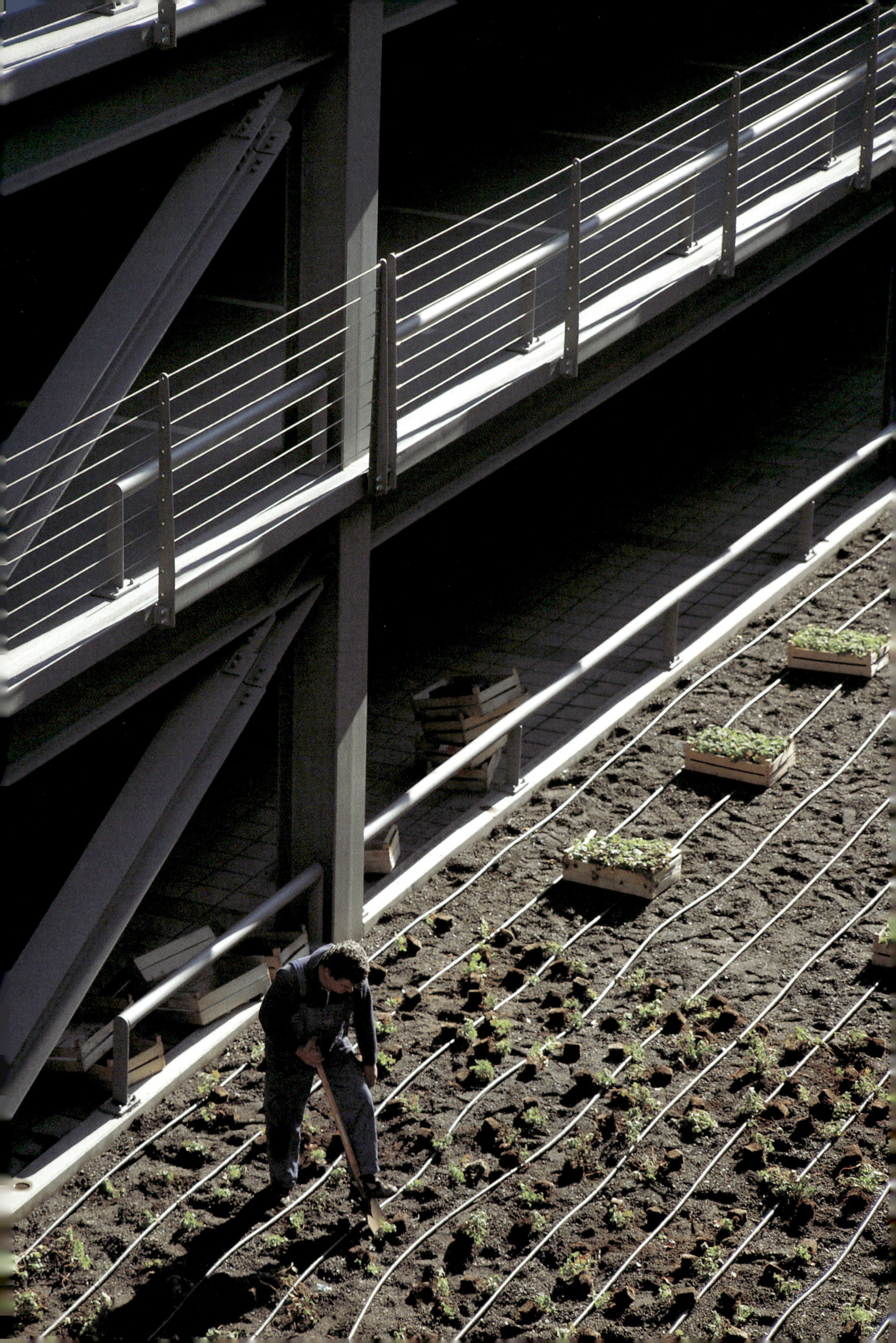

Linke Seite: Parkhaus 2, Detailaufnahme der Stahlkonstruktion der Treppenhäuser
Left: Car Park 2, detail view of the steel structure of the stairways

Eine Stütze zu dimensionieren ist trivial, aber alle Dinge so zu formen, daß sie zueinander passen und jeweils für sich richtig sind, darin besteht die Leistung.

KUHN: Beziehen Sie sich dabei auf eine bestimmte Tradition? Wen würden Sie als Ahnherren – auch Ihrer Zusammenarbeit – bezeichnen?

SOBEK: Das läßt sich für mich nicht so leicht beantworten, denn im Ingenieurwesen gibt es in dem Sinne keine Schulen. Man spricht zwar von einer Stuttgarter Schule, aber die ist eher durch die Haltung geprägt, wie man mit den Materialien umgeht im Bereich der Fügetechnik, der Verarbeitung und Berechnung. Das trifft aber nicht für den gestalterischen Umgang mit den Materialien zu. Zudem ist die Stuttgarter Schule auf wenige Werkstoffe fixiert: Stahlbeton, Holz, Stahl und ein wenig Mauerwerk. Erweitert man die Palette der Materialien auf Titan, Aluminium, Glas und ähnliches, dann gibt es keine Vorbilder mehr. Bezeichnenderweise gibt es bis heute im Ingenieurwesen keinen Stilbegriff.

JAHN: Natürlich könnte man auf die Frage nach der Herkunft eine konventionelle Antwort geben und mit Leuten wie Maillart, Nervi, Prouvé kommen oder an einen Vorläufer wie Paxton im Ingenieurwesen erinnern. Dennoch stimme ich Werner Sobek zu. Unser Bauen fängt eigentlich erst mit dem McCormick Palace an, bei dem es ebenfalls diese strukturelle Vorprägung gab. Gewiß, Prouvé hat mich interessiert wegen der Vorfertigungen.

Flughafen München Terminal 2 (Wettbewerb / Competition)

Das Terminal ist eine der radikalsten Formulierungen und einer der Höhepunkte in der Reihe von Bauten, die Helmut Jahn und Werner Sobek zusammen geplant haben. Ein großes ebenes Dach aus Stahlträgern schwebt über dem Terminal. Es wird nur durch wenige Stützen gehalten. Die Dachhaut besteht aus Metall und elektrochromatischem Glas, dessen Transparenz modifizierbar und somit den veränderlichen Lichtbedingungen der Atmosphäre anpaßbar ist. Optisch kaum noch wahrnehmbare senkrecht gespannte Seile halten eine vollkommen aus Glas bestehende Fassade.

This terminal is one of the most radical designs and certainly one of the most outstanding of the many architectural structures planned by the team of Helmut Jahn and Werner Sobek. A large, level roof of steel girders appears suspended above the terminal. It is held in place by a very few supports. The skin of the roof is made of metal and electrochromatic glass, which can be modified to exhibit varying degrees of transparency and thus adapted in response to changing atmospheric light conditions. Barely perceptible cables stretched in a vertical configuration stabilise a facade consisting entirely of glass.

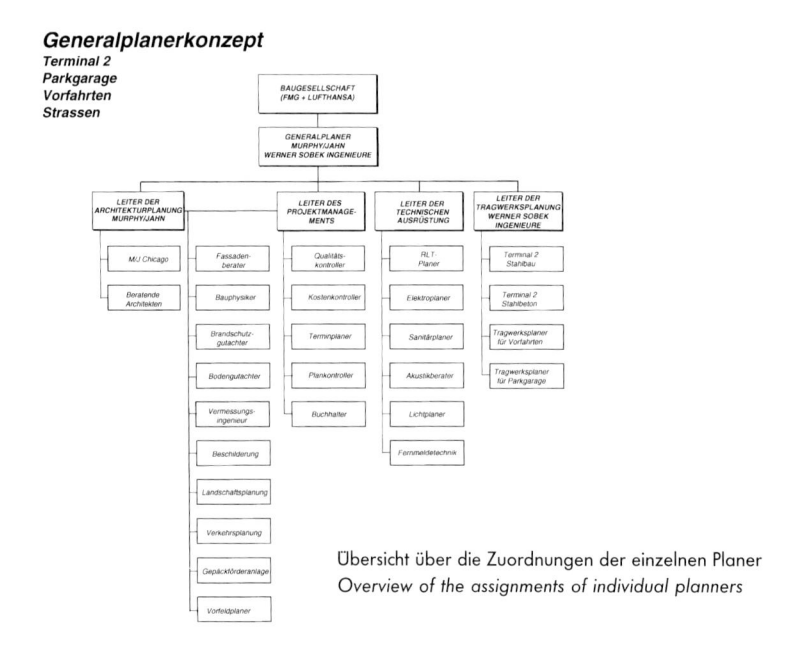

Übersicht über die Zuordnungen der einzelnen Planer
Overview of the assignments of individual planners

Aber letztlich muß diese Frage nach der Herkunft unserer Arbeit jemand anderer beantworten.

SOBEK: Im Grunde ist es auch weniger eine Schule, auf die man sich beruft, sondern es sind eher Menschen, die prägend sind: Frei Otto etwa oder Jörg Schlaich, für den ich mehrere Jahre gearbeitet habe, waren sicher prägend. Auch Jürgen Joedicke. Hinzu kommt der Einfluß der Verstorbenen, Maillart, Prouvé. Aber die haben keine Schule im klassischen Sinn geprägt. Für meinen Ansatz war vielmehr eine Unzufriedenheit mit dem bisherigen Repertoire an Lösungen, die es bislang im Bauingenieurwesen gab, ausschlaggebend. Das führte dann dazu, daß ich mich mit Flugzeug- oder Automobilkonstruktionen beschäftigt habe, etwa mit der Konstruktion eines Concorde-Flügels oder der Form eines Automobilkotflügels. Diese Technologien beherrsche ich heute. Und dieses Wissen, etwa wie man mit Dünnblech umgeht, kann ich auf den Bau mit dünnem Glas transferieren.

JAHN: Aber all das kommt nicht von einem Studium der Geschichte oder ihrer versuchten Fortsetzung, sondern es resultiert aus einer Kenntnis, über die unsere Vorgänger noch nicht verfügten. Ich glaube, jedes Mal, wenn man sich auf die Geschichte als Inspiration beruft, ist man verloren, verloren in Bezug auf den Fortschritt. Derjenige, der die Concorde entworfen hat, hat sich schließlich auch nicht damit auseinandergesetzt, wie die JU 52 geflogen ist.

SOBEK: Vor circa 15 Jahren begann das Thema der Ingenieurgeschichte zunehmend wichtiger zu werden.

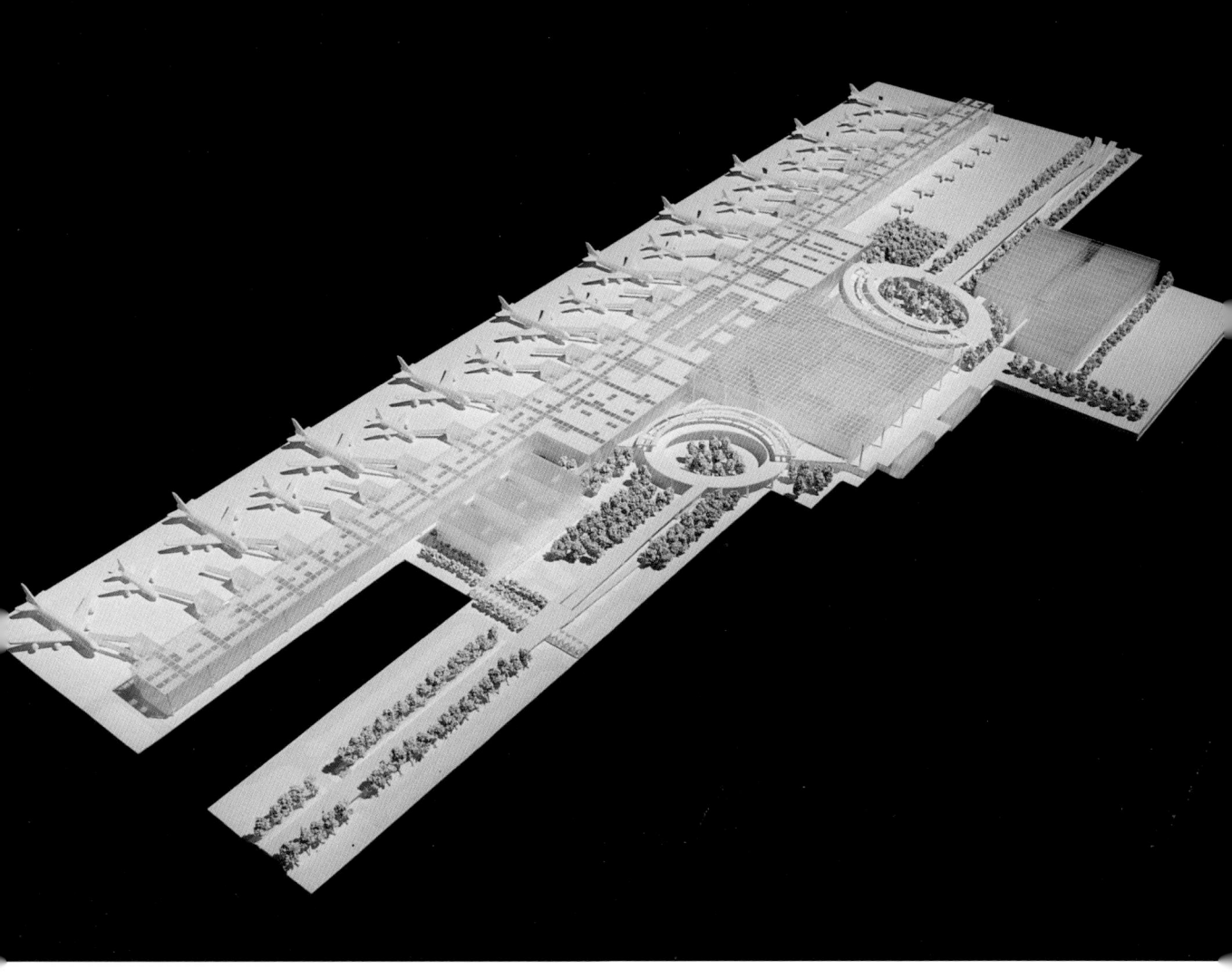

Gesamtansicht des Wettbewerbsbeitrages, Modellaufnahme
General view of the competition entry, model photo

Das war sicherlich ein unterstützenswerter Ansatz, um die Wurzeln zu erforschen und das eigene Berufsbild nachzuzeichnen. Andererseits resultierte die Beschäftigung mit der Ingenieurgeschichte bei einigen auch aus einer gewissen Ratlosigkeit, weil man den Stahl im Griff hatte, den Beton beherrschte, Holz und Mauerwerk als nahezu trivial empfand.

JAHN: Das berühmte Wort der 80er Jahre lautete dafür Postmodernismus. Damals habe ich auch mitgemacht. Aber wenn ich heute zurückblicke, funktionierte es nicht. Das hatte nicht die Kraft der Architektur, die wir zehn Jahre zuvor gebaut hatten, die heute noch gut aussieht, sogar erstaunlich gut. Doch heute ist diese Zeit endgültig vorüber, die Postmoderne ist tot. Die in dieser Zeit entstandenen Gebäude sehen aus wie Old Ladies mit zuviel Schmuck.

SOBEK: Ich habe da die Gnade der späten Geburt.

JAHN: In dieser Zeit wurde einfach nichts Bedeutendes produziert. Damals ging es der Wirtschaft hervorragend; die Steuern waren niedrig, die Leute haben gut verdient, bis die Bush-Jahre kamen. Das ist heute mit Clinton wieder so: Der Stockmarket geht hoch, die Menschen sind reich, geben ihr Geld aus, und wieder entsteht nichts Wichtiges. Leuten, die etwas Gutes gemacht haben, ist es ohnehin nie ums Geld, sondern um die Ideen gegangen. Deswegen finden sich in Amerika heutzutage auch so wenige gute Ideen in der Architektur, im Inge-

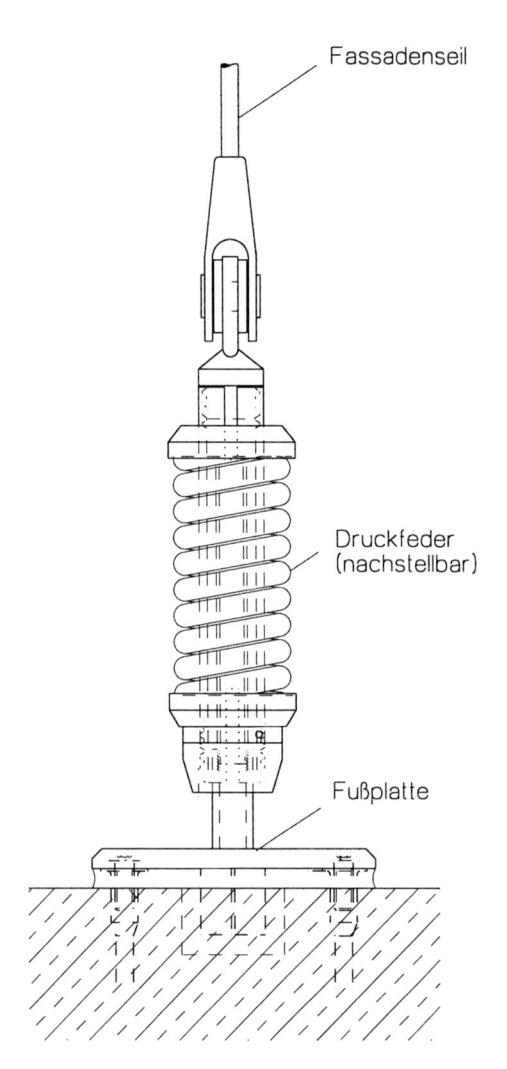

Konstruktionsdetail: Feder der an vertikalen Seilen aufgespannten Glasfassade
Structural detail: spring for the glass facade mounted on vertical cables

nieurwesen verwirklicht. Dort fehlt es nicht nur an der Akzeptanz für technologische Neuerungen, sondern auch an der Durchsetzbarkeit in der Industrie.

KUHN: Ihre gemeinsame Arbeit reflektiert auch die komplexer gewordenen Anforderungen an die Architektur heute, die in immer größeren städtebaulichen Dimensionen entsteht und diverse Funktionen abdecken muß. So befriedigen das Sony-Center in Berlin und das Campus Center IIT, auch die Messe Shanghai-Pudong vielfältige urbane Bedürfnisse und sind mittlerweile eigenständige städtische Gebilde.

JAHN: Bei Sony gab es einen Masterplan, einen städtebaulichen Plan, der eine Blockstruktur vorschrieb. So mußten wir einerseits die Anlage auf die 19.-Jahrhundert-Stadtstruktur zurückbringen, andererseits hatten wir durch die besonderen Grundstücks- beziehungsweise Besitzverhältnisse innerhalb des Terrains eine neue räumliche Ordnung zu schaffen. Wir wollten nicht nur Büros, kommerzielle Gebäude, Wohngebäude, sondern auch ein Entertainment-Center unterbringen, eine räumliche Ordnung also, die wie in einer typischen Stadtstruktur mehrfach benutzbar ist. Das Berliner Sony-Gebäude steht in der Nachfolge des State of Illinois Center in Chicago. Auch dort haben wir bis zu einem gewissen Grad einen Stadtraum geschaffen und ihn ins Gebäude geholt. Ich erinnere mich noch, als dort die Fassade fertig war, habe ich mir für das nächstes Mal vorgenommen, keine Fassade mehr davor zu setzen, so wie wir es jetzt in Berlin gemacht haben. Bei den Besprechungen in Chicago hieß

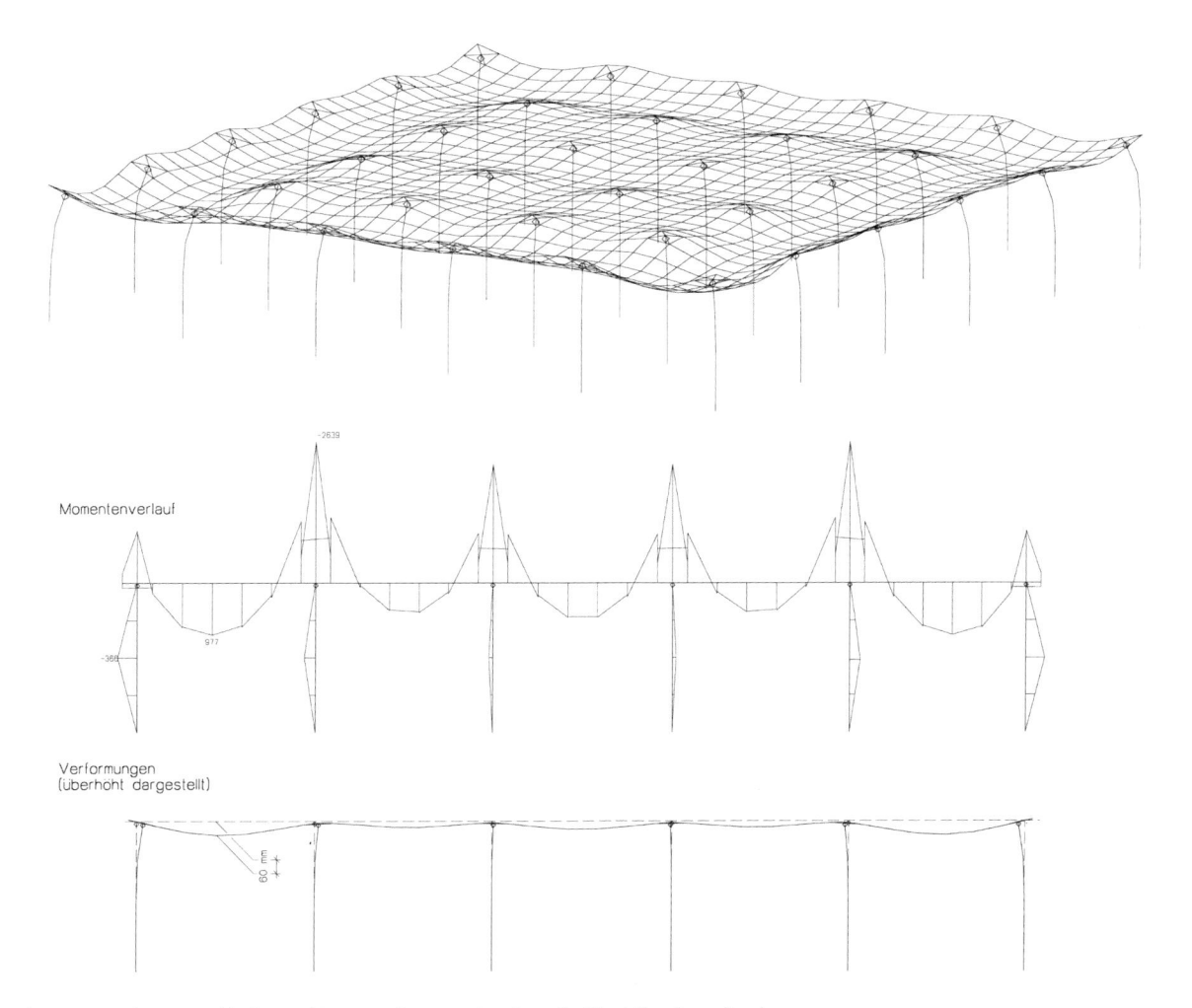

Deformationen des Terminaldaches und Beanspruchungen seiner Bauteile (überhöhte Darstellung)
Deformations in the terminal roof and resulting strain on roof components (exaggerated presentation)

es immer: »You have to put some doors there. There got to be doors, we got to control it.« Und in Deutschland denken alle, Sony sei eine typisch amerikanische introvertierte Mall. Das Gegenteil ist der Fall; es wird dort immer offen sein, und man kann jederzeit hineingehen. Das ist ein Merkmal vieler unserer Projekte – so auch beim Kranzler-Eck –, daß wir nach Möglichkeiten gesucht haben, den öffentlichen Raum in die Gebäude einzubinden. Selbst bei den Messeprojekten entsteht so etwas wie eine Stadtstruktur. Die Messe in Shanghai etwa mit ihrem Vorplatz, den Freiräumen, den Außenflächen für die Ausstellung – das ist wie ein richtiger Stadtraum.

KUHN: Ebenso bei den Flughäfen.

JAHN: Ja, etwa der Flughafen in München ist um einen solchen Stadtraum gruppiert. Ganz gleich wie er heute von vielen beurteilt wird. Es war die beste Entscheidung, die dort gefällt wurde – einen großen, freien Raum ins Zentrum zu setzen inmitten eines großen Gebäudes. Jemand hat das mit einer Kathedrale in einer Stadt verglichen, die auch ein Zeichen setzt, das Zentrum markiert. Je mehr von diesen Bauten entstehen, desto wichtiger wird das. Viele behaupten jetzt, das sei zu groß. Aber so sah es damals der Wettbewerb vor. Das Urteil der Geschichte kommt ohnehin hinterher.

SOBEK: Das ist ein typisch deutsches Argument: Etwas sei zu groß. Das hört man hier permanent.

JAHN: In Frankreich ist das anders. Dort gibt es zahlreiche interessante Gebäude. Doch wieviele Bauten sol-

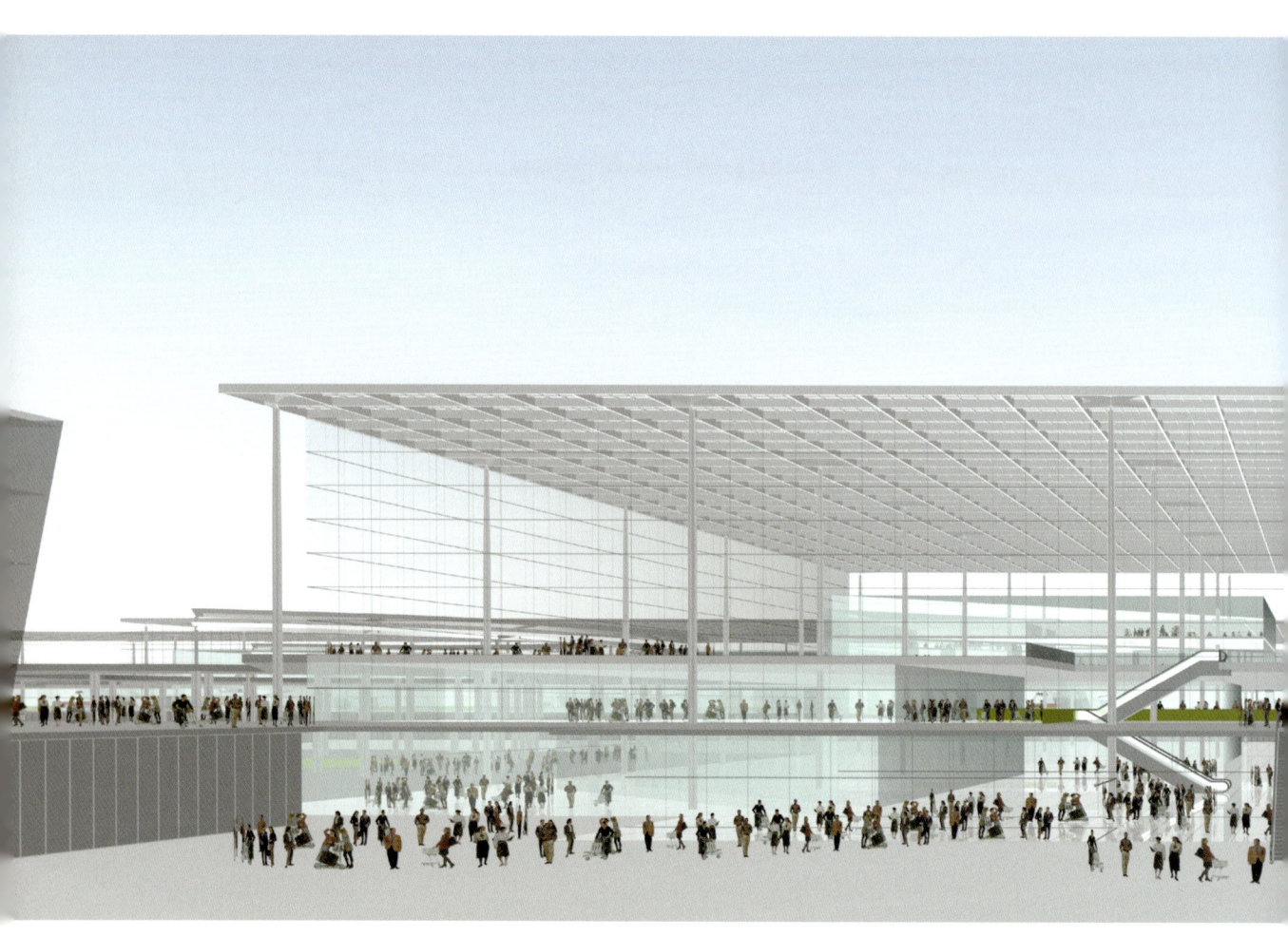

Gesamtansicht des Terminalgebäudes, Zeichnung
General view of the terminal building, drawing

cher Qualität entstanden in Deutschland im Laufe all dieser Wettbewerbe, die die gleiche Erkennbarkeit, die gleiche Zeichenhaftigkeit hätten? Nur sehr wenige. Das Olympiadach in München ist mit Sicherheit eines.

SOBEK: Oder der Deutsche Bundestag.

JAHN: Dann noch die Münchner Hypobank und das BMW-Hochhaus, …

SOBEK: …der Stuttgarter Fernsehturm. Und dann hört es schon auf. Neuere Düsseldorfer Bauten wie das Stadttor-Hochhaus, oder das RWE-Gebäude in Essen wären noch zu erwähnen.

KUHN: Für Ihre gemeinsame Arbeit ist interdisziplinäres Denken Voraussetzung. Schauen Sie dafür auch in andere Bereiche, zum Beispiel in die Musik? Schließlich soll Schelling gesagt haben, Architektur sei gebaute Musik. Was wäre denn demnach die passende Musik zu Ihrer Architektur?

JAHN: Vor zwei Jahren hat mich der Münchner Generalintendant August Everding zur Vortragsreihe »Aussagen über die Zukunft am Ende des 20. Jahrhunderts« unter anderem zusammen mit Christian Barnard und Henry Kissinger eingeladen. Ein Bestandteil der Veranstaltung war es, daß sich der Redner eine Musik wählte, die vorher gespielt wurde. Ich habe ein Stück von Philip Glass ausgesucht, das interessanterweise *Glassworks* hieß. Leider gab es aber niemanden, der das damals in München spielen konnte. Auf Vorschlag von Everding habe ich dann Luigi Nono als Einführungsstück genommen.

KUHN: Herr Sobek, welche Musik paßt zu Ihnen beziehungsweise zu Ihrer gemeinsamen Arbeit?

SOBEK: Ich habe seit meiner frühen Jugend ein Faible für elektronische Musik. Glass mag ich natürlich auch oder Alfred Schnittke.

JAHN: Ich glaube ohnehin nicht, daß man einen Zusammenhang zwischen Architektur und Musik herstellen kann. Musik hat doch eher mit Stimmungen zu tun.

KUHN: Sie beide teilen außerdem ein gemeinsames Interesse für Mode, für Stoff also. Hat dies auch Bedeutung für Ihre gemeinsame Arbeit?

SOBEK: Unbedingt. Zwar nicht erkennbar im trivialen Sinn, also daß wir Fassaden aus Stoff bauen, aber was die Geisteshaltung und die Wertschätzung gewisser Eigenschaften und Effekte betrifft. An der Universität forciere ich bei den Studien- und Diplomarbeiten das Bauen mit Stoff auch im Bereich der Gebäudehüllen sehr. Dabei entstehen Arbeiten, die mitnichten baubar sind, aber die Utopien langsam in den Bereich des Realisierbaren holen. Die Entwicklungsmöglichkeiten bei Textilien schätze ich ähnlich hoch ein wie bei Glas. So gibt es schaltbare Fasern, energiespeichernde Fasern, bei denen man per Knopfdruck beziehungsweise elektrischem Impuls Energie abrufen kann. Was beispielsweise im Bereich der Sport- oder Weltraumkleidung längst verwendet wird, ist für das Bauwesen noch vollkommen unentdeckt. Sicher gilt es im Bauwesen, diese Dinge noch weiter zu son-

Street Furniture Designer Line für J. C. Decaux

Die Entwurfsreihe besteht aus einer Haltestelle, einem Zeitungskiosk und einer Litfaßsäule, die vollkommen aus Glas sind. Nur wenige, sorgfältig gestaltete metallische Verbinder halten die einzelnen Glastafeln zusammen. Zurückgenommen in ihrer architektonischen Wirkung sind diese Elemente für die Stadt dazu gedacht, den städtischen Raum nie zu dominieren, sondern ihn, auch aufgrund ihrer eigenen hohen Gestaltqualität, zu unterstreichen.

This series of designs comprises a bus stop, a newspaper kiosk and an advertising column, all of which are constructed completely of glass. Only a very few carefully designed metal connectors hold the individual panes of glass together. Architecturally restrained, these elements of the urban setting are conceived in such a way that they never dominate urban space but emphasise it by virtue of their own inherent gestalt quality instead.

Vollständig aus Glas: Zeitungskiosk (oben), Litfaßsäule (rechts) und Bushaltestelle (folgende Seiten)
Full-glass constructions: Newspaper kiosk (above), advertising column (right) and bus stop (following pages)

dieren, aber in zehn bis zwanzig Jahren wird es solche Möglichkeiten geben. Man muß nur heute schon daran arbeiten.

JAHN: Für mich hat Mode genauso viel mit Material wie Stil zu tun. Jedes Jahr kaufe ich einen besseren Anzug, nicht dem Aussehen nach, denn das ist alles vergänglich, sondern von der Qualität des Stoffes her, der immer weniger knittert, weniger Raum einnimmt, sich im Sommer wie Winter tragen läßt. Das schätze ich an Materialien, genauso wie beim Bauen.

SOBEK: Die technologische Entwicklung beispielsweise von Textilien ist der eine Punkt. Von der Stuttgarter Schule ausgehend, insbesondere durch Frei Otto, gibt es eine Reihe wichtiger Beiträge für das Bauen mit Textilien im Sinne einer straff gespannten Haut. Helmut Jahn und mich interessiert aber nicht so sehr diese faltenlose monochrome Haut, der man ihre Abmessungen nicht mehr ansieht, sondern der künstlerische Umgang mit Textilien beim Bauen. Durch gezielte Faltungen, unterschiedliche Lichttransmissionen wird eine fast poetische Qualität ins Gebaute transferiert. Und so kommt die Mode wieder mit der Architektur zusammen.

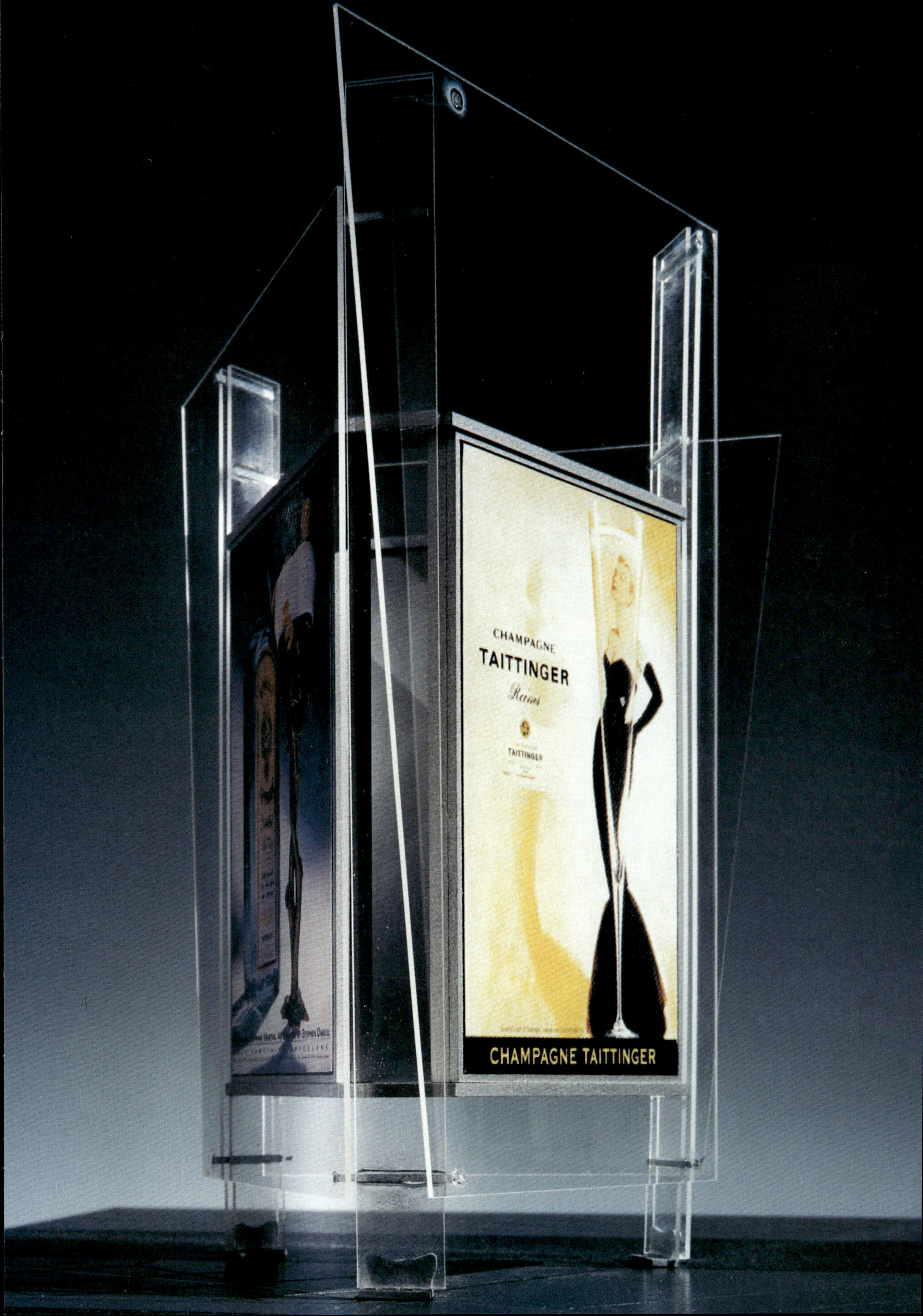
CHAMPAGNE
TAITTINGER
CHAMPAGNE TAITTINGER

CLK
SPORTSWEAR
FOR MEN AND WOMEN

Ab 14.6. bei Ihrem Mercedes-Benz Vertriebspartner.

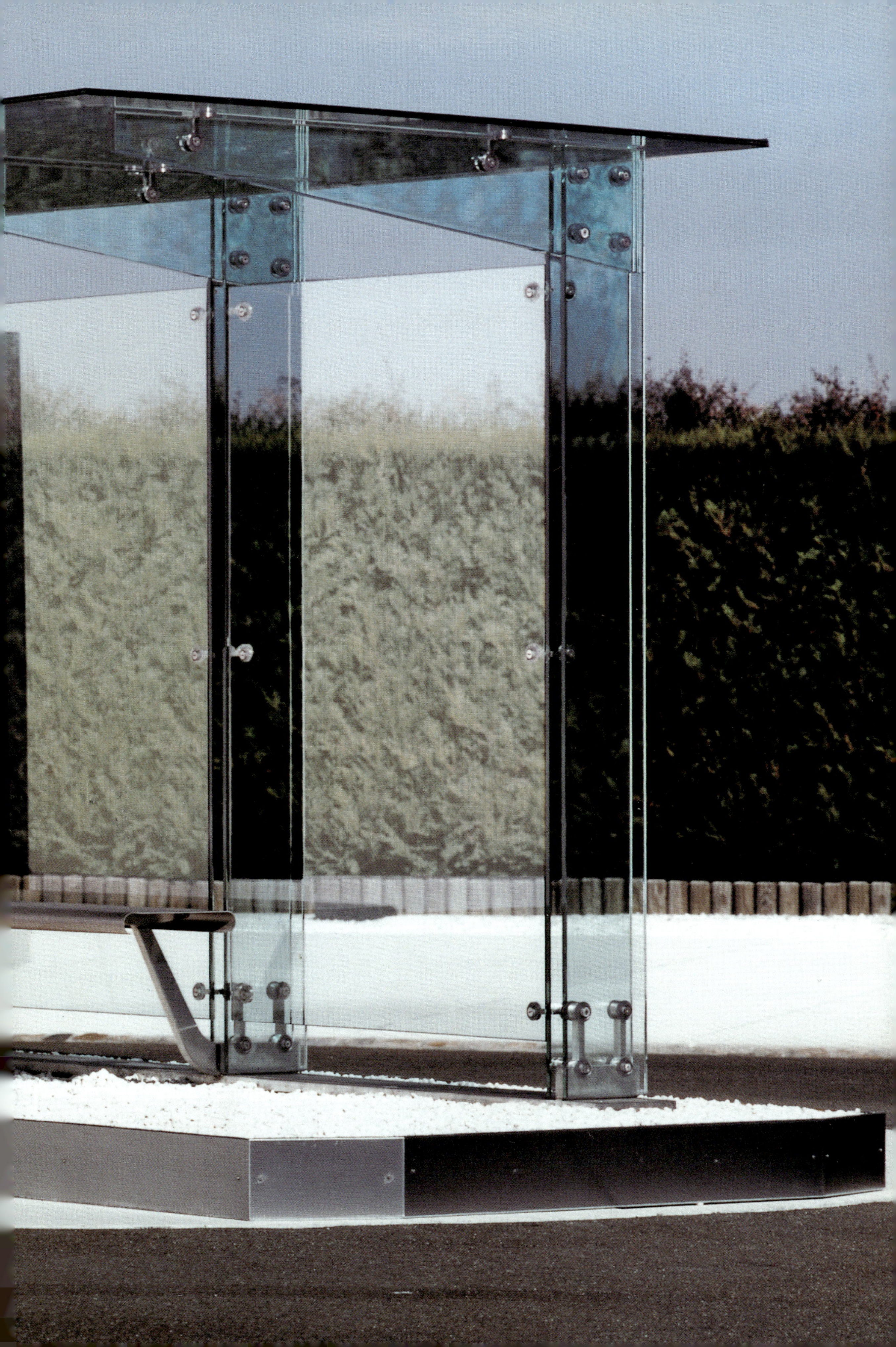

Nicola Kuhn in Conversation with Helmut Jahn and Werner Sobek

Architecture Today

KUHN: Architecture today, at the close of the twentieth century – What role does it play in society? And what part do architects and engineers play?

JAHN: Architecture's goal is to give form to the essential characteristics of a society and to translate that form into architecture. It responds to the spirit of the times and must deal with the technical resources available to it and the constraints imposed upon it at any given time. Unlike that of the modern period, today's architecture should not be expected to change society, I would think, but it can reflect its qualities and contribute to its betterment.

SOBEK: Architecture is shaped environment, and thus it is a mirror of society that reflects how it behaves and what it wants. This is also a theme in the current discussion regarding architecture as it is pertains to Berlin, for example, where there is a desire for projections of a city profile, retrospective projections on the last century.

KUHN: Isn't it the architect's duty to redirect attention to the future?

JAHN: That is part of a fundamental debate about how architects should respond to challenges or what means they should employ in doing so. Our architecture takes a very optimistic view. Werner Sobek and I both believe in progress and that innovation can engender positive development – not simply for the sake of creating something new, of course, but to improve buildings and thus the outer shells of our living situations as well. Glo-

balization has given us an entirely new situation today. Everything relates to everything else in a global context. One can travel around the world in just a few days. And that has engendered dispute: How far can one go as an architect? To what extent is it necessary to take a specific place into account? That stands in total contradiction to the way society and politics are behaving. People hide behind arguments in order to maintain the status quo and prefer to look back upon history. In Berlin, for example, people want to revive values that no longer exist in our society. History will show whether this is the right approach or not.

SOBEK: The quality of diversity counts as well, of course. Helmut Jahn and I are convinced that the mental attitudes of a human being are influenced by his architectural environment. Whether I live in a house with small windows, air-conditioned and completely walled-in by stone slabs, or in one that is nourished by solar energy and similar sources, a transparent, expansive house from which one can watch the changing of the seasons – such things help shape the attitudes of the people who live inside.

KUHN: Mr. Jahn, you once said that we are now in a phase you refer to as the second modern period. What, exactly, do you mean by that, and how does it affect your relationship with Mr. Sobek as an engineer?

JAHN: The first modern period was that of the Bauhaus and Mies van der Rohe. It was the beginning of a rational, technical kind of architecture that made use of modern materials and was actually always far ahead of

Illinois Institute of Technology, Campus Center (Wettbewerb/ Competition)

Der von Mies van der Rohe geplante und berühmte Campus des IIT soll um ein Gebäude, ein Campus Center, erweitert werden. In der zweiten Phase des internationalen Wettbewerbes, in der noch fünf Architekten verblieben waren, schlugen Helmut Jahn und Werner Sobek eine Gruppe aus vier großen Raumhüllen vor, die teilweise miteinander verbunden, teilweise durch die »Elevated« angeschniten werden. Die Dachflächen der Raumhüllen sind mit einer Vielzahl unterschiedlicher Zellen mit veränderlichen, schaltbaren physikalischen Eigenschaften belegt. Die Dachfläche wird somit zur Haut.

The famous ITT campus, designed by Mies van der Rohe, was to be expanded through the addition of a campus centre. In the second phase of the international competition, for which five architects had qualified, Helmut Jahn and Werner Sobek proposed a group of four large, partially connected spatial shells intersected at certain points by the Chicago "Elevated". The roof surfaces of the building shells are covered with a large number of different cells with variable, electrically controllable physical properties. Thus the roof surfaces acts as a kind of skin.

Beitrag zur ersten Stufe des Wettbewerbs: kein Entwurf, sondern ein Statement
Entry for the first phase of the competition: not a design plan, but a statement

the possibilities of its time in a conceptual sense. The apartment buildings designed by Mies van der Rohe were made entirely of glass and they had problems that no one would wish to deal with today. It got too hot in those buildings, and they let in the rain. But that is precisely what made Mies a genius. He managed to convince people that these things had to be modified to meet new needs, but that they worked. Above all, he persuaded industry to develop materials that would make such architecture possible. With this approach he achieved real progress on behalf of architecture. Today, during the second modern period, we have considerably greater technological possibilities, with respect to materials and in terms of production, calculation and simulation. We can go much farther and feel much more secure in pursuing a very similar approach. Yet one can't take the same kind of risks as these heroes of the first modern period today. In a certain sense, they were much like Alexander the Great or the medieval kings who rode into battle at the head of their armies. Today we are no longer vanguards, for we can rely upon knowledge that offers us more possibilities and permits us to move closer to the visions of earlier times with much greater certainty.

Hans Stimmann, Director of Construction for the Berlin Senate, said to me some time ago that there was too much glass in the Sony buildings on Potsdamer Platz and that that had nothing at all to do with Berlin, especially the tower. We showed him a photograph of the high-rise building Mies had planned for Friedrichstraße in 1919.

Blick über das Dach auf die City von Chicago
View of the city of Chicago over the building roof

And my response to Stimmann was, "That is Berlin, too, but it was never built." It is only now becoming possible to construct buildings with minimum technology and maximum transparency and make them comfortable at the same time. That is the link between the first and the second modern periods, but it is also the difference between them.

SOBEK: Industrialisation was introduced to architecture during the so-called first modern period. New materials such as huge glass panels, profile steel, anodised aluminium and the like were incorporated into the building process by Mies and others, although the level of technology in planning was totally inadequate, measured by today's standards. Mies could put up with a lot and was able to live with the fact that apartments overheated in the summer and icicles formed on the windows in the winter. That would be impossible today. As planners, we would be ruined after the very first malfunctioning building.

JAHN: Or take the concrete supports. They had a steel outside shell but were not insulated. We are a great deal more conscious of potential conflicts in our work today. Everything leads right to the process, so that we don't have to take risks. Everything has to be safe, the whole thing has to be perfect. The urge to try something new was much stronger back then. Builders used single-pane glass in those years, and that is no longer enough today. Air-conditioning was virtually unknown back then. Today we have to create a pleasant climate inside the

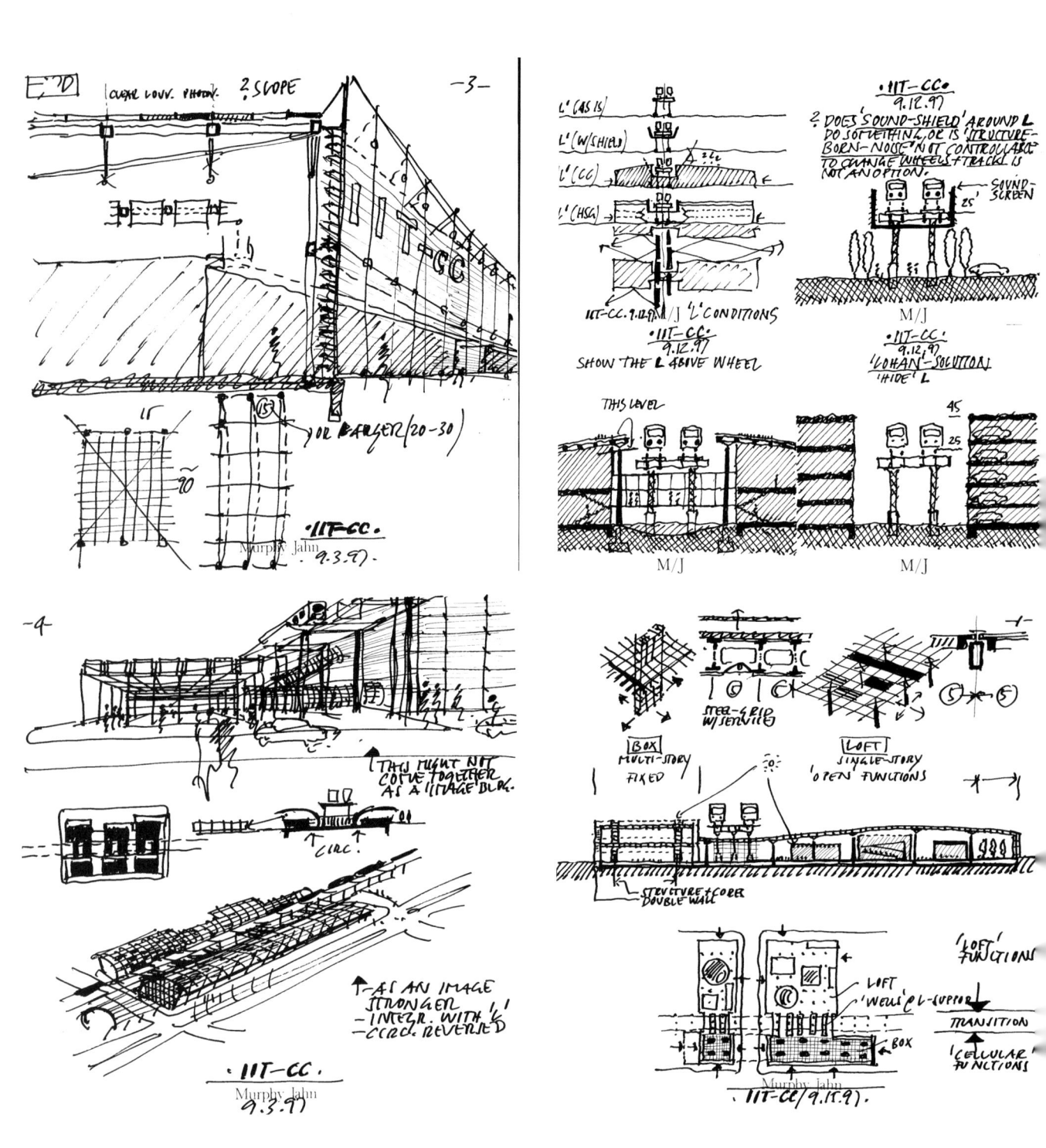

Entwurfszeichnungen zur Gesamtanlage und zur Integration der »Elevated«
Design drawing of the entire complex and the integration of the "Elevated"

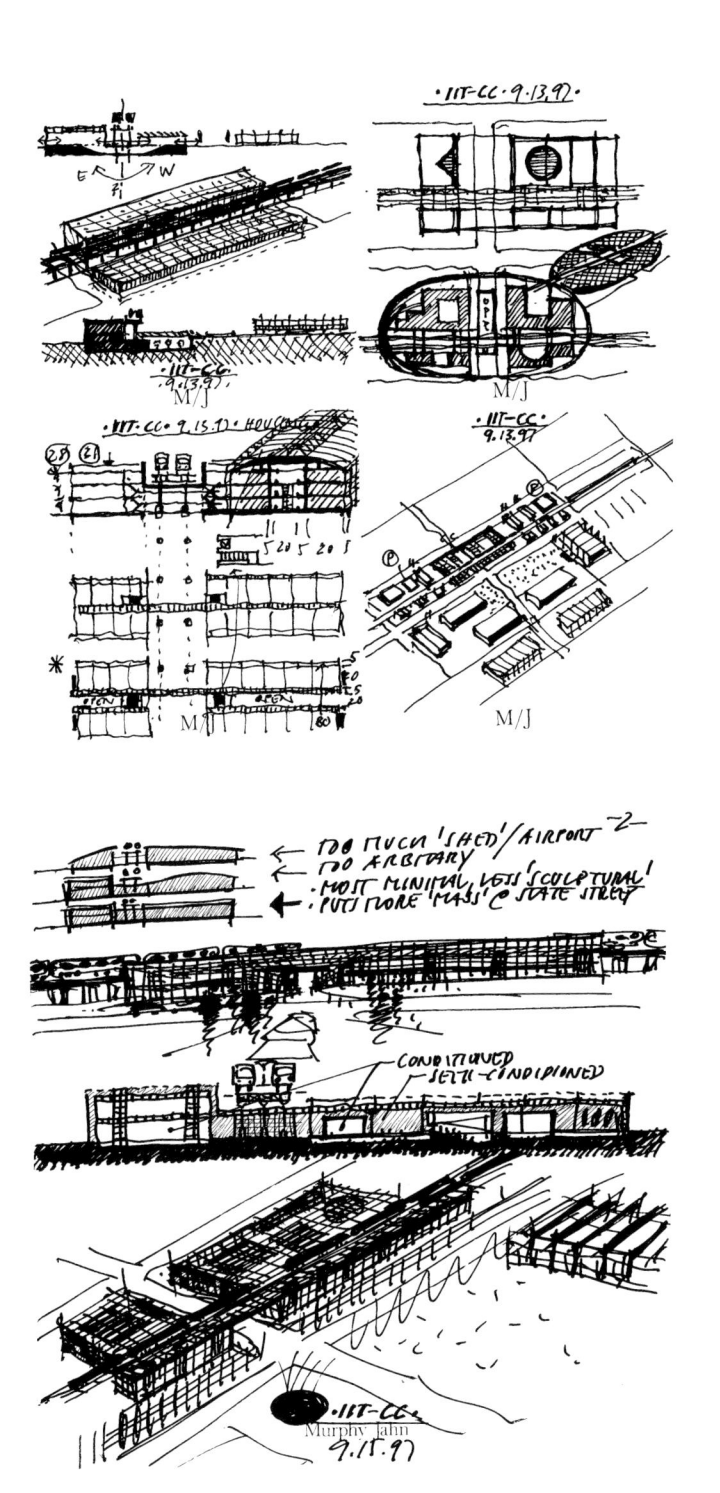

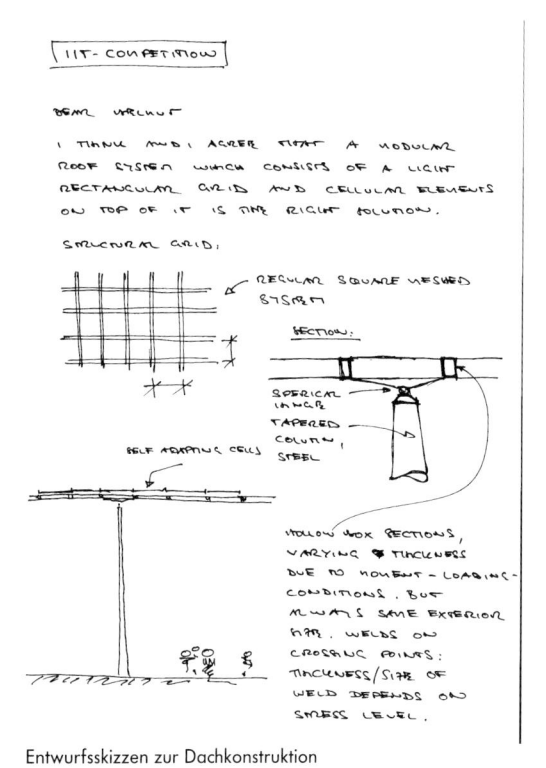

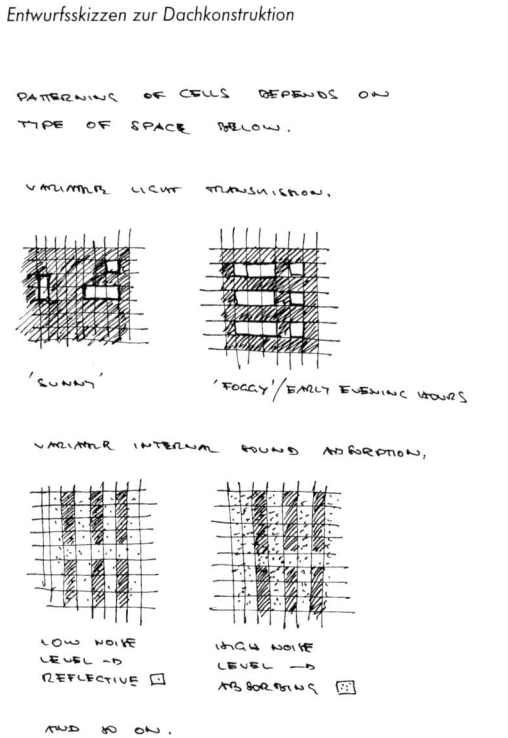

Illinois Institute of Technology, Campus Center

Entwurfsskizzen zur Dachkonstruktion
Entwurfsskizzen zur Dachkonstruktion

Entwurfsskizzen zum Layout der veränderbaren Zellen auf dem Gebäudedach
Design sketches for the layout of the variable cells on the building roof

Aufsicht auf den Gesamtkomplex, dessen Dachfläche durch die »Elevated« angeschnitten wird, Modellaufnahme
View of the entire complex, its roof surface intersected by the "Elevated", model photo

building. And that is what brings us – Werner Sobek and I – together. We both believe that architecture has a lot to do with finding solutions for technical problems and not just with aesthetics and form. Certainly, aesthetics and form are always a part of architecture, but a good engineer always considers the aesthetic consequences of his decisions, and a good architect always takes into account the technical consequences of the forms he creates. When Frank Gehry creates a building today, he uses a computer in every phase of the process, from design to manufacture to construction. The computer enables him to realise practically any conceivable form. With the aid of a computer, any form can be broken down into its individual component parts and then manufactured accordingly. In this case we use engineering to give concrete shape to an aesthetic idea.

SOBEK: We should explain how we arrived at this view. Our idea of architecture goes even further, especially in the newer buildings created with the help of others – Matthias Schuler, for example, a building energy specialist from Stuttgart. He brings building-energy concepts into the mix which go far beyond current standards. He works with solar energy systems, floor cooling and other such things, enabling us to reduce the volume of technical apparatus to a minimum. This minimum is so simple that it can also be installed with ease. Take the concrete ceilings, for example: Cold water flows through them, so that they function as large cooling surfaces in the building during the summer. It is no longer necessary to bring in cold air; the cooling slots are more or less

directly overhead. Consequently, there are no more suspended ceilings. That, in turn, leads to a kind of purism, meaning that the technical aspects of buildings are becoming increasingly simple. Our goal is to make things so simple that nothing more needs to be added or taken away. In some of the buildings that we still have on the drawing board – although neither of us uses a drawing board anymore – we have almost achieved that goal. Everything becomes very simple and easy to understand at the same time. The air doesn't come from a slit in the ceiling anymore, and then nobody knows why the air has become cool or warm, since everything is concealed. What we have instead is a double-skinned facade. One can open the window; there is a cooling ceiling and small heating ribs. That's all!

KUHN: Some prognosticators say that the next century will be the century of ecology, of nature conservation. What can architecture contribute, having apparently been on the other side up to now? Your design for the high-rise Deutsche Post building in Bonn has attracted a lot of praise as an example of ecological architecture, and you were awarded the "Internationale Trend-Preis Bauen mit Grün" by the European Landscape Contractors Association and the Bundesverband Garten-, Landschafts- und Sportplatzbau in February. That seems to show that ecological, environmentally sound building and a decidedly modernist kind of architecture can indeed go hand in hand.

Generaldirektion Deutsche Post AG, Bonn

Der Entwurf stellt einen neuen Typ des Bürohochhauses im Hinblick auf städtebauliche Einbindung, Funktion, Technik und Benutzerkomfort dar. Die Gesamtform, bestehend aus zwei im Grundriß gegeneinander verschobenen Ellipsenhälften, ist minimal und einprägsam. Zwischen den beiden Gebäudehälften spannen sich, über die Höhe gestaffelt, vier große Wintergärten auf. Die Gebäudehülle besteht aus einer Zweite-Haut-Fassade, die auch in den oberen Geschossen Fenster, die sich öffnen lassen, zuläßt und die integraler Bestandteil des mit minimalen Energiemengen arbeitenden Gebäudeenergiekonzeptes ist.

This design introduces a new type of office high-rise, viewed in terms of integration into urban architecture, function, engineering and user comfort. The overall form, consisting of two semi-elliptical shapes positioned immediately adjacent to one another at their bases, is minimal and striking at once. Four large glass "winter gardens" arranged one above the other bridge the gap between the two structures. The building shell is composed of a second-skin facade that also provides for windows that can be opened even on the upper floors and is itself an integral component of the building energy concept devoted to minimum energy consumption.

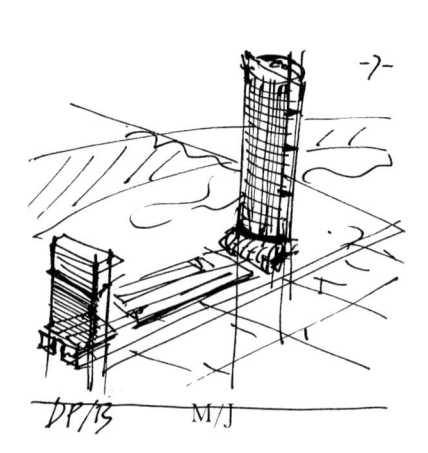

Entwurfsskizzen zur Korrelation des Neubaus mit dem »Langen Eugen«
Design sketches showing the correlation of the new buildings with the "Langer Eugen"

Lage des Neubaus relativ zum »Langen Eugen«
Location of the new building in relation to the "Langer Eugen"

JAHN: One could quote our slogan from the IIT Competition: "Mies was ahead of his time. He used materials and techniques which pushed the limits of available technologies." We also take the view that it is no longer enough just to use conventional materials like bricks and steel, that one needs to use others derived from innovative products and processes as well, materials that change, that generate energy and thus create a new aesthetics at the same time. These materials are highly technical, but that ultimately makes them simple again. The outcome is the total integration of architecture and engineering.

SOBEK: We are no longer concerned only with building shells or components with constant physical properties. Little by little, we have approached a position, and will continue to come closer to it in the future, where we can control these building shells. The shells will then react in a perfectly natural way to internal and external changes. But this means that they have to be built with a certain degree of technical sophistication that demands considerable engineering input and also has a significant impact upon architectural design. Handled masterfully, this technology leads to totally new solutions. Thus we now have self-darkening facades or facades that are capable of generating energy or double-skinned facades with as panels placed in front of the actual panes, making it possible to generate heat in the intervening space with the aid of solar radiation, which can in turn be directed into the inside of the building.

Ansichtszeichnung, die vollkommen aus Glas bestehende
Zweite-Haut-Fassade des Hochhauses
*Display drawing of the full-glass second-skin facade of the
high-rise building*

Generaldirektion Deutsche Post AG, Bonn

Presseausschnitte
Press clippings

JAHN: These components, these technical aspects, also determine the appearance of the building. The ability to control the shell engenders an aesthetics that is itself dynamic and changeable. And that is the essence of our belief that architecture is ultimately determined not only by aesthetics but by these other factors as well.

SOBEK: To return to the issue of ecology, it is certainly ecologically beneficial per se when we not only eliminate the air-conditioning system but reduce energy consumption at the same time by decreasing the need for cool air in the presence of higher outside temperatures and for heating when outside temperatures fall.

Another aspect that is close to my heart has become a part of our work together. While we continue to make things simpler, reducing them to the essential in terms of the way they function as well, we are using single-material components to an increasing degree. For example, a concrete ceiling that is cooled. So we can eliminated the suspended ceiling, the spray plaster, the wallpaper. The concrete ceiling is relatively easy to remove and can be recycled, unlike conventional ceilings that tend to fall into the category of hazardous waste. The latter are compound components that can no longer be broken down and thus cannot be recycled. Everything in our buildings can be easily assembled and dismantled, which makes everything much easier to modify and dispose of. That is not merely a positive side effect but reflects a fundamental ecological attitude.

JAHN: It is wise to avoid catchwords altogether. Ecology is one of these catchwords today. Architecture has

always had its share of such phrases, which represent a certain Zeitgeist. The only way to build ecologically is to design the building from the bottom up – plans, forms and systems – in such a way that it behaves in a responsible way with respect to its environment. And that is why we gather all the experts around the table: not just the architect and the engineer but the physicist as well. The conventional building systems technician would hardly be the right partner for us, since all he does is calculate how much air is needed. A physicist, on the other hand, assesses both the well-being of the human being and the quality of the shell. The window of opportunity for technical systems originates in the interaction between the well-being of the user, the building shell and the exterior and interior conditions. In reality, a building that is absolutely ecologically sound is one that needs no building technology whatsoever. But that requires an outstanding engineer. The ultimate goal would be to make both the engineer and the building systems technician superfluous.

KUHN: What you're describing is almost the endpoint of a development. Can we go back to the beginning of your work together? How did you get together?

SOBEK: Five years ago, John Durbrow, from Helmut Jahn's office, and Bill Baker, a friend of mine from Chicago, were talking one day, when the question came up as to who might be able to give Helmut a tip about building with glass. A small problem had arisen at the time. My friend called me and said, "Give Mr. Jahn a call. They

Generaldirektion Deutsche Post AG, Bonn

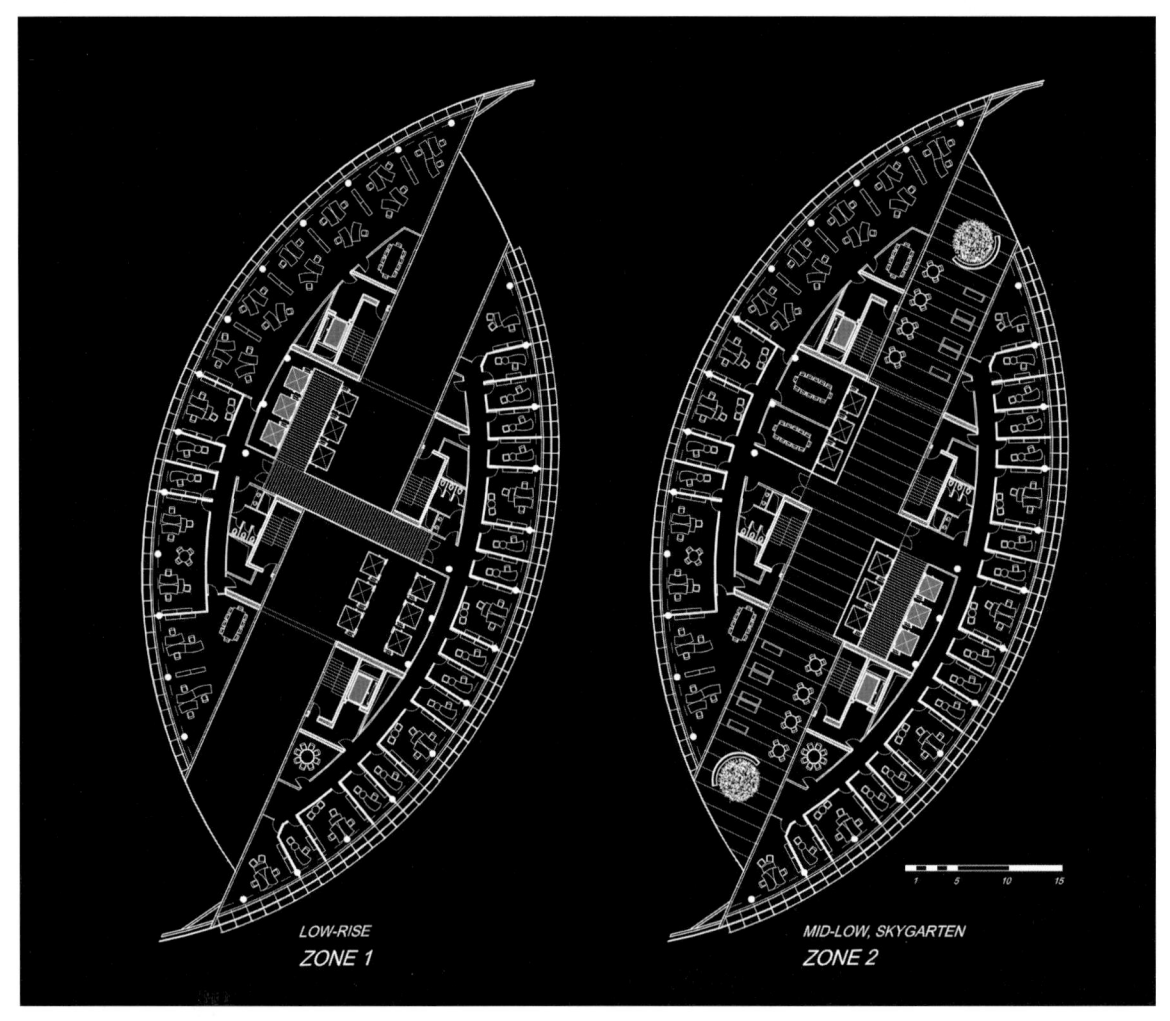

LOW-RISE ZONE 1

MID-LOW, SKYGARTEN ZONE 2

Grundrisse, auf dem linken Grundriß ist eines der nur durch Brücken durchquerten Atrien zu erkennen
Ground plans, one of the atria, crossed only by bridges, is seen on the ground plan on the left
Rechte Seite: Modellaufnahme, Hochhaus, aus zwei gegeneinander verschobenen Körpern bestehend, links daran anbindend der Flachbau
Right: Model photo, high-rise building comprising two units offset against each other, the low building connecting with them on the left

need help." When I did call I was told that everything had been taken care of. The problem had been solved. Three months later I happened to be visiting offices with students from my university in Chicago, and when we came to the Jahn office, I naturally wanted to say hello to Helmut.

JAHN: I didn't have much time that day. We only talked for about five minutes, but . . .

SOBEK: . . . three months later I got a fax from you.

JAHN: Things happened rather quickly after that. Actually, it was the airport terminal in Bangkok that brought us together. At the time we had already engaged the assistance of Matthias Schuler, the building energy specialist, through the good offices of Werner Sobek. Before Bangkok we had already done several detail jobs for Sony – the walls, the fixed-point cable and glass constructions. Aside from Sony, the Kranzler-Eck in Berlin and the Cologne-Bonn airport projects, in which we co-operated in a rather more additive sense, were encompassed within that first phase. The next steps we took together included the trade fair centre and the airport in Shanghai and then the Transrapid stations in Berlin, Hamburg and Schwerin. An especially important moment for us was the competition for the Campus Center of the Illinois Institute of Technology, in the course of which we developed a further refinement of the idea of the total integration of shell construction and architecture. We continued to pursue the idea of linking the supporting framework, building systems engineering and the shell

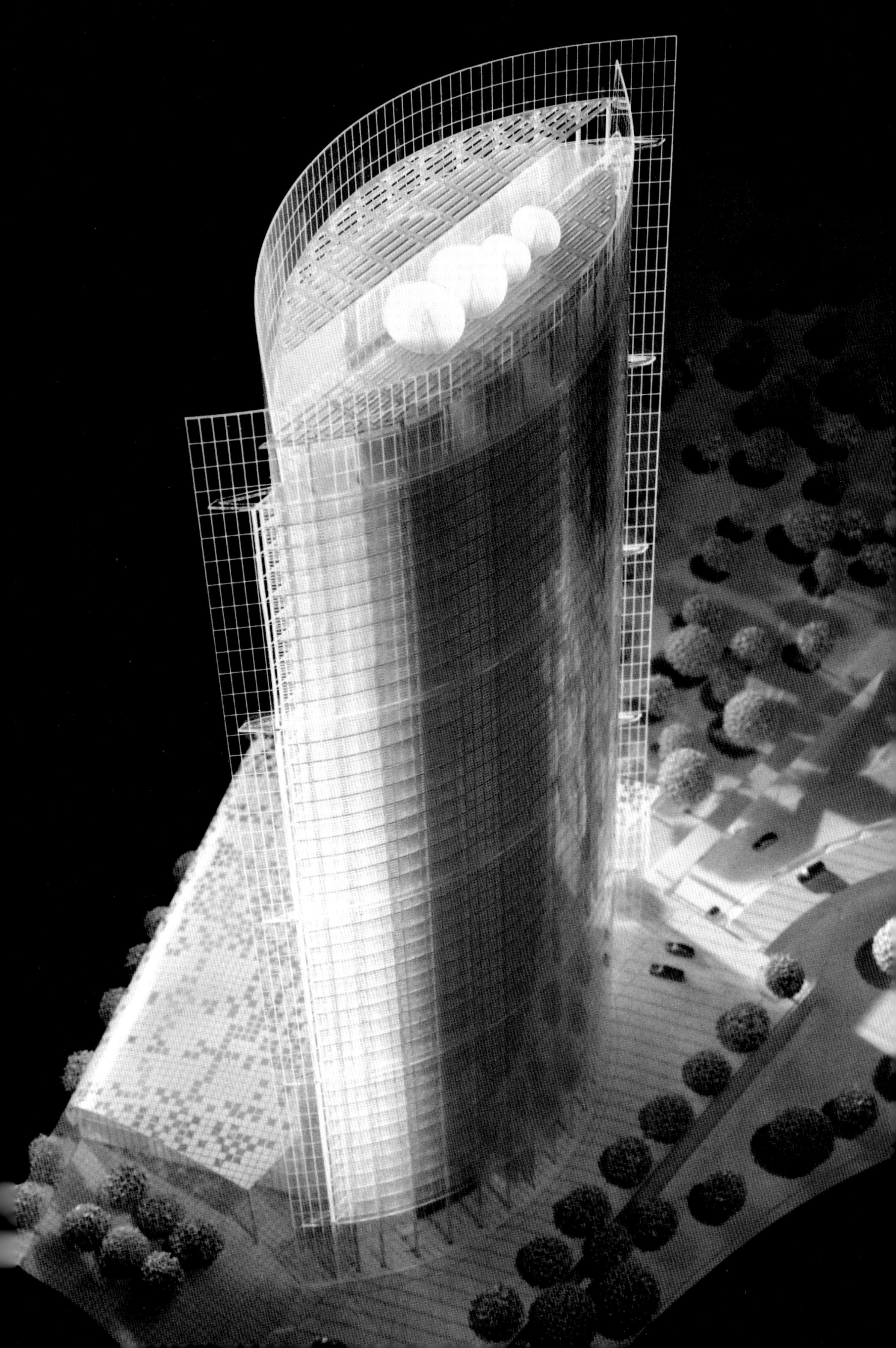

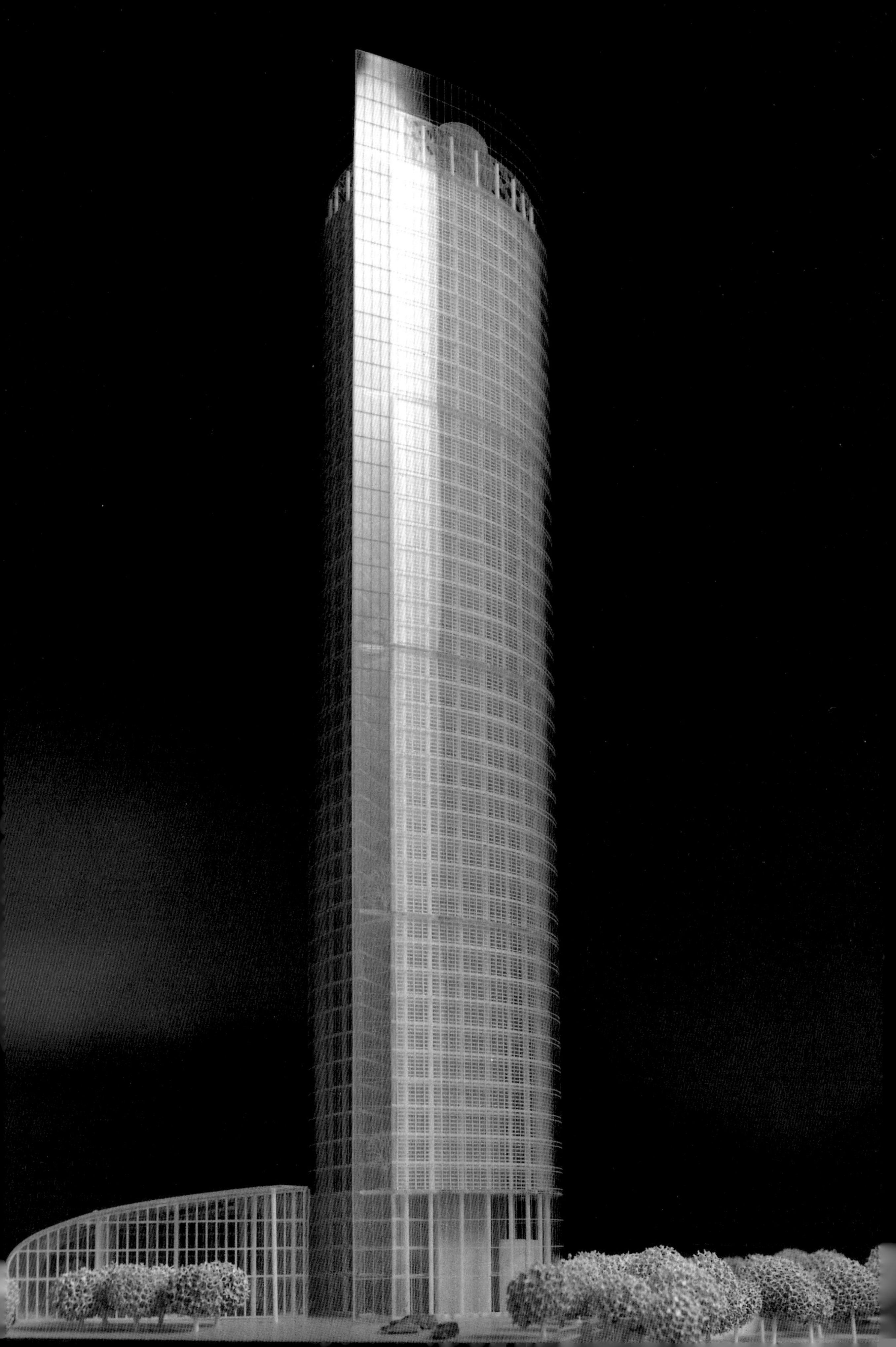

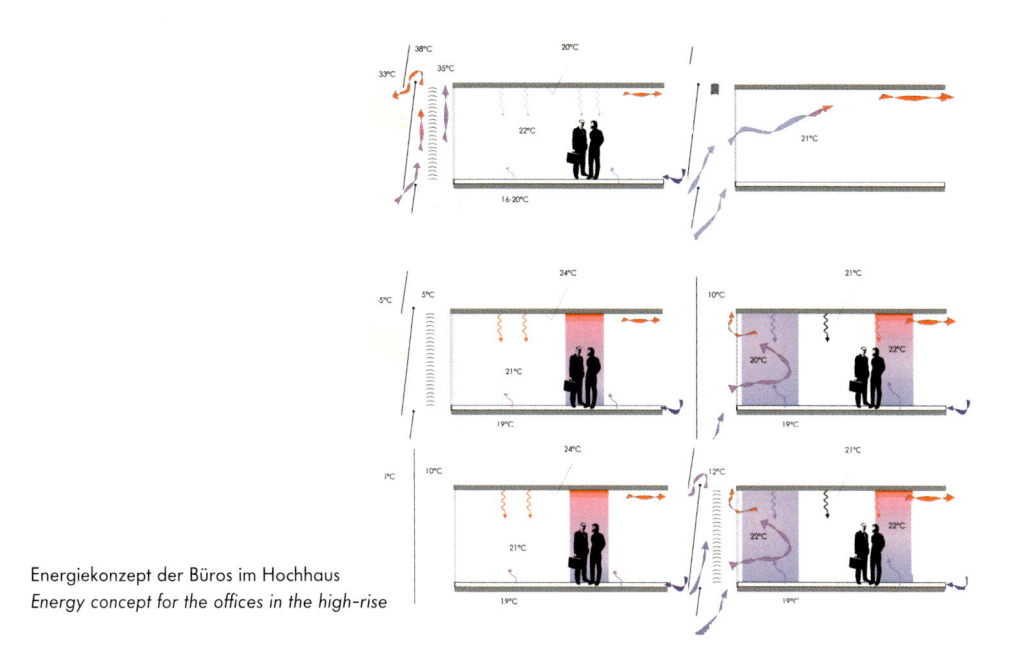

Energiekonzept der Büros im Hochhaus
Energy concept for the offices in the high-rise

Computerzeichnungen zur Fassade, Blicke von Außen nach Innen und umgekehrt
Computer drawing for the facade, view of the interior from outside and vice-versa
Linke Seite: Modellaufnahme, Hochhaus und Flachbau
Left: Model photo, high-rise and low building

together in the Kaufhof project in Chemnitz, the Andersen Consulting office building in Sulzbach, the headquarters of the Deutsche Post in Bonn, Bayer AG in Leverkusen and HA-LO in Chicago.

SOBEK: This perfect understanding, the totally natural communication via a simple phone call, grew stronger with each project. The first projects, including Sony, had already been formulated in architectural terms. There wasn't much left for me to change. I could only make a contribution and thus didn't have any fundamental influence on the whole. In the case of Bangkok, the competition had already been won, and the architecture had been planned roughly, though the details remained to be worked out – in the terminal building, for example, a glass cuboid for which Helmut Jahn wanted something absolutely non-material. We then developed that in Stuttgart. Because we understood one another so well, I was able to develop a concept that meet his architectural requirements. I also suggested other changes, somewhat cautiously in some cases, since we hadn't known each other so very long. But Helmut was completely open and never said anything but "Let's have those changes, as long as they make the thing better."

JAHN: Bangkok was a classical example of the way things had always gone before. We engaged the services of engineers for the competition, as architects usually do, without really sitting down and talking with them. The airport terminal was supposed to have a roof with a span of 126 metres, a 40-metre overhang and a down-

Neue Konzernzentrale der Bayer AG, Leverkusen

Der Neubau der Konzernzentrale der Bayer AG ist geprägt von einer Transparenz, die im bewußten Gegensatz zu den bestehenden Altbauten steht und die symbolhaft und zukunftsweisend für die Bayer AG im 21. Jahrhundert wirkt. Die Form des aus einer Halbellipse und einer langen »porte cochère« geschaffenen Gebäudes ist minimal und einprägsam. Durch die Integration von Struktur, Materialien und Konstruktion wird eine bewußte Komplexität erreicht, die Funktionen des Gebäudes sind wie ein Diagramm ablesbar und verständlich.

The new headquarters building for Bayer AG is characterised by a degree of transparency that stands in deliberate contrast to the existing older buildings and symbolises the future-oriented image of Bayer AG in the 21st century. The shape of the building comprising a semi-ellipse and a long "porte cochère" is minimal and visually striking. Structure, materials and constructive design are deliberately integrated to achieve a high level of complexity. The building's functions are made visible and comprehensible in the style of a diagram.

Ansicht der Gesamtanlage, im Vordergrund die Pergola
View of the entire complex, pergola in the foreground

ward arching fish-belly. It wasn't until after we had won the competition and begun working on the building that it dawned on me that the engineer really made no genuine contribution of his own, since he did nothing but carry out what we had put on paper. That attitude towards the relationship between the architect and the engineer is especially typical in America: The architect thinks something up, and the engineer carries it out . . .

SOBEK: . . . and in doing so, he influences the architectural idea as little as possible and would hardly attempt to modify it.

JAHN: He is the executor of the architect's wishes. The engineer might suggest putting in a little more steel here, a little more concrete there. It might even be that he really does have a better idea and doesn't recognise the possibilities that are available. After all, it is difficult to describe how a design takes shape in your own head when you're working with someone else.

I remember the competition for the Deutsche Post in Bonn very well: an open competition in which we were invited to participate. We asked ourselves whether we should even take part at all. There were hundreds of competitors. It's a lot like a lottery and luck is just as much a factor. Werner told me at the time that I would have to be careful in Bonn with the Siebengebirge [a range of hills near Bonn] and talked about all kinds of things I'd never heard about. He recommended doing something soft. During our conversation we drew circles and ellip-

Blick in einen Konferenzraum
View of a conference room

ses, and that is how the plan came to be. All it took was a single remark: "do something soft". At the time I was working on the Pudong tower; one needs a point of departure, after all. You said the tower had too many sharp edges and was simply not friendly enough. And that was what made our design so successful in the end – that certain softness, that mildness. Although the building is large, it isn't overbearing. It's rather more restrained, almost lyrical. Because of the light – you can see this in the drawings – its effect is not confrontational but conciliatory instead. This is precisely the point I was getting at before, that the engineer thinks like an architect and the architect, in turn, thinks like an engineer. That's the way it is in all good partnerships: you understand each other, complement each other and ultimately act as one.

SOBEK: In other words, the one speaks the other's language. What is special about our situation is that this also works at the conceptual level, so that ultimately just a few words – "not mild enough", "too sharp" – are enough. That also goes beyond the rational aspects of the proposed building. Normally, this kind of communication is very time-consuming. Yet we simply talk on the phone with the sketch in front of us, and we communicate with just two or three words that really describe only an atmosphere or a mood. I just say, "That is too wild somehow, or too hard," and Helmut answers, "Really? Yes, I think I know what you mean".

Aufsicht auf die Gesamtanlage, Modellaufnahme
View of the entire complex, model photo

And it's just the same the other way around. Unlike most architects, Helmut Jahn is an outstanding engineer and framework planner, which often prompts me to joke with him: "If you keep this up you won't need me much longer." Of course, this communication process requires that I learn the language of the other discipline, so that I can understand what the other person is trying to tell me. When I talk about stress or load situations, Helmut understands what I mean without my having to give him a long explanation.

KUHN: You have expressed that idea in a nutshell with the term "Archi-Neering". How did it come about?

SOBEK: I face the fundamental problem that there is no professional designation for what I do. I think "framework planner" covers only part of it; I'm not an architect in the usual sense; I'm a bit more of an engineer. The word "designer" has negative connotations in German, although that is really unjust. When I renamed my firm I briefly considered calling ourselves "Archineurs". It was exactly a year later that Helmut came up with the concept of archi-neering.

JAHN: We had already sat down together once before and ran some possibilities through our minds: architecture and technology, architecture and engineering, architecture and . . . this technology. All we knew was that it had to be something easy to remember . And since I'm a person who can think only while drawing or writing,

I kept trying it out on paper over and over again. The process produced the linking of the two concepts and eventually led to "Archi-Neering". It was as much a visual as an intellectual outcome.

KUHN: What is the general reaction to this almost intimate form of co-operation?

JAHN: The public, the press and the majority of architecture critics don't seem to think much of it. Our mutual goal of going to the limits, even blurring them sometimes, doesn't always gain us friends and applause. It makes many people nervous. When I do interviews in the US and talk about our work with the same enthusiasm and the same conviction as now, a lot of people get really anxious. They see me as a terrorist, a lunatic with a cause – regardless of whether it's religion or architecture and engineering. This is of no interest to anyone in Germany, either. People would rather have something sensational, a dramatic failure or a controversy like the one here in Berlin between Stimmann and the architects who wanted something different than he did.

Sony is a good example. It shows that it was possible to do something different. Some see that as good, while others will pass devastating judgements. But many people only want to have their own preconceived notions confirmed. The Sony building is not accepted for what it is; people want a re-presentation of history for Berlin. The situation with the new buildings in France is quite different: the library, the Fondation Cartier in Paris, the pyra-

Neue Konzernzentrale der Bayer AG, Leverkusen

Ansicht der neuen Konzernzentrale, vom Garten aus gesehen
View of the new corporate headquarters, seen from the garden

mid outside the Louvre. The only thing to criticise about the pyramid is that it is too small. It was originally planned as a larger structure; its present form is a compromise. The buildings I mentioned are the only ones in Paris that can stand up to the old ones. Everything in between lacks the quality.

SOBEK: That kind of thing is possible only with a client who identifies with what he plans to build. President Mitterand simply wanted to have the Grand Bibliothèque, and he protected the architects. Dominique Perrault was 26 years old when he was awarded the project. And everyone condemned him, of course, calling his design monstrous, too expensive, "library engineering lunacy". It took the assertive power of a president to see the project to its end. Much the same can be said of the Grand Arche or the Institut du Monde Arabe. You won't find such buildings anywhere in Germany. A project becomes truly unique only when it is backed up by courage and an unmistakable position. Then a structure of integrity comes to be, a building that is truly a statement.

KUHN: So the ideal client stands courageously behind the architect from the outset.

JAHN: As I always say, you don't need a different project but a different, good client. When I look back on the buildings we've done I see an exact correlation between the quality of the architecture and the support or the pressure, in a positive sense, exerted by the client to ensure that something outstanding is achieved. That is

why it is so difficult to realise a great project in the field of commercial architecture. All of the French structures we've mentioned are public projects. In most countries – and not just in Germany or the US – public architecture doesn't come close to matching this level of quality, because public authorities normally get cold feet when something begins to look expensive. If it's expensive, they think, then it can't be good.

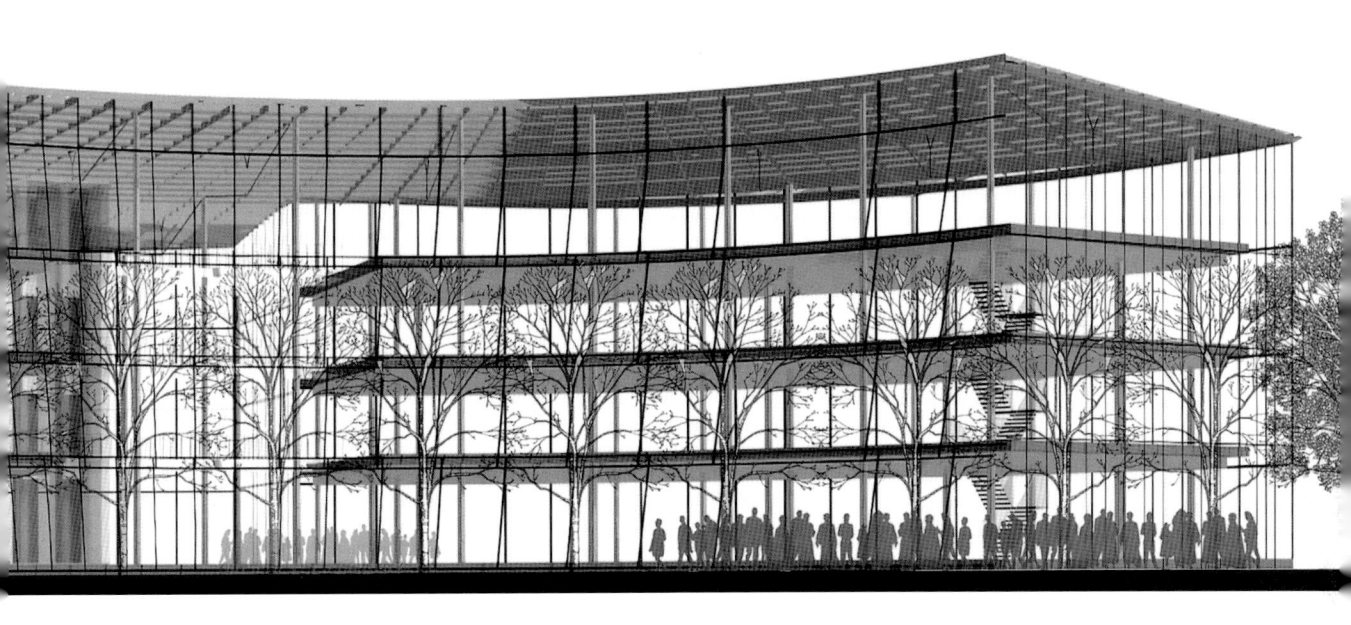

SOBEK: It's also true that there is a certain residual risk associated with these buildings: a cost risk, perhaps, or a building-energy risk or a utilisation risk. If there is a possibility that the temperature could rise to over 28° C in an office two days in a year, people get worried because the workplace law prescribes work stoppage when interior temperature exceeds 28° C. Then the lessee doesn't have to pay rent for the time in question. Then the problem comes back to the architect, whom the investor accuses of having made a planning miscalculation. We would prefer a private client who can afford and who is willing to accept the loss of, say, a month's rent once every twenty years or to allow his staff to take off their coats and ties. A committee client – a public client, for example – would never accept that small risk.

KUHN: You've described your idea of the ideal client. Don't you also have unfulfilled wishes with respect to architectural projects you would like to realise together?

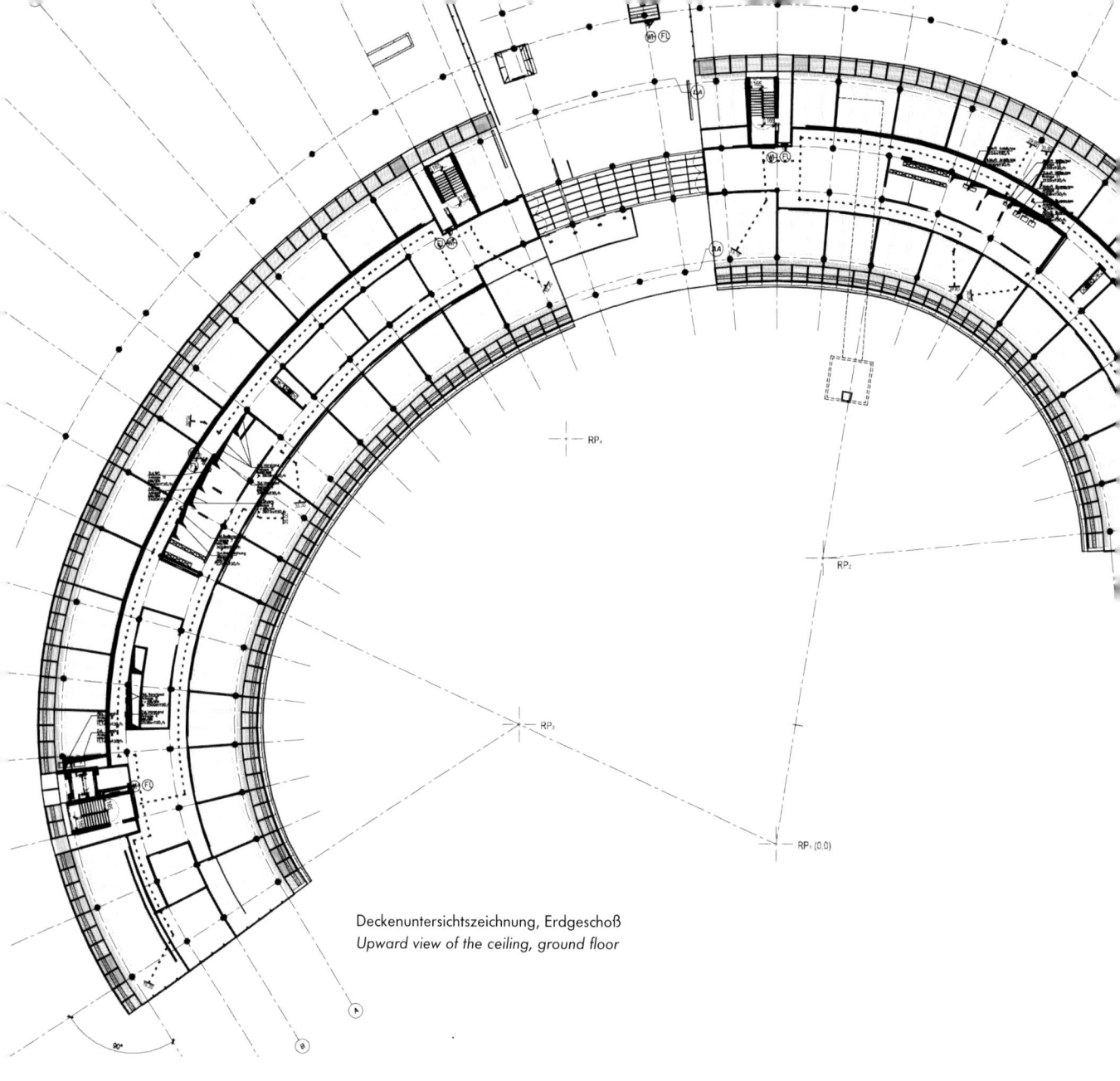

Deckenuntersichtszeichnung, Erdgeschoß
Upward view of the ceiling, ground floor

JAHN: I have never thought that I would have to build a certain kind of building, a church or a museum. This series of office buildings we have just completed – first the airport centre, then Sony and the Kranzler-Eck in Berlin and lastly the Bayer headquarters in Leverkusen and the office tower for the Deutsche Post in Bonn – represents the step-by-step refinement of our concept of the integration of architecture and engineering. It is the result of a certain natural understanding, an approach in which one is never satisfied with what one completed the day before. There is always the sense of obligation to create something better the next day. But that's possible only with the help of others, of engineers and industry. That is where progress lies.

This series of office buildings is much more interesting than if I had built a church here, a museum there, although we would also take on a number of these building projects as well. Or take the succession of airports, for instance: United Terminal in Chicago, the Cologne-Bonn airport, the Bangkok airport; that is all one line of development. I'm always saying somewhat sarcastically that the United Terminal is a nineteenth-century building, that Cologne is from the twentieth century and that Bangkok will perhaps be from the twenty-first century. I think the challenge and the real interest lies here, in shifting the boundaries, in raising the bar to a new height. Testing oneself in every area is much more dangerous. That's what the typical architect does, the kind I used to be. In his

Hauptverwaltung der Bayer AG, Leverkusen

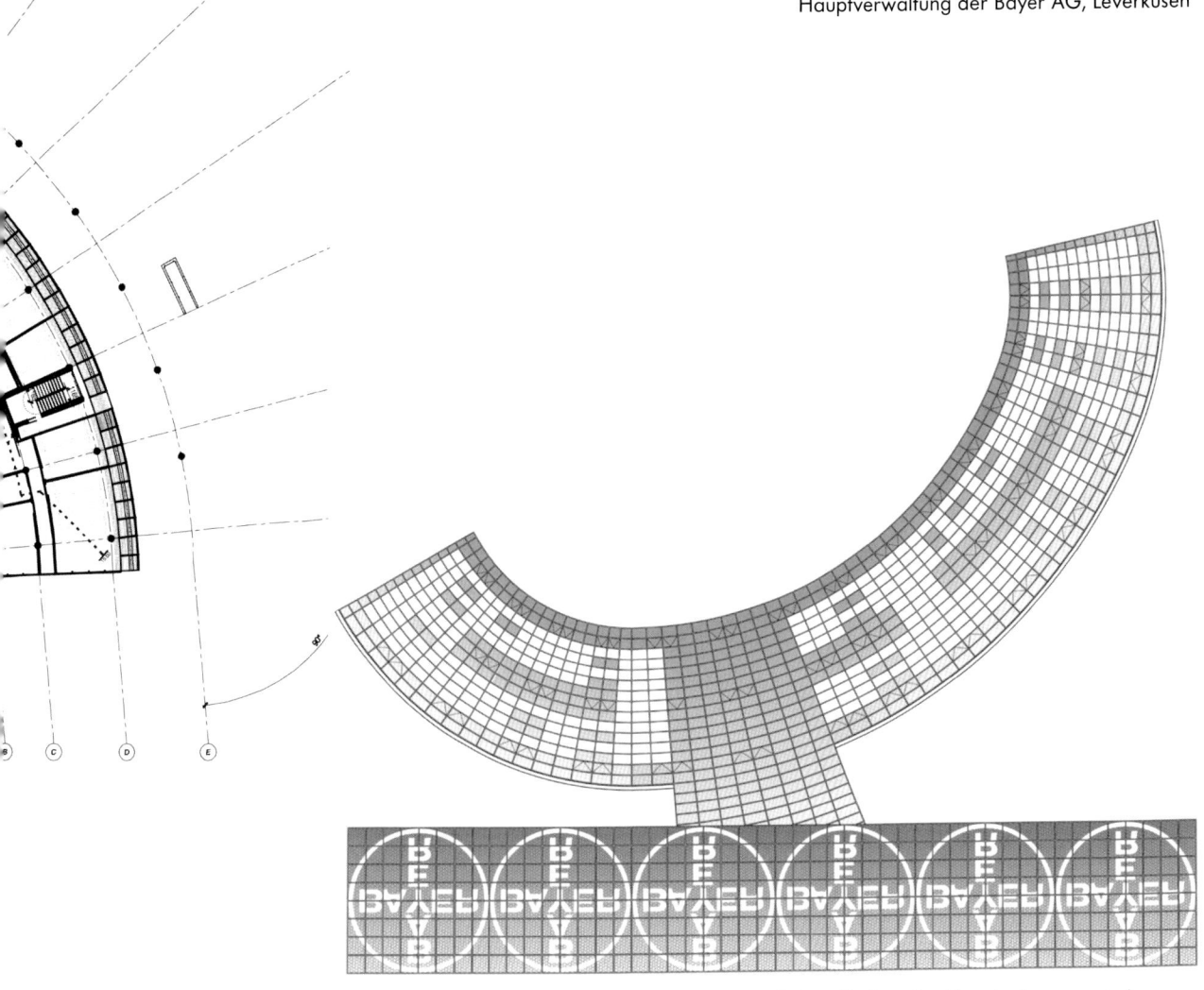

Dachaufsichtszeichnung mit den verglasten und den metallisch verkleideten Bereichen der Konzernzentrale
Roof view showing the glass and metal-covered sections of the corporate headquarters complex

arrogance and with his preconceived notions, he thinks he can do it all. We never used to involve consultants in the work of our Chicago office. We did everything ourselves, even the landscape planning, and we even told the engineer what he was supposed to do. In contrast, the quality of the buildings we do today is determined not only by the architect's input but by the framework, the building technology, the landscape planning.

Just this afternoon I attended a presentation by the French illuminationist Yann Kersalé for the lighting of the Sony building – for the roof, the portals and the high-rise. Kersalé's contribution complements, indeed enhances the architectural and spatial conception of the complex as a whole, the idea of a transition from the real city to the internal, virtual city. Of course I was immediately prompted to wonder how it would have been if I had gotten him involved as a consultant on the Munich airport centre project. Like any expert in his field, Kersalé has total command of his hardware, the resources with which he works, just as an engineer must know the limits of his materials or the building systems technician deals with the issue of comfort.

While the typical building systems technical merely measures the room temperature, our specialist Matthias Schuler looks at how the human being feels, asking about the perceived temperature and how heat radiates from the walls. Kersalé takes a similarly holistic approach with the Sony building. In his design, all the lights are out-

Hauptverwaltung der Bayer AG, Leverkusen

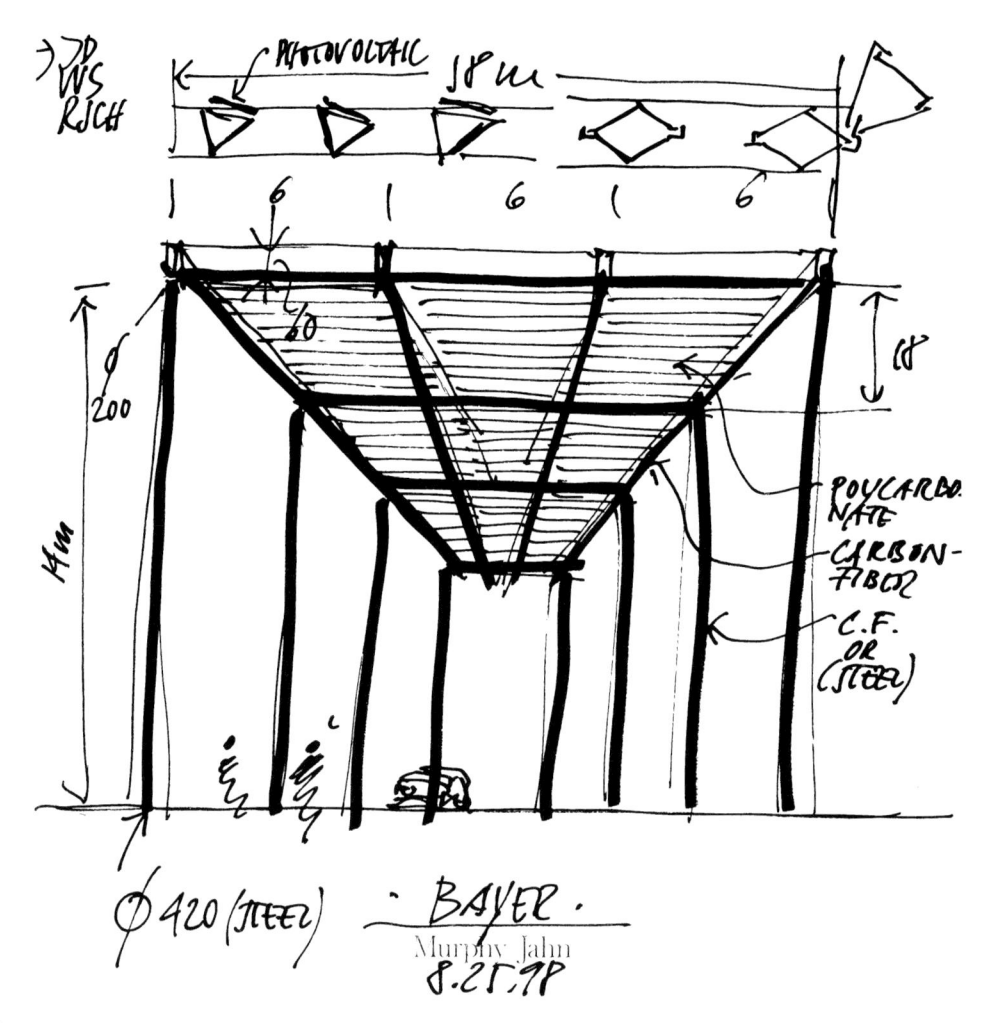

Erste Entwurfsüberlegungen zur Pergola
Initial ideas for the design of the pergola
Rechte Seite: Entwurfsskizzen zur Pergola und ihren Elementen aus Polycarbonat
Right: Design sketches for the pergola and its polycarbonate elements

side. They illuminate the roof like a huge lamp that shines from outside rather than inside and is translucent. As a result, the colours can be seen from the outside but hardly at all from the inside. They are created by a dichroitic glass, which he turns so that it shines red and blue on the one side and green and yellow on the other. So many artists have used this dichroitic glass, yet none of them like Kersalé. We believed him when he said how easy it was. If something is truly convincing, no one asks when it's finished why it is right. That is the art of finding a solution that really fits for a given situation.

SOBEK: We're not concerned with landing the commission for the highest building, the longest bridge or the largest hall. Instead, our goal is to perfect our work, through the involvement of others as well. We have gradually put together a team of people with a similar intellectual approach, people who have learned to understand the others' language. And all of a sudden the buildings we plan together are becoming clearer, simpler, more logical. They are improving in quality.

JAHN: At the beginning of the Sony project, during the serious planning stage in 1994/95, I simply didn't have the right engineers at my side. The engineers just didn't want to be challenged; they preferred to keep working in the old familiar way – as if saying, "If you don't try out new things, you can't make mistakes". That is kind

BAUER

n/fa
☒ br.
DIES SIND
DIE NÄCHSTEN
SCHRITTE ZU
BAUER

◻ CANOPY MIT KOHLEFASER GRID UND EINGEKLEMMTEN PC-ELEMENTEN

- 18m
- 18
- 6
- ± 500 ?!
- CARBON FASER
- CF / STAHL
- ⌀ 420 ZUGESPITZT AUF ⌀ 200
- 6000
- POLYCARBONAT-HOHLKÄSTEN

◻ SCHEIBEN ODER AUSPFOSTEN/FASERN:

- 8°
- 3.60
- 0.50
- 100 1600
- ESG 15 87?
- SSG 19
- 3200
- STÜTZ
- 100 t=10
- WIE WIRD EG ABGE-TRAGEN?

◻ TREPPEN + BRÜCKEN IM ATRIUM.

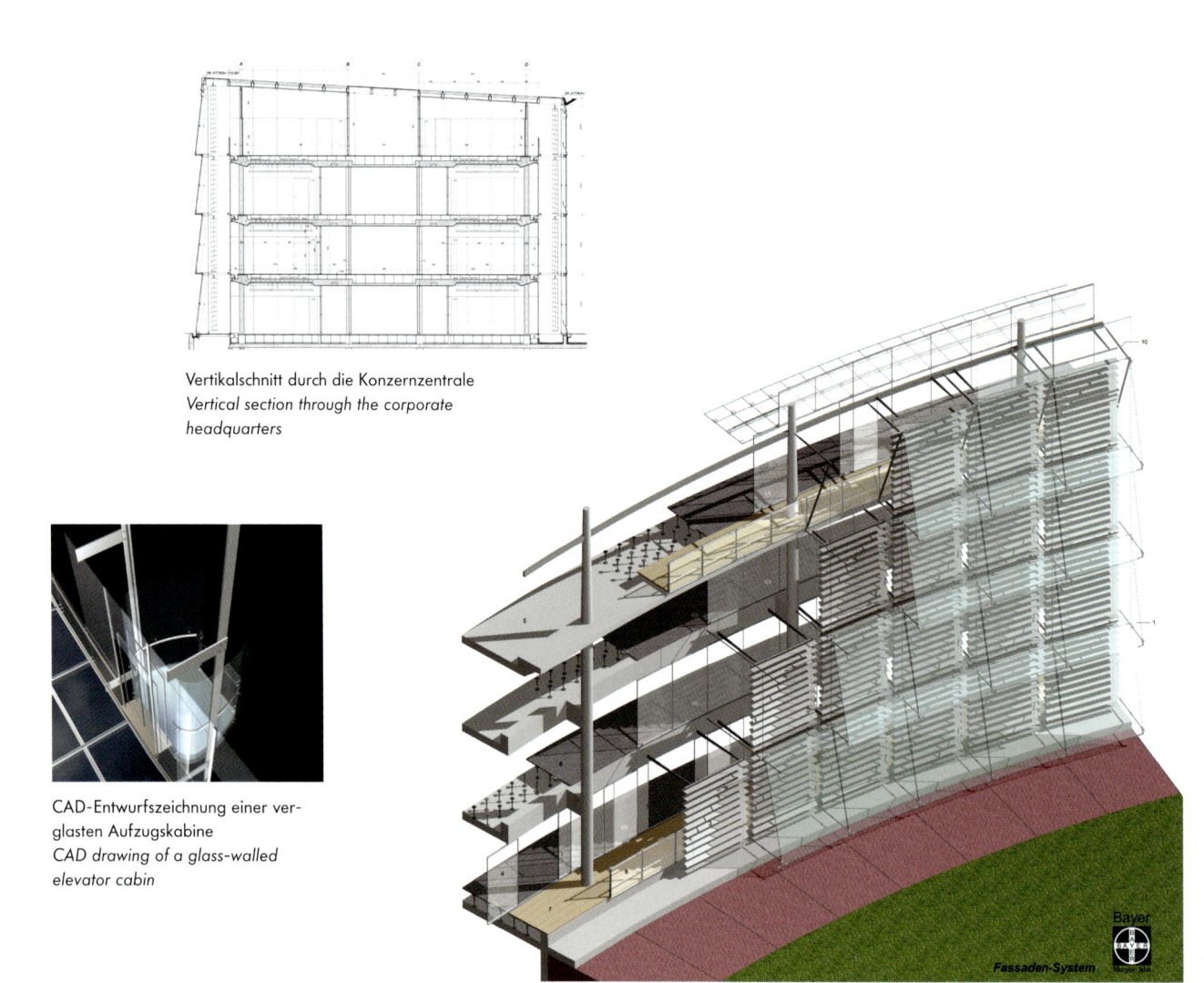

Vertikalschnitt durch die Konzernzentrale
Vertical section through the corporate headquarters

CAD-Entwurfszeichnung einer verglasten Aufzugskabine
CAD drawing of a glass-walled elevator cabin

Perspektivische Darstellung der Zweite-Haut-Fassade und ihrer Sonnenschutzelemente
Perspective view of the second-skin facade and its awning elements

of like the person who wants to climb a mountain without the right equipment; he won't reach the top. With those engineers I would never have been able to create these special walls for Sony. I remember how hard I tried to persuade them. All I ever heard was, "But this is a facade. You are the architect. You have to do the facade". And I always just said, "No, I can't do the facade". That was this traditional division of labour between the architect and the engineer, who actually only reacts. What we wanted was an engineer who would get involved. Only the typical architect feels threatened when he has to share with someone.

SOBEK: Clients are always coming to me and saying, "Mr. Sobek, I'd like you to build me one of those glass walls, too". The problem then often arises that although I may speak the architect's language, he can't converse in my language because he hasn't put any thought on these specific engineering aspects or doesn't care to do so.

JAHN: You can see the results of such communication problems in many buildings. Industry does the marketing work for that kind of thing, declaring, "We can produce a wall like that for you as well; you don't need Sobek at all; we can do the calculation just as well".

And then the building turns out accordingly – as if five different people had designed it. One did the canopy roof, the next the large glass wall in the lobby, the third the sunshades. But a building has real quality only if it comes from a single mould.

Hauptverwaltung der Bayer AG, Leverkusen

Die Pergola balanciert das Volumen der älteren Bauten aus
The pergola balances out the volumes of the older buildings
Folgende Seiten: Aufsicht auf die Gesamtanlage, Modellaufnahme
Following pages: View of the entire complex from above, model photo

Right now we're talking primarily about glass buildings, transparent, dynamic buildings. But the same applies to stone buildings. Things simply have to be assessed according to different rules, judged from a different standpoint. After all, people don't all have to believe in the same thing. But when I look at the new buildings at the Pariser Platz in Berlin, I can see that the architects have been forced to give way to some higher prevailing notion. The best buildings at this location are actually still the very simple ones on both sides of the Brandenburg Gate. In the others, which attempt to articulate a traditional vocabulary of forms, neither the old nor the new wins, although an effort was made to eliminate risks. The same goes for the Berliner Stadtschloß. If the idea is to rebuild it as it was, then we know exactly how it should look. But if they dare to do something different, many people will find the risk too high.

KUHN: Your team is not limited to large-scale projects. You also do things on a much smaller scale, like Street Furnitures.

JAHN: There is no major and no minor surgery. Every surgery is serious.

KUHN: Does that mean that you don't differentiate between large and small building projects?

JAHN: What is large, and what is small? The "Ku'damm-70" building covers only 800 square metres, while Sony fills 200,000. The Street Furnitures for Decaux were a pilot project devoted to an exploration of just how

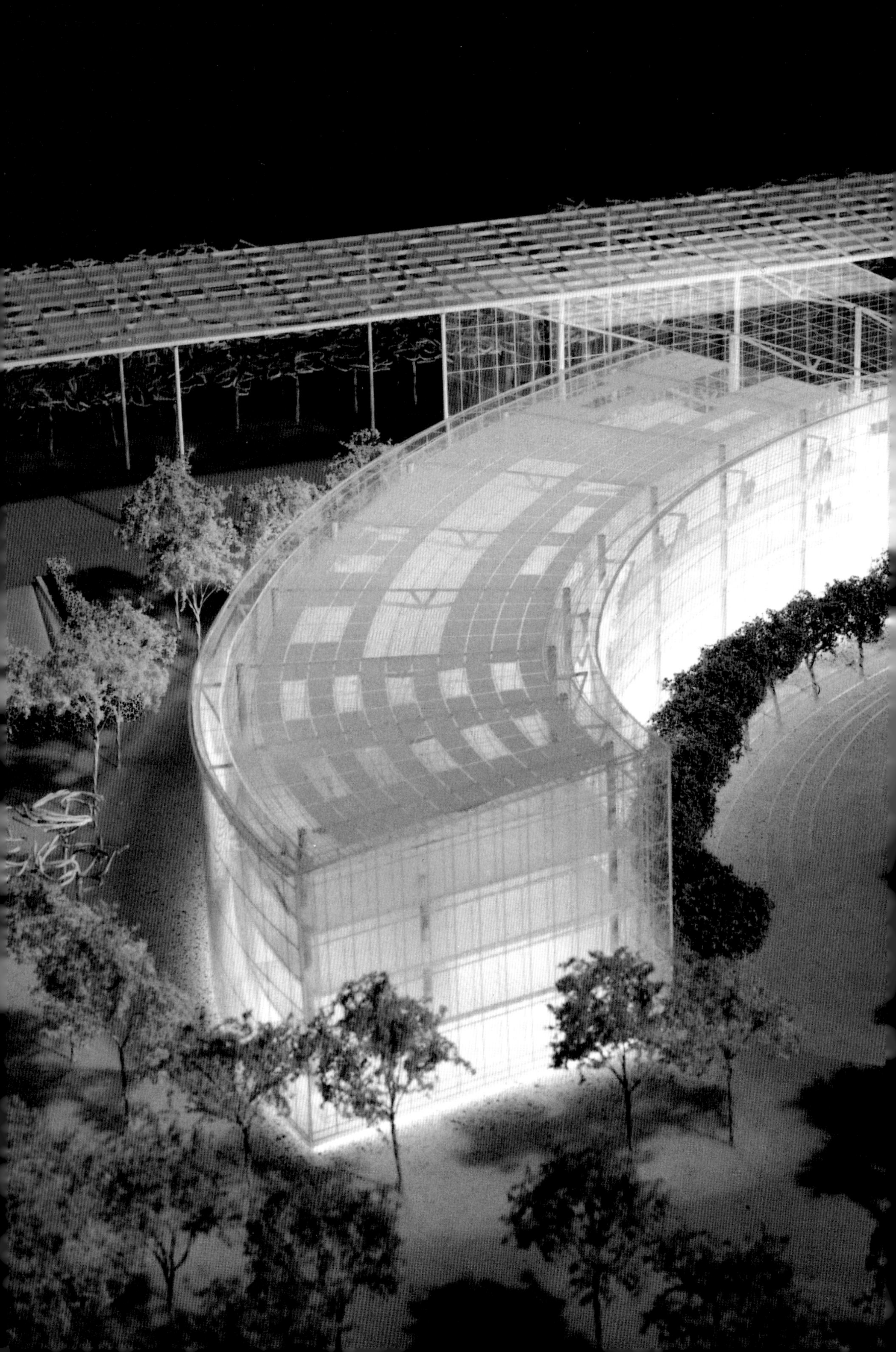

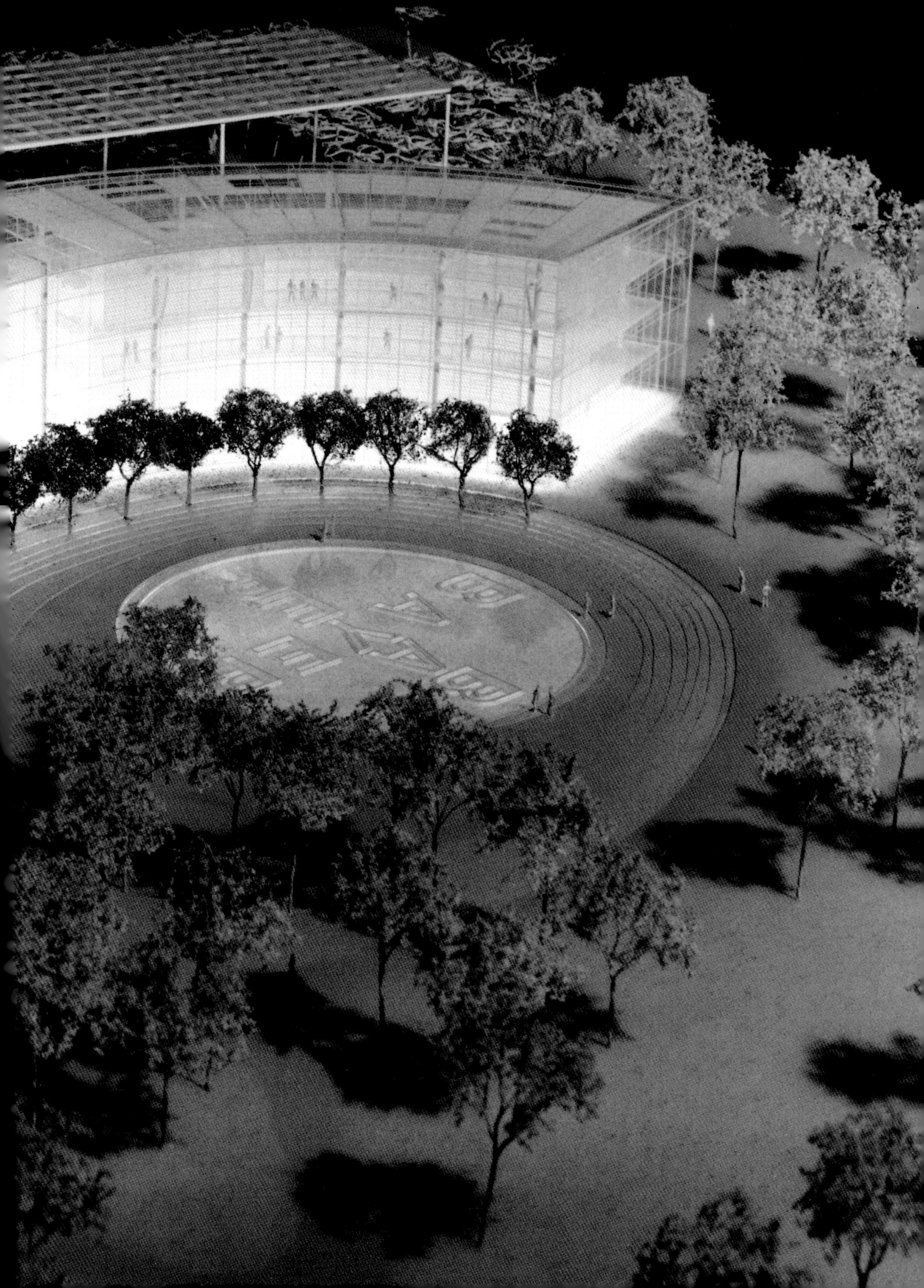

Transrapid-Stationen für Hamburg, Schwerin und Berlin

Das Grundprinzip des Entwurfes besteht darin, den Transrapid als Gestaltungselement der Station selbst einzubinden und als Station eine minimale und einfache Hülle zu schaffen. Weitauskragende Dächer und schwebende, an den Stützen der Fahrbahn angehängte Baukörper bilden das Gebäude. Zug und Hülle bestimmen die Architektur, deren Erscheinungsbild durch Struktur, Konstruktion und Materialien geprägt wird. Das Hauptinteresse gilt »Engineering und Performance« im Gegensatz zu »Design und Styling«.

The basic principle underlying this plan is the integration of the Transrapid as an element of station design and to create a station as a minimal, simple shell. Widely overhanging roofs and floating structures suspended on the columns supporting the railway line form the shape of the building. The train and the shell dominate the architecture, whose appearance is characterised by structure, construction and materials. The focus of interest is "Engineering and Performance" rather than "Design und Styling".

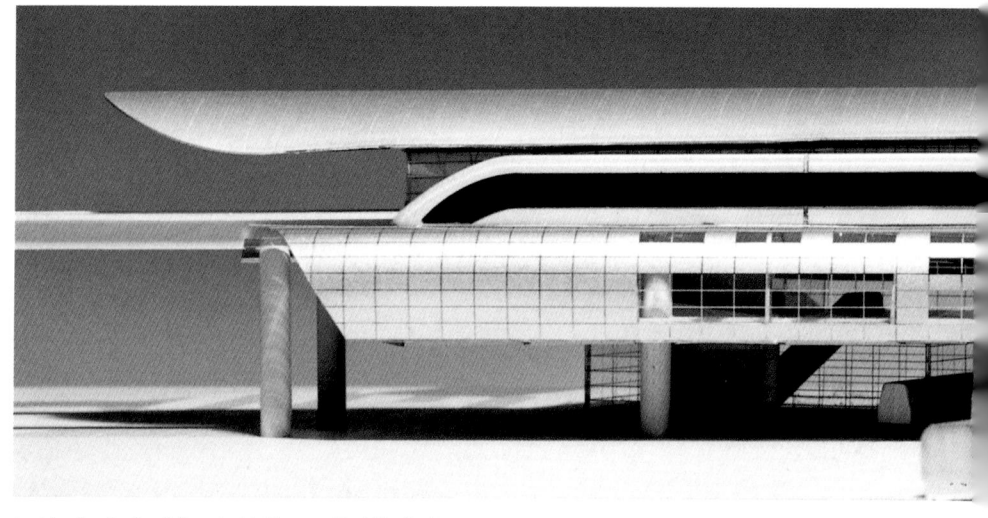

Ansicht der Station Schwerin-Holthusen, Modellaufnahme
View of the station Schwerin-Holthusen, model photo

far one could go with glass as a load-bearing material. We would do that quite differently today.

SOBEK: But it was the right thing to do at its time.

KUHN: Are these Street Furnitures – the bus stop, the advertising column, the newspaper kiosk – actually going to be built?

SOBEK: A bus stop has already been built.

KUHN: A relatively small object in comparison to most of your other architecture, which is typically characterised by its substantial height and thus has a significant impact on its urban surroundings.

JAHN: I have never regarded the height of a building as a kind of exhibitionism or a sign of gigantomania. The Frankfurt Messeturm [Trade Fair Centre Tower] was built so high because Walter Wallmann, mayor of Frankfurt at the time, wanted it that way. And Sony has so many floors because Debis is so high. I have always been rather apathetic when it came to deciding whether a building should have more or fewer floors. The quality, the posture of a building is much more important to me. I think that this discussion about high-rises has more to do with sensationalism. Together, the buildings on Potsdamer Platz set an urban-planning accent. People recognise them as a group and accept that they have a certain right to be there. Like a gateway, the mark the transition from Potsdamer Platz to Leipziger Straße.

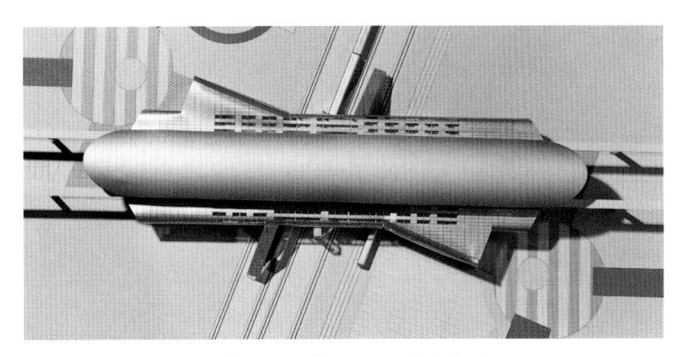

Aufsicht auf die Station Schwerin-Holthusen, Modellaufnahme
View of the station Schwerin-Holthusen from above, model photo

KUHN: With the Sony tower you have created a "point de vue", a prominent point within the city.

JAHN: A skyscraper – intentionally or otherwise – always sets an accent. That was precisely the objective in the case of the Messeturm in Frankfurt. This type of skyscraper was a symbol for Frankfurt, a kind of re-import, since the Bauhaus, which built these huge buildings, was forced to emigrate to America. The ones in Frankfurt are just a pale imitation of the American skyscrapers of the fifties and sixties. These old buildings are actually of better quality than those that were erected during the eighties: the Civic Center in Chicago, the old Mies van der Rohe Building, IBM, Olivetti, the Seagram's Building in New York. And that isn't likely to change for a long time, since the technological feasibility of the ideas we advocate is very low in the US. We're currently working on a building for HA-LO Corporate in Chicago, where we can realise only a fraction – in terms of materials and the integration of building technology – of what we are achieving here in Germany.

SOBEK: All in all, one gets his fill of problems working on this Chicago project.

JAHN: But to return to the Frankfurter Messeturm, that building has an almost figural effect. That was the desired design at the time, the Zeitgeist. Even back then we were trying to find a way to realise a traditional form in a modern, contemporary approach. The natural stone material became acceptable in my eyes only once we had discovered that the slabs did not have to be four centimetres thick but could be reduced to a thickness of two

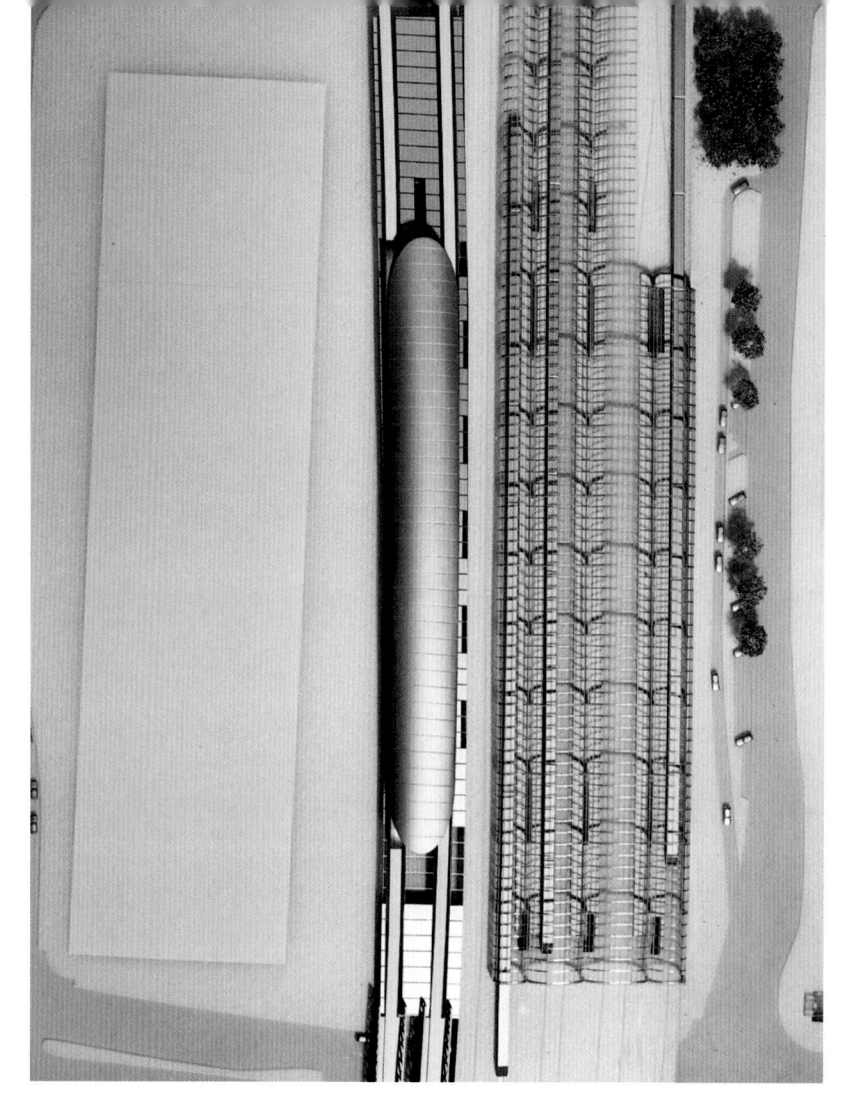

Aufsicht der Station Berlin-Spandauer Bahnhof, Modellaufnahme
View of the station Berlin-Spandau Railway Station from above, model photo

centimetres using new machines and even routed on the edges, allowing them to be installed in frames like panes of glass. You can clearly see these metal frames on the Messeturm. The whole thing was prefabricated in panels, which were fixed in place with four screws. And although the building has a more figural look – quite unlike Sony, which embodies a much more abstract aesthetics – the engineering approach is the same: to take advantage of all of the technical possibilities in dealing with the materials, in order to ensure that they are honest in their expression. This strategy always leads to minimisation, of course. The real art involved is that of leaving things out. The goal is achieved when you can leave something out.

SOBEK: Or, to be exact, when there's ultimately nothing more to leave out.

JAHN: We'll probably never reach that goal, though, for we can't possibly live long enough. We're looking for a shell that reacts dynamically, one that no longer consists of a cumbersome construction. We really want only a single panel, instead of the double-shelled facade in which the outer layer no longer does anything. But we still need cables and brackets to span the glass from one floor to another with the aid of winches. At some point, however, someone is going to develop a kind of glass that is either stronger or is capable of bending. It's only a question of time until we have unbreakable glass. But it will only come if someone demands it.

KUHN: Thus glass will be your most important building material in the future as well.

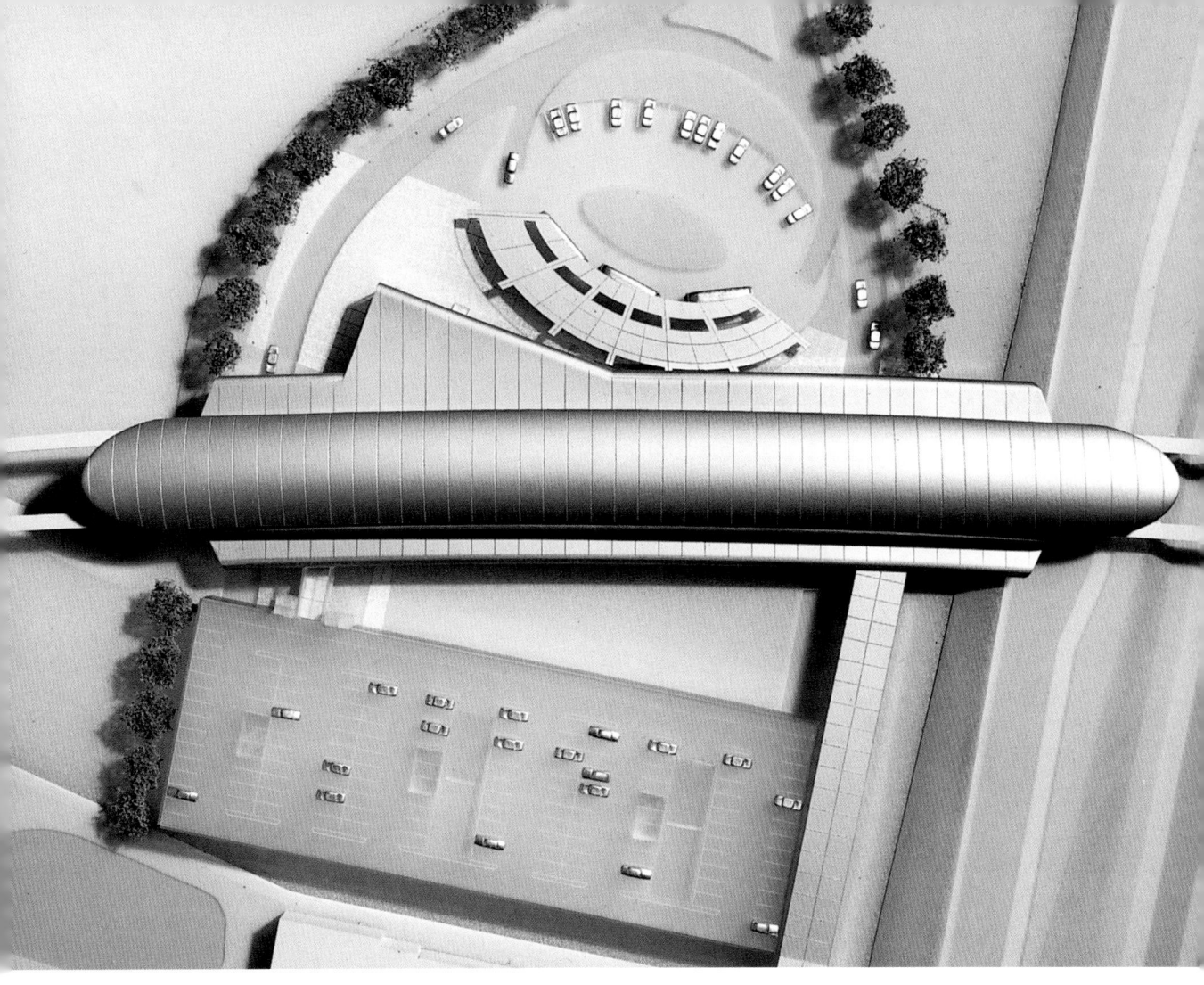

Aufsicht der Station Hamburg-Moorfleet, Modellaufnahme
View of the station Hamburg-Moorfleet from above, model photo

SOBEK: We work with glass for two reasons. The first is its transparency, and the second is its technological potential. That potential is going be developed much further than is has been to date. There will be switch-controlled glass, for example. Even now we can make a transparent pane opaque simply by pressing a button. Certain light frequencies, such as the infrared frequencies, no longer pass through but are reflected instead to prevent a building from absorbing heat during the summer. Or these same frequencies are allowed to pass through during the winter months to help heat the building. Besides textiles, which are not so easily incorporated into architecture, mainly because no one has yet learned to play their full repertoire perfectly, glass holds for the greatest potential for development.

JAHN: Clay has reached the end of its development, for example. It is perfect. Perhaps it could bear more weight, harden more quickly, be made stronger or easier to work, but the limits have been reached. Steel has its limits as well, as strong as it is being made today. Brick – to be honest – doesn't interest me either, because it is an outdated technology. That's a manual trade, laying stone upon stone. Yet buildings are still being erected today for which floor-sized brick panels are prefabricated by the manufacturer because the cost of paying a mason to lay bricks one by one can no longer be justified. This really amounts to desecration of brick, as such use is not in keeping with its material properties.

Ansicht der Station Hamburg-Moorfleet, Modellaufnahme
View of the station Hamburg-Moorfleet, model photo

SOBEK: One is prompted to ask why bricks are used at all today. The reason is visual habit. We still associate a great deal with brick. People used to build with brick because there was no technology available for the production of large-scale elements. Bricks produced in larger sizes split apart during the baking process. And there were no construction cranes. Bricks had to be carried up to the scaffolding – well into the sixties. Since today's cranes were unknown then, incredible effort was invested into the development of small-component construction modules. Now the technology is available, which is why it makes no sense to use module sizes that no longer match the technology we have.

KUHN: You work with glass in order to create transparency. Does that have a symbolic meaning for you, in the sense of "democratic architecture" perhaps?

JAHN: About twenty years ago there was a symposium in Frankfurt on democratic architecture. Everybody was talking about transparency and history. I was the only one who got booed when I said that good architecture is always monumental. Oh my, were they up in arms! Yet ultimately it is true. All of the great architectural works – the Greek temples, the pyramids in Egypt, the Coliseum in Rome or the train stations – are monumental. Not that some architect or an engineer was trying to erect a monument to himself, it was simply appropriate to the situation. Democratic architecture is just another way of dealing with the past, of suppressing consciousness.

SOBEK: The approach is also highly populistic, since the idea is all too easily articulated. Some people are still building on the basis of these concepts.

JAHN: They use them as marketing tools.

KUHN: So the equation of glass or transparency with democratic architecture or the open society is no longer valid?

SOBEK: Fortunately. There are certain fundamental rules that are so trivial that they needn't even be mentioned. But when, for example, someone builds a Bundestag like Behnisch, where visitors descend into the building, then people enter a room in a completely different way. You look down from above at what comes up to meet you – in complete contrast to the Reichstag, where you have to ascend a number of steps with bowed head before entering. Those are the old tricks used in the architecture of power: having people arrive breathless and bowing when they arrive.

KUHN: Let us look at another kind of material – wood. Mr. Sobek, I know that you are an admirer of wood. Wouldn't it be another material you could use in your work with Mr. Jahn? Or doesn't it fit in?

SOBEK: Of course. But it depends upon how wood is used. Four materials are used in classical engineering: steel, concrete, wood and masonry. If you visited any standard engineering office in Germany, even one of the

Kaufhaus Kaufhof in Chemnitz

In seiner wichtigen Lage, begrenzt von Neumarkt, Marktplatzarkaden, Bahnhofstraße und Rathausstraße, wird das Kaufhof-Projekt zu einem entscheidenden Bestandteil der Wiederverdichtung und damit der Reparatur der Stadt Chemnitz. Die Grundstücksfläche wird mit einer Blockbebauung überbaut, eine Galeria trennt das Kaufhaus von der Parkgarage. Das vollkommen transparente Gebäude erlaubt Blickbeziehungen von Innen nach Außen und umgekehrt, es schafft durchgehende Räume und erlebbare Verbindungen.

In its important position surrounded by the Neumarkt, the town market arcades, Bahnhofsstraße and Rathausstraße, the Kaufhof project represents a major contribution to the reconcentration and thus to the reconstruction of the city of Chemnitz. The lot is to be covered with a block-style structure, and a gallery will separate the department store from the parking garage. The entirely transparent building opens views from inside to outside and vice-versa, creating continuous spaces and perceptible interconnections.

Chemnitz, Innenstadt
Chemnitz, city centre

better qualified ones, and suggested an aluminium construction, they would all probably say, "Interesting, but that's not our field". If you wanted something built with glass, you would probably find a few who can do that, but by no means all of them. If you wanted a facade done in titanium, you'd get no answers, nor would you find takers for a carbon-fibre construction. Even as a student I made it my goal to make use of all possible materials – wood, bamboo, carbon-fibre, titanium, concrete or whatever. And I vowed to use them in a way that is always appropriate for the site and the planned architecture. At the same time I want to use the materials and combine them in such a manner that they meet state-of-the-art technological standards and that they can be dismantled and recycled easily. This single-material concept – assembling, joining and dismantling, composing and decomposing – is important to both of us.

Wood naturally plays an important role in this context, not least of all because of its strong tactile quality. It has excellent weight-bearing characteristics in certain areas. In addition, wood is attractive from the standpoint of energy utilisation as heat and noise insulation. Used properly in architecture, wood offers notable environmental benefits as a renewable raw material that is comparatively easy to recycle or dispose of, as long as it is impregnated with environmentally safe chemicals or not impregnated at all. The big problem with wood is that it is a very strong building material along one axis – parallel to the grain – but has virtually no strength at

Chemnitz, Innenstadt
Chemnitz, City centre

Zeichnung, Zufahrt zum Parkhaus und Kaufhof
Drawing, access road to car park and Kaufhof

all along the second axis running perpendicular to the wood fibres, which are hollow and collapse like a sponge. That has consequences for assembly techniques. There is practically nothing worse one can do than pound a nail into wood or drive a screw into it. One cannot remove loads from soft materials at discreet points. Wood is a very effective building material, but only if forces are applied and removed in a completely homogeneous manner.

KUHN: Does that mean that you wouldn't consider wood in joint projects with Mr. Jahn?

SOBEK: My office is involved in intensive work on the development of connection techniques appropriate for wood. The method most commonly used today – connecting a series of wooden rods with large-scale steel elements – is unacceptable to us. For some buildings, the A-Motion Pavilion for DaimlerChrysler, for instance, we have incorporated large wooden elements with very appealing formal qualities. Ultimately, however, there is still a metallic shield that is fastened with bolts in keeping with the principles of steel construction. If we ever come up with a satisfactory solution for joining wooden components, I can imagine that Mr. Jahn would also be willing to build with wood.

JAHN: I've always thought that wood, as a natural material, was too precious. But perhaps I don't know enough about wood and the way wooden elements are connected.

HA-LO Corporate Headquarters in Chicago

Das Gebäude für die Hauptverwaltung einer Sportmarketingfirma ist bewußt selbst Zeichen, die Firma stellt sich im Atrium des Gebäudes bewußt zur Schau. Gleichzeitig leistet das Gebäude hinsichtlich seiner Transparenz, seiner Minimalität in der Verwendung der Mittel, seiner konsequenten Zusammenführung von Gestalt und Technik und seinem minimalen Energieverbrauch bei gleichzeitig hohem Benutzerkomfort einen wichtigen Beitrag im Bauschaffen Nordamerikas der letzten Jahre.

The headquarters building for the sports marketing company is intended to serve as a symbol. The company deliberately displays itself in the atrium. At the same time, the building makes a significant contribution to recent North American architecture by virtue of its transparency, its minimal use of resources, its consistent integration of form and technology and its combination of starkly reduced energy consumption with a maximum of user comfort.

Typischer Büroraum
Typical office

KUHN: Apparently, the building of the future will be characterised not only by greater flexibility of use but by the aspect of motion in general. At least that is what some of your works seem to suggest, Mr. Sobek. Does that hold another vision for the architecture of the twenty-first century, which will be developed through the association of the architect and the engineer?

SOBEK: To an increasing extent, the aspect of motion is becoming a necessary part of our work – making a roof that can be flexibly opened and closed, for instance. But I'm testing a number of things outside the context of our work together, in the area of trade fair stands, for example, since they are usually in place for only a week or a month and clients tend to be more willing to accept a certain amount of risk. Things don't have to be absolutely watertight, and you have an opportunity to build something with carbon fibres or test a wooden construction. These are experiments designed to establish a degree of certainty before we propose such things on a large scale to a building client who is going to invest millions of marks, putting his existence on the line, and for whom they are going to have to function properly for the next fifty years.

Helmut Jahn and I are also carrying out similar experiments together. In Stuttgart, four of us – Helmut and I along with the building systems physicist Matthias Schuler and an acoustics specialist – had a wooden container built for the purpose of studying light transmission through different layers of material. Of course it is possible to

Blick in das längsseits aufgeschnittene Gebäude
View into the building, cut open on its long side

calculate how much light passes through a certain number of layers of material. But what does the figure 1.5 per cent really tell us? So we wanted to experience the effects for ourselves. We spent a afternoon inside the container for the purpose of finding out how light intensity changes in a room.

JAHN: We now have a world-wide patent on this triple-shelled construction with one membrane on the outside, one on the inside and acoustic absorbers in the centre.

SOBEK: Of course there is never only the one solution. You develop a whole repertoire of so-called correct solutions. The key to the art, then, is opening up the drawers of the this repertoire and knowing which solution to combine with the other solutions in a building in order to ensure that the style is consistent through and through. Calculating the dimensions of a support is a trivial problem, but shaping all of the elements in such a way that they fit together and each is right for itself – that is the real accomplishment.

KUHN: Do you relate to a specific tradition? Whom would you refer to as forebears – of your co-operative work as well?

SOBEK: That is not an easy question to answer, since there aren't any schools in that sense in engineering. People speak of a Stuttgart School, but it is characterised more by an approach – the way materials are dealt with respect to connection techniques, processing and calculation. It doesn't relate to the creative handling of

Neue Messe Shanghai-Pudong

Wichtige Entwurfsüberlegungen für das auf einem annähernd dreieckigen Grundriß befindliche, neu zu bauende Messegelände waren dessen städtebauliche Einordnung, seine Funktionalität und die zur Anwendung kommenden Technologien. Hieraus entstand das Konzept eines aus Messehallen, Eingangsbauwerk und Hotel bestehenden Gebäudekomplexes, der in mehreren Phasen errichtet werden wird. Zunächst entstehen vier Messehallen, deren weitgespannte Dächer mit einfachen technischen Mitteln bei gleichzeitig minimiertem Aufwand einen lichtdurchfluteten Innenraum schaffen.

Important aspects considered in the design of the new trade fair centre to be build on a practically triangular ground plan were integration into existing urban architecture, its functionality and the technologies to be incorporated into it. On this basis, the concept of a building complex consisting of trade show halls, an entrance building and a hotel was developed which is to be erected in successive phases. The first phase calls for construction of four trade show halls, whose expansive roofs will create a light-flooded interior using simple technical resources and minimum efforts.

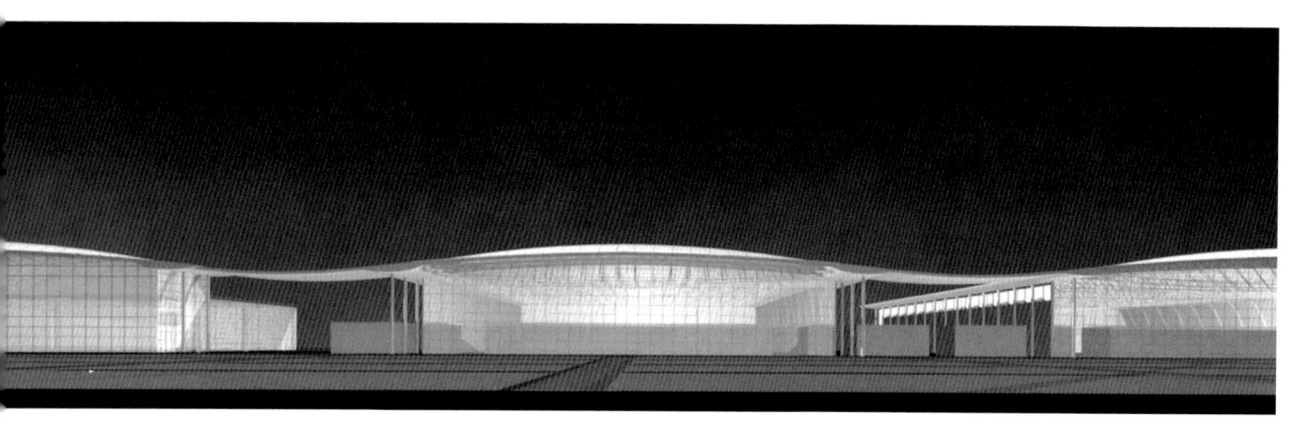

Blick auf die Stirnfassade einer Messehalle
View of the front facade of an exhibition hall

materials. Too, the Stuttgart School has fixed its interest on only a few specific materials: reinforced concrete, wood, steel and a little masonry. If we expand the palette to include titanium, aluminium, glass and the like, then we have no forebears at all. Typically, there is still no concept of style in engineering today.

JAHN: Of course we could answer the question about our origins with a conventional response, citing people like Maillart, Nervi, Prouvé or calling to mind pioneer figures like Paxton in engineering. But I tend to agree with Werner Sobek. Our kind of building really has its origins in the McCormick Palace, which also had this same prior structural influence. Ultimately, however, someone else will have to find the answer to the question of the roots of our work.

SOBEK: Basically, we would tend not to refer to a school but instead to people who had an influence: Frei Otto and Jörg Schlaich, for instance, for whom I worked for several years, were surely influential. Jürgen Joedicke also. Add to this the influence of the deceased, Maillart, Prouvé. But they did not influence a school in the classical sense. What ultimately shaped my approach was my dissatisfaction with the existing repertoire of solutions that engineering had to offer. And that led me to the study of aircraft and automobile designs: the construction of a wing on the Concorde or the shape of an automobile fender. I still have command of these technologies today. And I can transfer that knowledge, about working with thin sheet metal, for example, to the con-

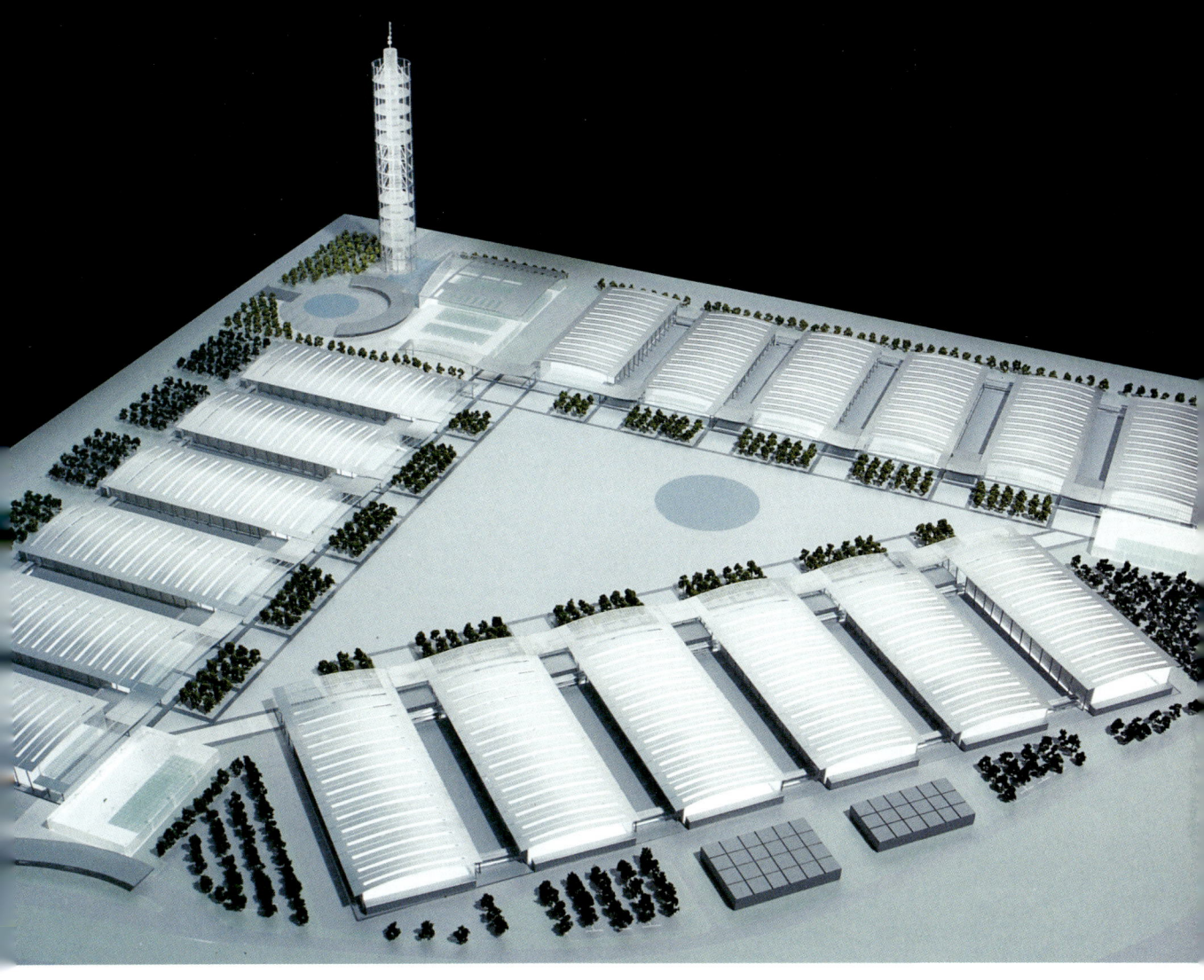

Aufsicht auf die Gesamtanlage nach Fertigstellung aller Bauphasen
View of the entire complex from above following completion of all phases of construction

text of building with thin glass.

JAHN: But none of that comes from a study of history or from attempts to pursue it further. It is the product of knowledge that our predecessors did not have. I think that we get lost every time we cite history as the source of our inspiration – lost with respect to progress. After all, the engineer who designed the Concorde didn't spend his time studying the flight behaviour of the JU 52.

SOBEK: The subject of engineering history began to take on increasing importance about fifteen years ago. The efforts towards exploring our roots and tracing the development of the engineer's profession were certainly worth supporting. Yet for many, this focus on engineering history was the product of a certain helpless "where-do-we-go-now" feeling, since we had gotten a hold on steel, mastered concrete and now found wood and masonry almost trivial.

JAHN: The famous word coined in the eighties for that is "postmodernism". I rode that wave, too, back then. But when I look back today, I realise that it didn't work. It didn't have the power of the architecture we had built ten years before, which still looks good today, amazingly good, in fact. That's all over today, though, and postmodernism is dead. The buildings erected during those years look like old ladies with too much jewellery.

SOBEK: I was fortunate to have been born too late.

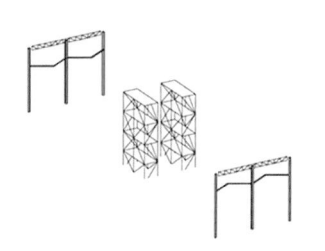

ERECTION SEQUENCE 1

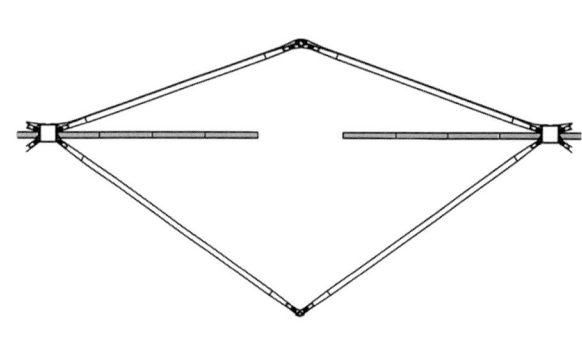

TRUSS FRAME DETAIL

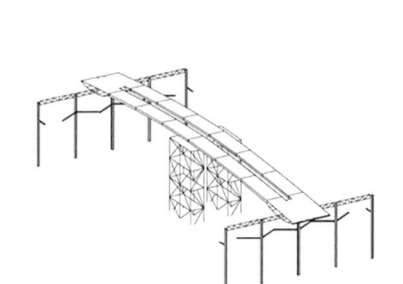

ERECTION SEQUENCE 2

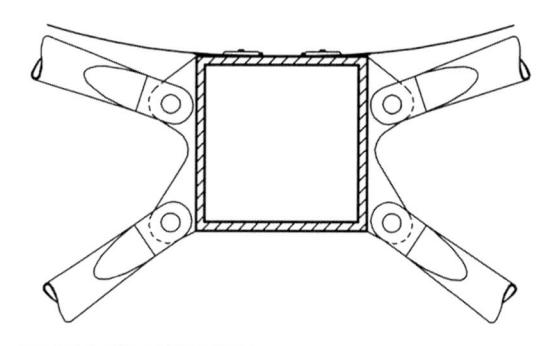

TRUSS FRAME DETAIL

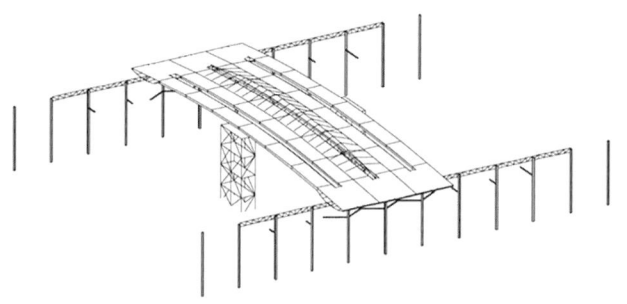

ERECTION SEQUENCE 3

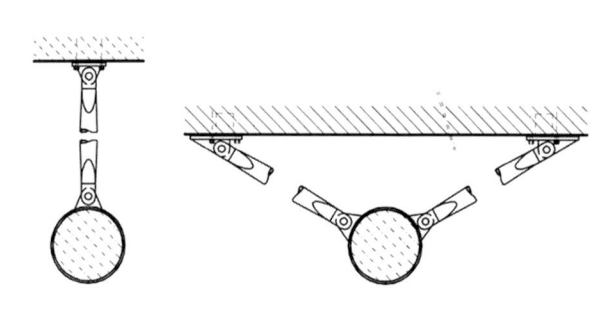

COLUMN DETAIL

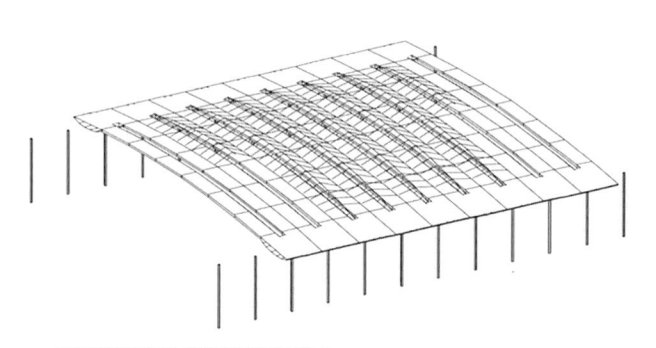

ERECTION SEQUENCE 4

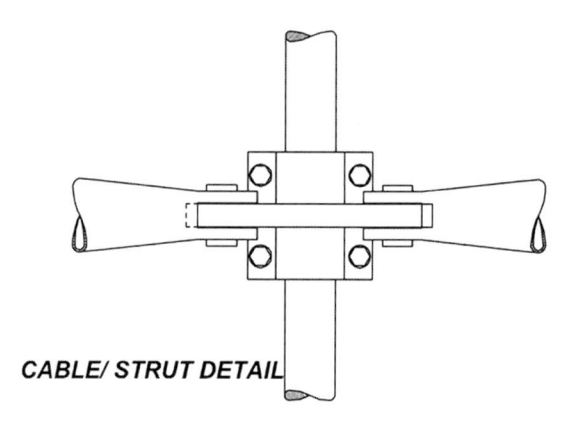

CABLE/ STRUT DETAIL

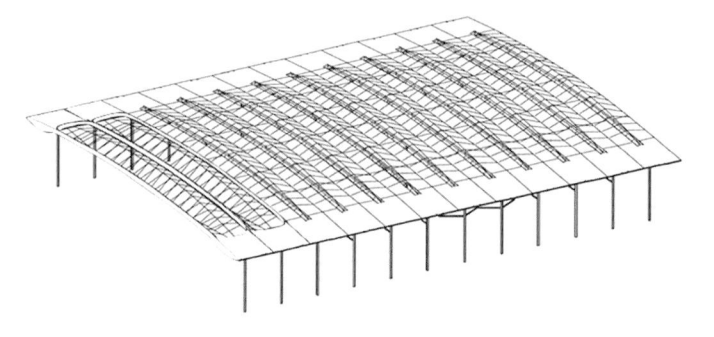

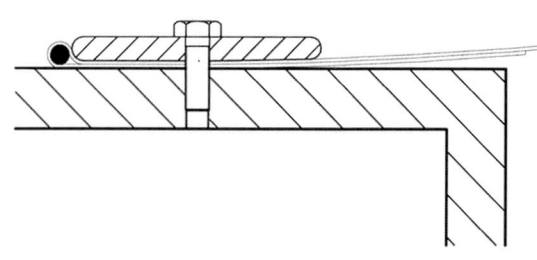

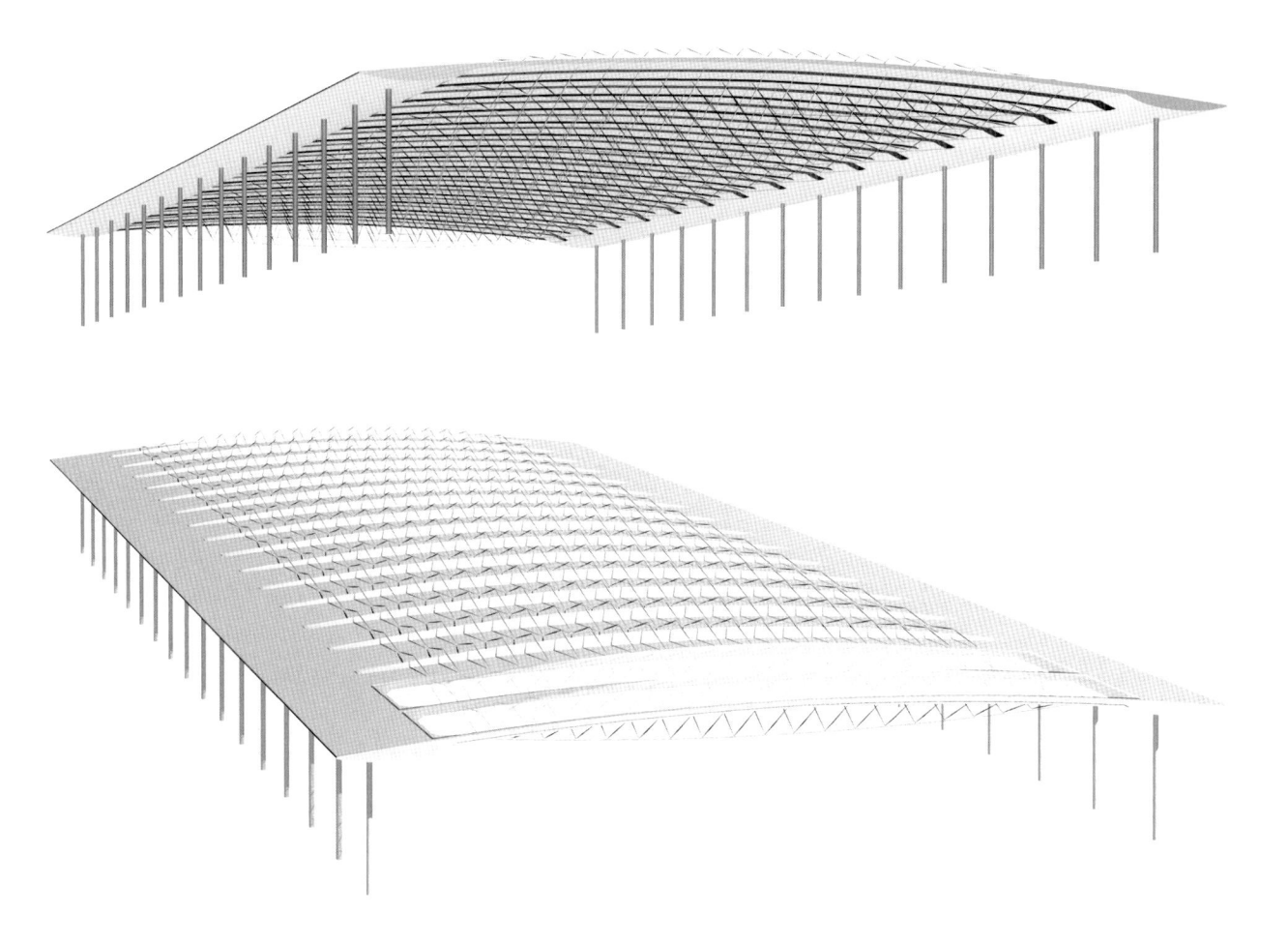

Konstruktionszeichnungen zum Dachtragwerk der Hallen
Structural drawings for the supporting roof framework of the halls
Linke Seite: Überlegungen zur Montage, Konstruktionsdetails
Left: Assembly considerations, structural details

JAHN: There was simply nothing significant produced during that period. The economy was in great shape back then; taxes were low, people's incomes were good – until the Bush years came. And it's the same with Clinton today. The stock market is soaring, people are rich and spending money, and nothing of importance is being created. The people who have accomplished something good have never been concerned with money but with ideas. And that is why you find so few good ideas realised in architecture or in engineering in America today, where the level of acceptance for innovation is at low ebb and industry is resistant to change as well.

KUHN: In your work together we also find reflections of more complex challenges to today's architecture, which takes form in increasingly larger urban-development contexts and must fulfil a wide range of functions. Thus the Sony Center in Berlin, the IIT Campus Center and the Shanghai-Pudong trade fair satisfy a variety of urban needs and have also become autonomous urban forms in their own right.

JAHN: There was a master plan for the Sony project, an urban-development master plan that prescribed a block structure. That meant that we had to restore the nineteenth-century urban configuration of the whole, on the one hand, and create a new spatial order within the confines of the terrain due to the particularities of the property and ownership situation. We wanted to accommodate offices, commercial buildings, residential buildings and even an entertainment centre – in other words, to establish a multi-purpose spatial order of the kind

Blick durch die Stirnseite in eine Messehalle
View through the front face into an exhibition hall

found in a typical city structure. The Berlin Sony building is a successor to the State of Illinois Center in Chicago. There as well, we created urban space to a certain degree and incorporated it into the building. I remember saying to myself when the facade was completed that I wouldn't put up another facade like that the next time, as we have now done in Berlin. During the discussion in Chicago people kept saying, "You have to put some doors there. There's got to be doors; we've got to control it". And in Germany everyone thinks that Sony is a typical introverted American mall. But quite the opposite it true. The place will always be open, and people will be able to go in any time they wish. That is a feature of many of our projects – of Kranzler Eck as well – the fact that we have searched for ways to incorporate public space into the buildings. You'll find something akin to an urban structure even in the trade fair projects. Look at the trade fair in Shanghai with its front square, the open spaces, the outside areas for exhibitions. That's just like a real city section.

KUHN: The same goes for the airports.

JAHN: Yes. The airport in Munich is grouped around such an urban area. No matter what many people think of it today, it was the best decision made there – putting a large, open space right in the centre, in the middle of a large building. Someone once compared it to a city cathedral, which also sets accents and marks the location of the centre. The more these buildings appear, the more important that will become. Many people are now say-

ing that it's too big. But that was what the competition foresaw. The judgement of history comes later, in any case.

SOBEK: That is a typically German argument – claiming that something is too big. You hear that here all the time.

JAHN: Things are different in France. There are many interesting buildings there. But how many buildings of that quality are built in Germany in the course of all of these competitions, buildings with such a high recognition factor, with that kind of symbolic character? Not very many. The roof of the Olympic Stadium in Munich is certainly one.

SOBEK: Or the German Bundestag.

JAHN: And the Munich Hypobank and the BMW building, . . .

SOBEK: . . . the Stuttgart TV tower. And that's about it. Buildings recently erected in Düsseldorf, such as the Stadttor high-rise, or the RWE building in Essen might be worth mentioning.

KUHN: Interdisciplinary thinking is an prerequisite for your work together. Do you investigate other fields, such as music, for instance? After all, Schelling is reputed to have said that architecture is music in building form. What music would you think fitting for your architecture?

JAHN: Two years ago, the Munich Theater and Music Director August Everding invited me and others,

Bürogebäude für Andersen Consulting in Sulzbach

Eine sehr ruhige, nur durch die Baustoffe Beton, Stahl und Glas geprägte Gesamtkubatur prägt die Erscheinung dieses Bürogebäudes, das in der Erfüllung der Anforderungen von Einzelbüros und Kombibüros einen neuen Typus darstellt. Die vollständige Verglasung mit hochwertigen Gläsern, teilweise weit auskragende Dachflächen und ein über zehn Geschosse verglastes Atrium verbinden das Innen mit dem Außen.

A very calm, overall cuboid form constructed entirely of concrete, steel and glass characterises the appearance of this office building, which, in meeting the requirements of both single offices and office complexes, represents a new building type. The full-glass construction using high-quality glass, the partially overhanging roof surfaces and a glass atrium extending over ten storeys connect the interior to the exterior.

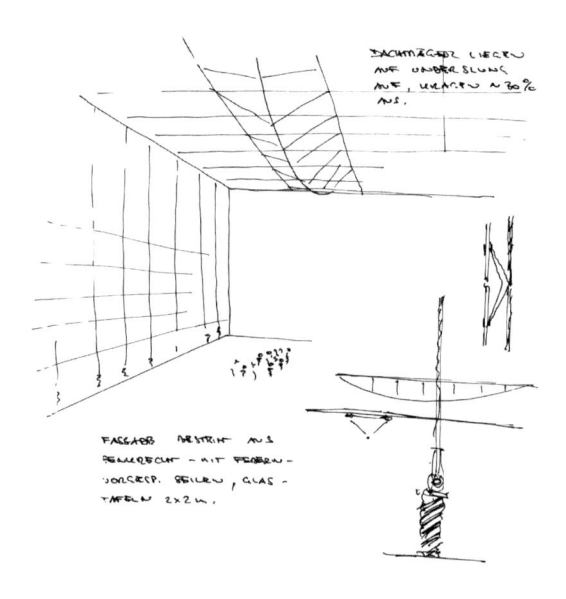

Entwurfsskizze zur tragenden Konstruktion des zehngeschossigen Atriums
Design sketch for the supporting framework of the ten-storey atrium

including Christian Barnard and Henry Kissinger, to participate in the lecture series entitled "Visions of the Future at the End of the 20th Century". One of the features of the presentations was that each speaker would select a piece of music to be played before his address. I chose a composition by Philip Glass entitled, interestingly enough, "Glassworks". Unfortunately, no one capable of playing it could be found in Munich. I then took Everding's suggestion and selected Luigi Nono as my introductory piece.

KUHN: Mr. Sobek, what kind of music would be appropriate for you or your work together?

SOBEK: I've had a weakness for electronic music since my early childhood. I like Glass, too, of course, or Alfred Schnittke.

JAHN: But I really don't think it's possible to create a link between architecture and music. Music has more to do with moods.

KUHN: You both also share an interest in fashion, in fabrics. Does this play any role in your work together?

SOBEK: Absolutely. It's not immediately apparent in the trivial sense, as if we were to build facades out of fabric. But it's there in terms of our intellectual approach and our appreciation for certain characteristics and effects. At the university I promote the concept of the use of fabrics in building shells among students doing semester and diploma projects. I have seen projects that were impossible to build but which bring these utopias

Gebäude und Landschaft
Building and surrounding landscape

a step closer to the realm of the feasible. I would say that the potential for development in textiles is as great as that of glass. There are switch-controlled fibres, energy-storing fibres from which energy can be drawn by pressing a button or emitting an electrical impulse. What has been in use for some time in the field of sports and space clothing has yet to be discovered in architecture. Of course it is important to explore these areas further, but such possibilities will be available to us in ten or twenty years. We just need to begin working on them today.

JAHN: In my view, fashion has as much to do with material as with style. I buy a better suit every year, not in terms of looks, since that is all transitory, but in terms of the quality of the fabric, which is steadily becoming more wrinkle-resistant, less space-consuming and can be worn both summer and winter. I appreciate that in fabrics and in architecture as well.

SOBEK: Technological development, in fabrics, for example, is one point. Based on work done by members of the Stuttgart School, especially by Frei Otto, a series of significant contributions on the subject of building with textiles as a kind of tightly stretched skin has appeared over the years. Helmut Jahn and I are less interested in this perfectly smooth, monochrome skin, whose dimensions are no longer evident to the eye, than in the creative use of textiles in building. Deliberately calculated folds and varying degrees of light transmission give buildings a fast poetic quality, and thus fashion joins hands with architecture once again.

Catalogue Raisonné

Bauwerk / project: Flughafenerweiterung Köln / Bonn
Gebäudetyp / building category: Flughafen / Airport
Ort / location: Köln / Cologne
Bauherr / client: Flughafen Köln / Bonn GmbH
Planungsbeginn / start of planning: 1992
Baubeginn / start of construction: 1997
Fertigstellung / completion: 2000

Bauwerk / project: Neues Kranzler-Eck Berlin
Gebäudetyp / building category: Bürogebäude / Office building
Ort / location: Berlin
Bauherr / client: DIFA Deutsche Immobilien Fonds AG
Planungsbeginn / start of planning: 1992
Baubeginn / start of construction: 1998
Fertigstellung / completion: 2001

Bauwerk / project: SONY Center
Gebäudetyp / building category: Büros, Kino, Museum, Wohnungen / Offices, cinema, museum, apartments
Ort / location: Berlin
Bauherr / client: SONY Corporation, TishmanSpeyer Properties Deutschland GmbH, Berlin
Planungsbeginn / start of planning: 1993
Baubeginn / start of construction: 1996
Fertigstellung / completion: 2000

Bauwerk / project: Charlemagne European Union Headquarters
Gebäudetyp / building category: Ministeriengebäude / Ministerial building
Ort / location: Brüssel / Brussel
Bauherr / client: S. A. Cofinimmo N.V.
Planungsbeginn / start of planning: 1994
Baubeginn / start of construction: 1995
Fertigstellung / completion: 1998

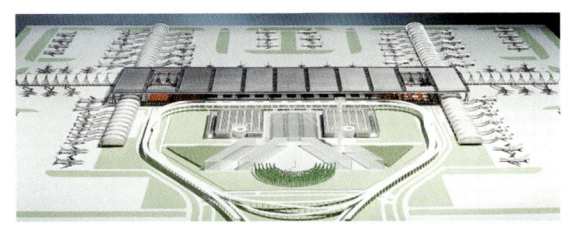

Bauwerk / project: New Bangkok International Airport
Gebäudetyp / building category: Flughafen / Airport
Ort / location: Bangkok
Bauherr / client: New Bangkok International Airport Co. Ltd. Bangkok
Planungsbeginn / start of planning: 1995
Baubeginn / start of construction: 1998
Fertigstellung / completion: 2004

Bauwerk / project: PB 6
Gebäudetyp / building category: Bürogebäude / Office building
Ort / location: Paris
Bauherr / client: Hines Interests Limited Partnership
Planungsbeginn / start of planning: 1995

133

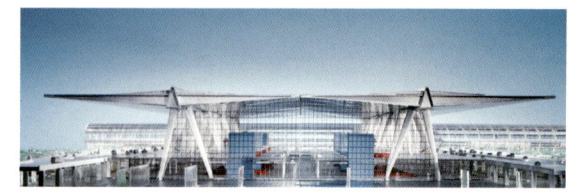

Catalogue Raisonné

Bauwerk / *project*: Shanghai Airport
Gebäudetyp / *building category*: Flughafen / *Airport*
Ort / *location*: Shanghai
Bauherr / *client*: Shanghai Pudong International Airport Corp.
Planungsbeginn / *start of planning*: 1995

Bauwerk / *project*: Flughafen München, Terminal 2
Gebäudetyp / *building category*: Flughafen / *Airport*
Ort / *location*: München / *Munich*
Bauherr / *client*: Flughafen München GmbH
Planungsbeginn / *start of planning*: 1996

Bauwerk / *project*: Flughafen Düsseldorf
Gebäudetyp / *building category*: Flughafen / *Airport*
Ort / *location*: Düsseldorf
Bauherr / *client*: Düsseldorf Airport Authorities
Planungsbeginn / *start of planning*: 1996

Bauwerk / *project*: Street Furniture
Gebäudetyp / *building category*: Stadtmöbel / *Street furniture*
Bauherr / *client*: J. C. Decaux
Planungsbeginn / *start of planning*: 1997
Fertigstellung / *completion*: 1998

Bauwerk / *project*: Hauptbahnhof Stuttgart
Gebäudetyp / *building category*: Bahnhof / *Train station*
Ort / *location*: Stuttgart
Bauherr / *client*: Deutsche Bahn AG
Planungsbeginn / *start of planning*: 1997

Bauwerk / *project*: Suyoung Bay Tower
Gebäudetyp / *building category*: Hotel, Apartments, Büros, Ausstellungsflächen / *Hotel, boarding house, offices, exhibition space*
Ort / *location*: Pusan
Bauherr / *client*: Daewoo Corporation
Planungsbeginn / *start of planning*: 1996

Bauwerk / *project*: Hauptbahnhof Dortmund
Gebäudetyp / *building category*: Bahnhof / *Train station*
Ort / *location*: Dortmund
Bauherr / *client*: Stadt Dortmund
Planungsbeginn / *start of planning*: 1997

Catalogue Raisonné

Bauwerk / project: Toronto Airport
Gebäudetyp / building category: Flughafen / Airport
Ort / location: Toronto
Bauherr / client: Greater Toronto Airport Authority
Planungsbeginn / start of planning: 1997

Bauwerk / project: Columbus Circle
Gebäudetyp / building category: Büros, Geschäfte, Wohnungen / Offices, shops, apartments
Ort / location: New York
Bauherr / client: TishmanSpeyer Properties
Planungsbeginn / start of planning: 1997

Bauwerk / project: Stralauer Platz 35
Gebäudetyp / building category: Bürogebäude / Office building
Ort / location: Berlin
Bauherr / client: Projektentwicklungsgesellschaft Stralauer Platz mbH & Co.
Planungsbeginn / start of planning: 1997

Bauwerk / project: YTL-Tower
Gebäudetyp / building category: Bürogebäude / Office building
Ort / location: Kuala Lumpur
Bauherr / client: YTL Corporation
Planungsbeginn / start of planning: 1997

Bauwerk / project: South Point
Gebäudetyp / building category: Bürohochhaus, Hotel, Wohnungen, Parkhaus / Office tower, hotel, apartments, parking space
Ort / location: Miami
Bauherr / client: The Continuum Company, LLC
Planungsbeginn / start of planning: 1997

Catalogue Raisonné

Bauwerk / *project*: Stralauer Platz 33/34
Gebäudetyp / *building category*: Bürogebäude / *Office building*
Ort / *location*: Berlin
Bauherr / *client*: Projektentwicklungsgesellschaft
Stralauer Platz mbH & Co.
Planungsbeginn / *start of planning*: 1997

Bauwerk / *project*: Mercedes Benz of North-America
Gebäudetyp / *building category*: Verwaltungsgebäude /
Administration building
Ort / *location*: Orangetown, N.Y.
Bauherr / *client*: Mercedes-Benz AG
Planungsbeginn / *start of planning*: 1997

Bauwerk / *project*: Constantini Museum
Gebäudetyp / *building category*: Museum
Ort / *location*: Buenos Aires
Bauherr / *client*: Constantini Museum
Planungsbeginn / *start of planning*: 1997

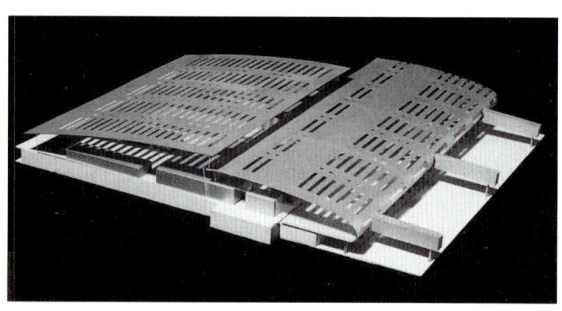

Bauwerk / *project*: Flughafen Stuttgart
Gebäudetyp / *building category*: Flughafen / *Airport*
Ort / *location*: Stuttgart
Bauherr / *client*: Flughafen Stuttgart GmbH
Planungsbeginn / *start of planning*: 1997

Bauwerk / *project*: Campus Center IIT (Illinois Institute of Technology)
Gebäudetyp / *building category*: Universitätsgebäude /
University building
Ort / *location*: Chicago
Bauherr / *client*: Illinois Institute of Technology
Planungsbeginn / *start of planning*: 1997

Bauwerk / *project*: MAC West Glasdecke, Glasboden
Gebäudetyp / *building category*: Sonderkonstruktion /
Special structure
Ort / *location*: München / *Munich*
Bauherr / *client*: MGF Delta KG
Planungsbeginn / *start of planning*: 1997
Baubeginn / *start of construction*: 1998
Fertigstellung / *completion*: 1998

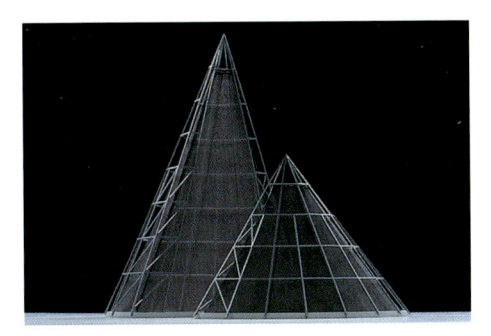

Catalogue Raisonné

Bauwerk / project: DIFA – Neues Kranzler-Eck, Volière
Gebäudetyp / building category: Volière
Ort / location: Berlin
Bauherr / client: DIFA Deutsche Immobilien Fonds AG
Planungsbeginn / start of planning: 1997
Baubeginn / start of construction: 1998
Fertigstellung / completion: 2001

Bauwerk / project: Kaufhof Chemnitz
Gebäudetyp / building category: Kaufhaus, Parkhaus, Zentrale Straßenbahnhaltestelle / Department store, parking, central street car station
Ort / location: Chemnitz
Bauherr / client: Kaufhof Warenhaus AG
Planungsbeginn / start of planning: 1998
Baubeginn / start of construction: 1999
Fertigstellung / completion: 2000

Bauwerk / project: Hauptverwaltung Deutsche Post
Gebäudetyp / building category: Verwaltungsgebäude / Administration building
Ort / location: Bonn
Bauherr / client: Deutsche Post AG
Planungsbeginn / start of planning: 1997
Baubeginn / start of construction: 2000
Fertigstellung / completion: 2001

Bauwerk / project: Transrapid-Stationen
Gebäudetyp / building category: Bahnhof / Station
Ort / location: Hamburg, Schwerin, Berlin
Bauherr / client: Magnetschnellbahn Planungsgesellschaft mbH
Planungsbeginn / start of planning: 1998
Baubeginn / start of construction: 2000
Fertigstellung / completion: 2004

Bauwerk / project: Neue Bayer-Konzernzentrale
Gebäudetyp / building category: Verwaltungsgebäude / Administration building
Ort / location: Leverkusen
Bauherr / client: Bayer AG
Planungsbeginn / start of planning: 1997
Baubeginn / start of construction: 1999
Fertigstellung / completion: 2001

Bauwerk / project: Hochhaus Lehrter Bahnhof
Gebäudetyp / building category: Bürogebäude / Office building
Ort / location: Berlin
Bauherr / client: TishmanSpeyer Properties
Planungsbeginn / start of planning: 1998

Catalogue Raisonné

Bauwerk / project: Dallas Arena
Gebäudetyp / building category: Stadion
Ort / location: Dallas
Bauherr / client: Hillwood Group
Planungsbeginn / start of planning: 1998

Bauwerk / project: Messe Shanghai-Pudong
Gebäudetyp / building category: Ausstellungshallen / Exhibition halls
Ort / location: Shanghai
Bauherr / client: Messe München International, Messe Düsseldorf Asia Pte Ltd., International Exhibition & Fair Service (IMAG)
Planungsbeginn / start of planning: 1998
Baubeginn / start of construction: 1999
Fertigstellung / completion: 2001

Bauwerk / project: HA-LO Corporate Headquarters
Gebäudetyp / building category: Verwaltungsgebäude / Administration building
Ort / location: Niles
Bauherr / client: Center Point Properties
Planungsbeginn / start of planning: 1998
Baubeginn / start of construction: 1999
Fertigstellung / completion: 2000

Bauwerk / project: Andersen Consulting
Gebäudetyp / building category: Bürogebäude / Office building
Ort / location: Sulzbach
Bauherr / client: CMC Projektmanagement
Planungsbeginn / start of planning: 1998
Baubeginn / start of construction: 2000
Fertigstellung / completion: 2002

Bauwerk / project: Canon Headquarters
Gebäudetyp / building category: Bürohochhaus / Office tower
Ort / location: Tokio / Tokyo
Bauherr / client: Obayashi Corp.
Planungsbeginn / start of planning: 1998

Bauwerk / project: 21st Century Tower
Gebäudetyp / building category: Bürogebäude / Office building
Ort / location: Shanghai
Bauherr / client: Shanghai 21st Century Center Real Estate Co., Ltd.
Planungsbeginn / start of planning: 1998
Baubeginn / start of construction: 1999
Fertigstellung / completion: 2001

Bauwerk / project: MAC Pavillon
Gebäudetyp / building category: Kiosk
Ort / location: München / Munich
Bauherr / client: MFG Delta KG
Planungsbeginn / start of planning: 1998
Baubeginn / start of construction: 1999
Fertigstellung / completion: 1999

Bauwerk / project: Konferenzzentrum Shenzhen
Gebäudetyp / building category: Konferenzzentrum / Convention center
Ort / location: Shanghai
Bauherr / client: Shenzhen Convention & Exhibition Center
Planungsbeginn / start of planning: 1999
Baubeginn / start of construction: 2000
Fertigstellung / completion: 2002

Biographien/Biographies

Helmut Jahn

1940 Geboren in Nürnberg

1960 – 1965 Architekturstudium an der Technischen Hochschule, München

1965 / 1966 Arbeitete mit P. C. von Seidlein, München

1966 / 1967 Abschlußstudien am Illinois Institute of Technology, Chicago bei Myron Goldsmith und Fazlur Kahn

1967 – 1973 Assistent von Gene Summers, C. F. Murphy Associates, Chicago

1973 Geschäftsführer und Direktor für Planung und Design, C. F. Murphy/Associates, Chicago

1975 Corporate Member of American Institute of Architects
Registrierter Architekt bei NCARB und in zahlreichen Staaten der USA
Mitglied der Deutschen Architektenkammer Hessen

1980 Honorary Degree Doctor of Fine Arts – St. Mary's College, Notre Dame, Indiana

1981 Principal Murphy/Jahn
Universität von Illinois Circle Campus, Chicago, Visiting Professor at Design Studio
Harvard Universität, Elliot Noyes Professor of Architectural Design

1982 Präsident, Murphy/Jahn

1983 Präsident und Hauptgeschäftsführer, Murphy/Jahn
Yale Universität, Davenport Visiting Professor of Architectural Design

1987 Fellow American Insitute of Architects

1989 – 1993 Illinois Institute of Technology, Thesis Professor

Werner Sobek

1953 Geboren in Aalen, Württemberg

1974 – 1980 Studium Bauingenieurwesen an der Universität Stuttgart

1978 – 1980 Architekturstudium an der Universität Stuttgart

1980 – 1986 Wissenschaftlicher Mitarbeiter am Sonderforschungsbereich 64 »Weitgespannte Flächentragwerke« an der Universität Stuttgart

1984 Mitarbeit bei Skidmore, Owings und Merrill, Chicago und San Francisco sowie am Illinois Institute of Technology, Chicago

1987 – 1991 Mitarbeiter im Ingenieurbüro Schlaich Bergermann und Partner, Stuttgart

1988 Lehrauftrag für Entwerfen von Tragwerken an der Fakultät für Bauingenieurwesen der Universität Stuttgart

1990 Ruf an die Universität Hannover (Nachfolge Bernd Tokarz)

1991 Gründung eines eigenen Ingenieurbüros
Professor und Leiter des Instituts für Tragwerksentwurf und Bauweisenforschung der Universität Hannover

1994 Ruf an die Universität Stuttgart (Nachfolge Frei Otto)

1995 Professor an der Universität Stuttgart
Direktor des Instituts für Leichte Flächentragwerke
Direktor des Zentrallabors des Konstruktiven Ingenieurbaus

1998 Benedictus Award Special Merit, San Francisco
Mitglied des Vorstandes der Ingenieurkammer Baden-Württemberg
Ernennung zum Prüfingenieur für Baustatik für alle Fachrichtungen

Helmut Jahn

1940 Born in Nürnberg

1960 – 1965 Degree course in architecture at Technische Hochschule, Munich

1965 / 1966 Worked with P. C. von Seidlein, Munich

1966 / 1967 Graduate studies, Illinois Institute of Technology, with Myron Goldsmith and Fazlur Kahn

1967 – 1973 Assistant to Gene Summers, C. F. Murphy Associates, Chicago

1973 Executive Vice President and Director of Planning and Design at C. F. Murphy Associates, Chicago

*1975 Corporate Member of American Institute of Architects
Registered Architect NCARB; state registrations in numerous states
Member of German Chamber of Architects, State of Hessen*

1980 Honorary Degree Doctor of Fine Arts – St. Mary's College, Notre Dame, Indiana

*1981 Principal, Murphy/Jahn
University of Illinois Circle Campus, Chicago, Design Studio
Harvard University, Elliot Noyes Professor of Architectural Design*

1982 President, Murphy/Jahn

*1983 President and CEO, Murphy/Jahn
Yale University, Davenport Visiting Professor of Architectural Design*

1987 Fellow American Institute of Architects

1989 – 1993 Illinois Institute of Technology, Thesis Professor

Werner Sobek

1953 Born in Aalen, Württemberg

1974 – 1980 Degree course in civil engineering at Stuttgart university

1978 – 1980 Degree course in architecture at Stuttgart university

1980 – 1986 Post-graduate fellow in Special Research Project 64 "Wide-span Lightweight Structures" at Stuttgart university

1984 Worked for Skidmore, Owings and Merrill, Chicago and San Francisco as well as at the Illinois Institute of Technology, Chicago

1987 – 1991 Worked for Ingenieurbüro Schlaich Bergermann & Partner, Stuttgart

1988 Teaching fellowship for Designing Load-bearing Structures at the civil engineering faculty of Stuttgart university

1990 Appointed professor at Hannover university (successor to Bernd Tokarz)

*1991 Founded his own engineering consultancy
Professor and director of the Institute for Structural Design and Study of Building Methods of Hannover university*

1994 Appointed professor at Stuttgart university (successor to Frei Otto)

*1995 Professor at Stuttgart university
Director of the Institute for Membrane Structures
Director of the Central Laboratory for Civil Engineering*

*1998 Benedictus Award Special Merit, San Francisco
Board member of the Chamber of Engineers of Baden-Württemberg
Appointment as Structural Approval Engineer for all professional disciplines*

Bibliographie / Bibliography

Helmut Jahn (Auswahl / *Selection*)

Blaser, Werner: Helmut Jahn. Transparency/Transparenz, Basel/Boston/Berlin 1996
Blaser, Werner: Furniture as Architecture. A Parallel between Building and Furniture Design, Zürich 1985
Blaser, Werner: Mies van der Rohe. Continuing the Chicago School of Architecture, Basel/Boston/Berlin 1981
Chicago and New York: Architectural Interactions, Ausst.Kat. The Art Institute of Chicago, Chicago 1984
Guiheux, Alain (Hrsg.): Lieux de Travail, Paris 1986
Kloos, Maarten (Hrsg.): An Architectural Lesson, Amsterdam 1989
Klotz, Heinrich (Hrsg.): Vision der Moderne. Das Prinzip Konstruktion, Frankfurt a. M. 1986
Klotz, Heinrich (Hrsg.): Die Revision der Moderne. Postmoderne Architektur 1960–1980, München 1984
Krantz, Les (Hrsg.): American Architects, New York 1989
Landers, Sam/Maday, Tom (Hrsg.): Great Chicago Stores, New York 1992
Mardaga, Pierre (Hrsg.): Biennale de Paris Architecture 1985, Paris 1985
Mierop, Caroline: Skyscraper and Higher, Brüssel 1995
Miller, Ross/Knopf, Alfred A.: Here's the Deal, New York 1996
Miller, Nory: Helmut Jahn, New York 1986
Thorndike, Joseph J.: Three Centuries of Notable American Architects, New York 1981

Werner Sobek (Auswahl / *Selection*)

Blaser, Werner: Werner Sobek. Art of Engineering – Ingenieur-Kunst, Basel/Boston/Berlin 1999
Schittich, C./Staib, G./Balkow, D./Sobek, W./Schuler, M.: Glasbau Atlas, Basel/Boston/Berlin 1998
Sobek, Werner: »Der Kubus«, in: Auf den Spuren einer Tour, hrsg. von der Daimler Benz AG, Stuttgart 1998
Sobek, W./Haase, W.: »Selbstanpassende Systeme in der Gebäudehülle«, in: Berichtsband IBK-Symposium »Außenwände und Fassaden 2000«, Darmstadt 1997
Sobek, Werner: »Leichte und selbstanpassende Konstruktionen«, in: Konstruktion. Ereignis und Prozeß, Tagungsband Internationales Symposium Architektur und Stahl, Berlin 1997
Sobek, Werner: Transluzent/Transparent/Selbstanpassend, Jahresbericht des Vereins der Freunde und Förderer der Universität Stuttgart, 1996
Sobek, Werner: Wandelbare Überdachungen aus textilen Werkstoffen, Frankfurt a.M. 1993
Sobek, Werner: Schalungen aus pneumatisch vorgespannten Membranen zur Herstellung von Überdachungen, Speicherbehältern und Leistungssystemen, 2. Internationales Techtextil Symposium, Frankfurt 1990
Sobek, Werner: Auf pneumatisch gestützten Schalungen hergestellte Betonschalen, Stuttgart 1987
Sobek, Werner: Untersuchungen zum Problem der Randausbildung mechanisch vorgespannter Membrankonstruktionen, Stuttgart 1980

Wahrnehmung (Auswahl) / *Perception (Selection)*

Burckhardt, Martin: Metamorphosen von Raum und Zeit. Eine Geschichte der Wahrnehmung, Frankfurt a. M./New York 1994
Ferguson, Eugene S.: Das innere Auge. Von der Kunst des Ingenieurs, Basel/Boston/Berlin 1993
Goldstein, E. Bruce: Wahrnehmungspsychologie, Heidelberg/Berlin/Oxford 1997
Gumin, Heinz/Meier, Heinrich (Hrsg.): Einführung in den Konstruktivismus, München 1998
Schiemann, Gregor (Hrsg.): Was ist Natur? Klassische Texte zur Naturphilosophie, München 1996
Schmidt, Siegfried J. (Hrsg.): Der Diskurs des Radikalen Konstruktivismus, Frankfurt a. M. 1996
Strasser, Peter: Journal der letzten Dinge, Frankfurt a. M. 1998
Zajonc, Arthur: Die gemeinsame Geschichte von Licht und Bewußtsein, Reinbek 1997

Architektur (Auswahl) / *Architecture (Selection)*

Addis, Bill: The Art of the Structural Engineer, London 1994
Baccini, Peter/Oswald, Franz (Hrsg.): Netzstadt. Transdisziplinäre Methoden zum Umbau urbaner Systeme, Zürich 1998
Berger, Horst: Light Structures – Structures of Light: The Art and Engineering of Tensile Architecture, Basel/Boston/Berlin 1996
Cerver, Francisco Asensio: The Architecture of Glass: Shaping Light, New York 1997
Compagno, Andrea: Intelligente Glasfassaden, Basel/Boston/Berlin 1996
Dalland, Todd/Goldsmith, Nicholas: FTL – Softness Movement and Light, London 1997
Daniels, Klaus (Hrsg.): Hohe Häuser, Stuttgart 1993
Heinle, Erwin/Leonhardt, Fritz: Türme aller Zeiten – aller Kulturen, Stuttgart 1997
Jesberg, Paulgerd: Die Geschichte der Ingenieurbaukunst, Stuttgart 1996
Kahn, Louis I.: Licht und Raum, Basel 1993
Die gläserne Kette – Visionäre Architekturen aus dem Kreise um Bruno Taut 1919–1920, Ausst.Kat. Städtisches Museum Leverkusen Schloß Morsbroich/Akademie der Künste Berlin, o.J.
Graefe, Rainer (Hrsg.): Zur Geschichte des Konstruierens, Stuttgart 1989
Knaack, Ulrich: Konstruktiver Glasbau, Köln 1998
Krewinkel, Heinz W.: Glasarchitektur. Material, Konstruktion und Detail, Basel/Boston/Berlin 1998
Kronenburg, Robert: Houses in Motion, London 1995
Neumann, Dietrich: Die Wolkenkratzer kommen, Braunschweig/Wiesbaden 1995
Profitopoli$ oder: Der Mensch braucht eine andere Stadt, Ausst.Kat. Die Neue Sammlung, Staatliches Museum für angewandte Kunst München, Niedernhausen 1971
Rice, Peter/Dutton, Hugh: Transparente Architektur. Glasfassaden mit Structural Glazing, Basel/Berlin/Boston 1995
Robin, Tony: Engineering a New Architecture, Massachusetts 1996
Rowe, Colin/Slutzky, Robert: Transparency, Basel/Boston/Berlin 1997
Schock, Hans-Joachim: Segel, Folien und Membranen. Innovative Konstruktionen in der textilen Architektur, Basel/Berlin/Boston 1997
Stadtgestalt. Monotonie und Vielfalt, Ausst.Kat. Städtisches Museum Leverkusen Schloß Morsbroich, Leverkusen 1977
Teichmann, Klaus/Wilke, Joachim (Hrsg.): Prozeß und Form »Natürlicher Konstruktionen«, Berlin 1996
Vandenberg, Maritz: Cable Nets, Chichester 1998